Origins of the Dream

UNIVERSITY PRESS OF FLORIDA

Florida A&M University, Tallahassee
Florida Atlantic University, Boca Raton
Florida Gulf Coast University, Ft. Myers
Florida International University, Miami
Florida State University, Tallahassee
New College of Florida, Sarasota
University of Central Florida, Orlando
University of Florida, Gainesville
University of North Florida, Jacksonville
University of South Florida, Tampa
University of West Florida, Pensacola

Origins of the Dream

Hughes's Poetry and King's Rhetoric

W. Jason Miller

UNIVERSITY PRESS OF FLORIDA

Gainesville/Tallahassee/Tampa/Boca Raton
Pensacola/Orlando/Miami/Jacksonville/Ft. Myers/Sarasota

This book may be available in an electronic edition.

20 19 18 17 16 15   6 5 4 3 2 1

Library of Congress Cataloging-in-Publication Data
Miller, W. Jason, author.
Origins of the dream : Hughes's poetry and King's rhetoric / W. Jason Miller.
pages cm
Includes bibliographical references and index.
ISBN 978-0-8130-6044-6
1. Hughes, Langston, 1902–1967—Influence. 2. King, Martin Luther, Jr., 1929–1968.
3. American poetry—African American authors. 4. African Americans—History.
5. Civil rights movements—United States—History—20th century. 6. African American
poets—20th century. I. Title.
PS3515.U274Z6844 2015
818'.5209—dc23   2014031882

The University Press of Florida is the scholarly publishing agency for the State University
System of Florida, comprising Florida A&M University, Florida Atlantic University,
Florida Gulf Coast University, Florida International University, Florida State University,
New College of Florida, University of Central Florida, University of Florida, University
of North Florida, University of South Florida, and University of West Florida.

University Press of Florida
15 Northwest 15th Street
Gainesville, FL 32611-2079
http://www.upf.com

Contents

Figures

Acknowledgments

Many people helped to bring this project to fruition. I benefited from the kind services of research librarians Natalia Sciarini at the Beinecke Library at Yale University and Ryan Hendrickson at the Howard Gotlieb Library at Boston University. Elaine Hall assisted me in locating important documents housed in Atlanta's Martin Luther King, Jr. Center, and the associates at the Robert W. Woodruff Library of the Atlanta University Center provided crucial assistance.

Of course, research takes time and funding. No one has been more supportive of this project than Antony Harrison, head of the English Department at North Carolina State University. Dr. Harrison approved various research stipends allowing me to travel to some of the country's most distinguished archives. Critical to this project's success was an off-campus scholarly assignment I received in the spring of 2013. I express my deepest gratitude to Dr. Harrison for helping me secure that assignment.

North Carolina State University also provided me access to exceptional research facilities at both the D. H. Hill and Hunt Library locations, where Cynthia Levine and Jason Evans-Groth provided timely insights and services. I thank all those at the African American Cultural Center, including Dr. Sheila Smith McKoy and Ms. Toni Thorpe. In my own department, Dick Reavis provided invaluable insight regarding King and his inner circle.

Permission to reprint "Mother to Son," "Youth," "Militant," and "I Dream a World," from *The Collected Poems of Langston Hughes* by Langston Hughes, edited by Arnold Rampersad with David Roessel, associate editor, copyright © 1994 by the Estate of Langston Hughes. Used by permission of Alfred A. Knopf, a division of Random House. These poems are also reprinted with electronic rights worldwide and UK/Commonwealth by permission of Harold Ober Associates Inc. I would like to thank those at the Beinecke Library at Yale University for assisting me in reprinting images from the Hughes papers in the James Weldon Johnson Collection. Finally, some of the ideas in chapter 1 were published earlier in a different form, and I am grateful for the permission granted by the *African American Review* to develop them further here.

I could not have asked for better experts to review the manuscript than John A. Kirk and Donna Akiba Sullivan Harper, who took time to loan me their eyes and offered insights and necessary correctives. I am grateful for their critical efforts on my behalf. I also thank Jonathan Lawrence for contributing his editorial expertise.

I received much assistance in my research. Christine Elizabeth Cross located information on important cultural contexts alluded to by King himself. Danielle Fuentes's research enabled me to better understand Hughes's popularity around the world. Rebecca le Roux helped with gathering primary source material. Megan Myers helped with research on the reception of *A Raisin in the Sun*. Jessica Odom ensured that my information about the marches through Alabama in 1965 was accurate. William Tolbert's keen ear ensured that every word of King's address in Rocky Mount was transcribed accurately. Amber Woolsey enabled me to better understand the relationship between Hugh Wooding and Hughes. Finally, Angie Oberg offered critical editorial advice as she reviewed sections of the manuscript.

Notwithstanding all these efforts, any mistakes that remain are mine alone.

One of the highlights of this project was getting to know some of the residents of Rocky Mount, North Carolina. I thank Reuben Blackwell, Helen Gay, Dr. Tolokun Omokunde, Rachel Smith, Charlene Tenny, Traci Thompson, Herbert Tillman, and JoEvelyn Williams for their time, resources, and kindness. Rebecca Cerese's belief in this work helped immensely in documenting these engagements.

For their wise counsel, I would like to thank Kim Andersen of the State Archives of North Carolina, Skip Elsheimer of AV Geeks, and Michael Hill at the North Carolina Office of Archives and History. Thanks to George Blood for meeting with me on a Sunday to digitize old audio. These efforts will be appreciated more as these ideas reach other media.

Chris and Meredith Barringer generously afforded me long retreats to turn my ideas into words, as this book was literally begun and finished at their cabin.

My wife, Sherri, and son, Austin, have contributed more than I could ask. Austin offered editorial advice, patience, and curiosity. Sherri knows how much she means, allowing me to do the work of two. To you, my thanks are forever and legion.

Introduction

Giving New Validity to Old Forms

Poets are the unacknowledged legislators of the world.

PERCY BYSSHE SHELLEY, "A DEFENSE OF POETRY"

Langston Hughes's poetry hovers behind Martin Luther King's speeches and sermons the way watermarks show through bonded paper when it's held up to light. King acknowledged how often he used the poems of his contemporary in a letter he wrote to Hughes: "My admiration for your works is not only expressed in my personal conversations, but I can no longer count the number of times and places, all over the nation, in my addresses and sermons in which I have read your poems. I know of no better way to express in beauty the heartbeat and struggle of our people."[1] However, what was common knowledge for these two men during their lifetimes has somehow gone uncharted in formal scholarship. In 1959, King's first biographer, Lawrence Reddick, noted that King "likes to quote the more communicable poets in his speeches and sermons. He reads Negro writers—especially James Weldon Johnson, Richard Wright, and Langston Hughes" (4). Twelve years later, Hortense Spillers implied a connection between King and Hughes when she suggested that King spoke "for the South and the black man's 'deferred dream' of civil rights" (22).[2] Again, without analyzing the depths of their interrelatedness, Richard Barksdale suggested that each of these men "courted and articulated the same dream" (245).

Hughes's biographer Arnold Rampersad notes that many of Hughes's friends pointed out that King's "I Have a Dream" address bore similarities with some of Hughes's own poems on dreams (2: 367). It has even been said that Hughes himself believed that his own poetry had inspired King's "I Have a Dream" speech (Ghosh 38–39). More than fifty years have passed since King gave this speech. During this time, several Langston Hughes scholars have suspected that King's dream was related to Hughes's poetry.[3] This study confirms their suspicions. It charts how Hughes's poetry became a measurable inflection in the voice of Martin Luther King.[4] More specifically, this book traces the origins of King's dream back to Hughes's poetry. This is not a speculative work: King's engagements with Hughes's poetry are made undeniably visible.

Though they are connected, King's metaphors and Hughes's poems were intentionally distanced from each other. The complex story of this distancing has created the critical need for this study. However, in finally allowing their ideas to be reunited, I do not suggest that King's ideas were not original. I am not arguing that Hughes should be privileged because his poems serve as points of origin. Rather, I have two goals in exploring these connections. First, reuniting Hughes's poems with King's speeches helps us understand the fullest resonance of King's metaphors. Second, King's engagements with Hughes's poems resulted in the twentieth century's most visible integration of poetry and politics.

A better understanding of the forces that led King to redeem metaphors from Hughes's poetry and then reactivate them in the political arena reveals a subversive element within King's rhetoric. King's subversive rhetoric reveals his determination to model resistance as well as engage his own poetic sensibilities. King flourished in a rich nexus of culture, politics, and art. The redemptive work of King shows how he negotiated a political climate that sought to silence a subversive voice like Hughes's. Because King separated Hughes's identity from his poems, the nation unconsciously embraced traces of his poetry.

For example, King's intimate knowledge of Hughes's poem "I Dream a World" represents King's earliest engagement with the metaphor of dreaming, and this fact alters our understanding of how King's dream became more inclusive as it expanded. King eventually stitched together his own garment of dream images. Seeing how the first piece of cloth came from this Hughes poem allows us to chart the growth of King's poetic sensibilities. Most remarkably, and unseen until now, this study reveals that King's first national presentation of "I Have a Dream" was literally in the form of a poem. This poem was masquerading as prose. Charting this metaphor's connection to

Hughes's poem enables us to amplify the previously undetectable inflections of cultural pride and political subversion underlying the speech King delivered at the March on Washington. Instead of quoting Hughes's poetry, King in his Washington, D.C., address was recalling lines from his own poetry. Read chronologically, this book documents King's own development as a poet.

Documenting the intertextual connections between these two artists brings to light four other critical discoveries. First, King redeemed metaphors from Hughes's poetry and transformed them so that they became the emblems of many of his own most significant principles. By linking Hughes's ideas with his own principles, King's rhetoric simultaneously exhibited redundancy and rebirth. King redeemed metaphors from Hughes's poetry to communicate the directive to "keep going," extend the resonance of "midnight" and "daybreak," create culturally relevant associations for "shattered dreams," shape a representation of the "beloved community," and generate a lasting resonance for his own "dream." This study reveals the significance of having Hughes's vehicles muted within King's song.

Second, Hughes's complex reputation accounts in part for why definitive links between the two men have been so difficult to establish. Hughes was simultaneously revered in African American culture for his status as a successful man of letters and reviled by the dominant culture as a subversive Communist. This tension can still be measured today when Hughes's name or poetry is referenced in overtly political contexts. King's willingness to integrate yet conceal Hughes's texts within his own voice demonstrates that King often spoke truth to power through a voice that power thought it had silenced. Metaphors are inherently untraceable. Severing them from Hughes's poetry allowed them to pass through careful surveillance.

Third, unlike what we see in other studies that often document inspiration and influence, the creative exchange between King and Hughes was reciprocal. Although this study primarily concerns Hughes's influence on King, portions of it identify King's influence on Hughes. As figure 1 reveals, this reciprocal influence is shown in the archival retrieval of Hughes's creation of one aria, four poems, and a play as a result of King's influence.

Fourth, and finally, in contrast to his handling of so many other sources, King personally sought out, revised, and incorporated Hughes's works into his addresses. In other words, King did not merely recycle and reinvent Hughes as he had heard him invoked in sermons by other preachers; instead, King purposefully selected Hughes's poetry with measurable intentionality.

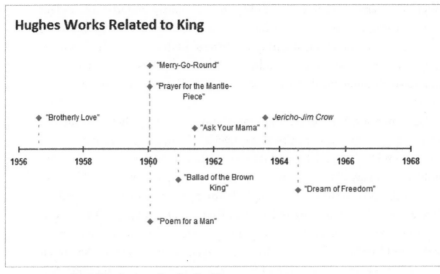

Hughes Works Related to King

- ◆ "Merry-Go-Round"
- ◆ "Prayer for the Mantle-Piece"
- ◆ "Brotherly Love"
- ◆ Jericho-Jim Crow
- ◆ "Ask Your Mama"

1956   1958   1960   1962   1964   1966   1968

- ◆ "Ballad of the Brown King"
- ◆ "Dream of Freedom"
- ◆ "Poem for a Man"

Figure 1. A timeline of Hughes's works related to King.

His choice to embed Hughes's poetry speaks directly to his personal investment in the primary works of Hughes's oeuvre.

King's incorporation of Hughes's poetry is highly significant. It demonstrates the highly educated preacher's desire to simultaneously connect with the heart of his African American audience and his own cultural roots. Furthermore, it affirms that when Hughes's poetry was transformed, performances of African American literature could move dominant culture. King gave Hughes's poems hundreds of public hearings that earned acceptance precisely because they had been separated from their derogatory labels as emblems of black culture. King's attraction to Hughes's poetry reveals an essential element of King's cultural heritage. As Lewis Baldwin suggests in *There Is a Balm in Gilead*, "King's cultural heritage must be carefully studied before we get a full portrait of the man, the movement, the message, and the legacy" (6).[5] Keith Miller's exhaustive scholarship, presented in *Voice of Deliverance,* has enabled us to see how King reinvented what he inherited from other preachers as he created his public identity. Richard Lischer has meticulously reconstructed the rich experience of hearing King preach with his critical study *The Preacher King.* I extend each of these studies in important ways to show that Hughes was the most appropriate poet for King to engage. Personally selected from King's cultural roots and then incorporated with uncommon care and intentionality, Hughes's poetry is precisely the source material that audiences unconsciously wanted to hear King preach.

In addition to his roles as preacher and prophet, King was also a revisionary poet. His philosophical approach to rewriting source material can best be understood from his own testimony. Speaking to an audience at Spelman College, King said: "Originality is a basic part of education. That does not mean that you think something altogether new; if that were the case Shakespeare wasn't original, for Shakespeare depended on Plutarch and others for many of his plots. Originality does not mean thinking up something totally new in the universe, but it does mean giving new validity to old forms" (Carson 5: 412). Extending this thought to King's own case, the speaker's dynamic personality is invoked in his or her ability to present and revise ideas, not to create original materials. By redeeming metaphors from Hughes's poetry, King infused his own rhetoric with an accessible, inspirational, visionary, and subversive vitality. His rhetoric establishes a historical continuity with the past in order to make it present and alive.

King deeply engaged with Hughes's poetry by memorizing and rewriting it on numerous occasions. In these instances, King intentionally altered Hughes's poetry—sometimes changing a key phrase, at other times using Hughes's organizational structures to create his own lines. King also rewrote an entire poem by Hughes and incorporated it seamlessly into his speeches on several occasions. Figure 2 charts how King gave new validity to old

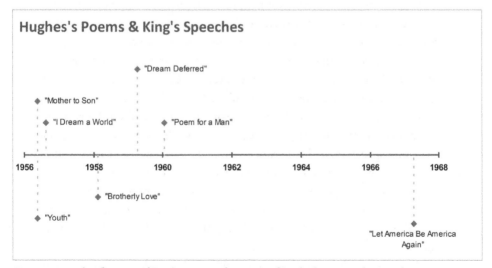

Figure 2. A timeline for some of King's most significant uses of Hughes's poetry in his speeches.

forms of poetry by consistently invoking Hughes's poems "Mother to Son," "Youth," "Let America Be America Again," "Dream Deferred," "Brotherly Love," and "I Dream a World" throughout his career. The vast majority of these poems were invoked for the first time in a three-month period from May 13 to August 11, 1956. In fact, on August 11 alone, King alluded to four different Hughes poems. As J. T. Porter, a member of King's congregation, would attest, "Everything else was a spin-off of what I heard the first year" (qtd. in Lischer, *Preacher King* 81). Invoking Hughes repeatedly during this formative period in his preaching career ensured that Hughes would forever remain a measurable inflection in King's voice. The pattern that emerges after this era is one in which King reworded, rewrote, and disguised Hughes's poetry.

Why did King rewrite Hughes's poetry in his addresses? The decision to rewrite rather than simply paraphrase or recite Hughes's poetry results in the creation of King's poetic persona. A poetic persona was important for several reasons. First, it allowed King to validate his prophetic persona. Poetry is a co-requisite to prophecy. We realize that we have forgotten this when we recognize that the Old Testament prophets presented their visions in poetic form. In these inherited models, prophecy trespasses into poetry. Without the gift of lyrical expression, King's declarations of the future would lack the rhetorical authority of scripture. Second, in sermons and addresses, reinventing another writer's ideas eliminates the need for disruptive referencing that can wake the dreamer. Driving for an effect sometimes bordering on incantation, allusive connections to other texts maintain the listener's hypnosis as they "get gone" right along with the preacher. This need is often intensified at the end of a speech as the rhetoric climbs in intensity. Hughes's metaphors consistently appeared in the final moments of King's oratory. Third, the rhetorical demands of the speech often dictate the elimination of some references. In the case of rewriting Hughes's verses, King often had to be careful to avoid triggering animosity as a result of Hughes's subversive reputation. Furthermore, as a teacher, King often sought to model the subject matter of his speeches through his rhetorical strategies. This sometimes resulted in brilliant displays where the rhetorical demands of the speech called for either reinvention or integration of his inherited sources. Fourth, and finally, the deep personal engagement that results from rewriting source material results in a genuine ownership of the new material. There is no need to reference something so intimately lived and deeply transformed that it has truly become one's own.

King's deep engagement with Hughes's poetry highlights his own poetic sensibilities. Although I am not alone in identifying King's poetic sensibilities, I do intend to amplify them. Andrew Young, King's longtime aide and close associate, said of King: "He was a poet, and poets work on speeches until every little syllable is right." John Lewis, another close confidant of King's from the civil rights era, reflected on one of King's speeches and concluded: "Yes, this is poetry."[6] Asked why he maintained such a rigorous speaking schedule amid all his other obligations, King replied: "An artist should never be denied his means of expression" (Carson 5: 178). King saw himself not only as a preacher but also as an artist. This self-identification can be traced to traits exhibited in his youth. The young Martin "came along with sensitivities" that only his mother could "investigate and soothe" (Baldwin, *Balm* 107). During his youth, his uncommon intensity led him to jump out a window after he believed that he and his brother had inadvertently killed his grandmother Jennie, who soon revived after being knocked unconscious (109–10). In addition to his love of music, exhibited at Morehouse by his membership in both the glee club and chorus, he also minored in English (32, 25). Coretta, the woman King ultimately married, was a singer and had envisioned a career on the concert stage (130). It is important to remember that songs are simply poems set to music.

Having read "numerous books about black history and the black experience," the young King "also developed a love for music and poetry, and was fascinated by the sounds and power of words" (Baldwin, *Balm* 115). Such traits belong as much to the occupation of a poet as they do to a preacher. King's drive for eloquence and his early desire for what he called "big words" have often been stated in poetic terms that need not be read as a means to simply rate his skill with language. They are comments on the genre he first admired and later mastered. His addresses featured "rhythmic eloquence and poetic speech" (276). Rev. Hosea Williams, King's contemporary, once declared that King "reminds me of David because he was a poetic man. His speeches are alive with a Psalm-like beauty of expression" (qtd. in Baldwin, *Balm* 245). King's poetic sensibilities were not confined to the persona he projected to the world. Although the constant tension and death threats were more than enough to produce a melancholy attitude in King, "SCLC [Southern Christian Leadership Conference] aide William Rutherford asserts that his malaise was based more on 'intellectual and spiritual' considerations than personal ones" (Lischer, *Preacher King* 170). Such melancholy has long been associated with poets.

The word *poet* was not merely bestowed on King to communicate his rhetorical prowess or eloquence. The term captures the literal genre of poetry that he included in his speeches. No one has made this clearer than Richard Lischer, who has faithfully transcribed some of King's pronouncements from audiotapes and presented them visually as poetry. Oral delivery blurs the boundaries between prose and poetry, and I extend Lischer's belief that King's "genius was poetic in nature" as he "practiced the creativity of a preacher and a poet" (*Preacher King* 10). We should also note that the greatest actors connect their performance with something they carry deep inside themselves. King's poetic sensibilities help us account for the dramatic success in delivering his metaphors. In addition to the extemporaneous riffs he was able to deliver, King also handwrote many of the scripts for the speeches he delivered. These scripts reveal intentional patterns where he wrote and rewrote poetry. Some of these compositions exhibit a high degree of originality and complexity. King's poetry is critically analyzed and visually reproduced in these pages with an ear tuned to its prosody. Too often, poetry now comes to us as printed words on paper, whereas poets have usually been expected to be both the writer and the performer of their verse. Like poems, speeches do not live on paper.

King's poetic sensibilities sharpened throughout his life. During King's time at Boston University, his handwritten notes reveal the type of journaling that often precedes the composition of a poem. Between 1948 and 1954, King documented some of his thoughts by turning a weekly planner into a journal. Ignoring columns meant for scheduling events, calculating time, and documenting expenses, King filled this book with words that often exhibit a deft use of rhyme. This document provides insight into his personality. One entry in this planner reads: "Karl Marx and his machine-man defined society by its economic character and left God out of consideration altogether" (Carson 6: 560). Rhyming "character" with "altogether" gives way to even subtler repetitions: "May God be with you as you walk the pathways of life. May he support and strengthen you until the lengthened shadows gather" (6: 560). Here, the "th" sounds in "strengthen" and "lengthened" are literally joined with the image of "pathways" as King enables these hopes and sounds to meet in "gather." He accomplishes this through a gradually quickening pace of well-placed rhymes to compress time. Poetry's medium is sound, just as the painter's medium is color. Such repetitions and rhythms are not just pleasing to the ear: their effects represent the ideas themselves. Poetry does not simply elevate the authority of the speaker: it deepens our understanding of the speaker's thoughts. Poetry's aim is not merely eloquence: it turns an idea into something unforgettable so that we can act on what we've remembered. Even when writing for an audience of one, King understood these things as he reveled in the expressive play of words and wrote them as poetry.

Langston Hughes

Born in 1902, Langston Hughes is best known as a central figure of the Harlem Renaissance, where his poetry and aesthetics helped shaped the African American music, art, culture, and literature that emerged from Harlem in the 1920s. However, Hughes wore many hats. Though best known for his poetry, he also wrote librettos and plays, children's literature, two novels, two autobiographies, and a weekly column in the *Chicago Defender* for twenty-four years. Hughes wanted to make his living as a writer, and he achieved this goal. However, it came at a price. Paid less as an African American, Hughes sometimes wrote inferior work to pay the bills. Though remarkably accomplished, he even wrote under a pseudonym as he worked to earn a living. Facing the barriers of this and even greater racial bigotry, Hughes embraced a Communist ideology throughout his life as he sought ways to address America's hypocritical stance on the freedom and justice advertised in its democracy. This stance still colors his reputation today.

Scholarship has done well to remember that Hughes published the first of his many canonical poems in 1921. It has proved much harder to remember that Hughes died in 1967, less than a year before King's assassination. Though Hughes was older than King, the two men were contemporaries. Not so coincidentally, and of crucial importance to the development of King's dream, Hughes has been linked with dreams "from the start of his career," as dreams became "the central motif of his poetry" (Rampersad 2: 152). Many of Hughes's most famous poems speak of dreams. Linking himself with many of his earliest poems on dreams in 1932, he titled one of his most popular books of poetry *The Dream Keeper*. As Steven Tracy writes, "Dreams have always figured prominently in the works of Langston Hughes. . . . Hughes's work is devoted to outlining, celebrating, and agitating on behalf of the dreams of oppressed and marginalized peoples worldwide, with particular focus on the dreams of African Americans" (223).

Hughes knew how often his poems were used by Martin Luther King. We can see this in Hughes's response to a letter from the stage actor Frederick O'Neal. In 1967, O'Neal wrote Hughes a belated confession: "I read one or two of your poems at Knoxville College and again last Wednesday at Hampton Institute in a lecture there. I don't know how much Royalty is due, but if this is not sufficient please let me know." O'Neal enclosed a check for ten dollars. Hughes responded the same day with equal parts astonishment and gratitude: "You may not believe me when I tell you that this is the *first* time in my natural life that anybody ever sent me *anything* just for reading or reciting a few of my poems. . . . I am so amazed and delighted at your thoughtfulness and courtesy that I feel as if I should repay YOU ten times over. . . . All I can say is, 'You're a gentleman and a prince!'"[7] Then, as if revealing something that had been on his mind for years, Hughes offered his own confession: "I don't know why Martin Luther King comes to mind (and it never occurred to me to hold it against him) but he has used a poem of mine or two in almost all of his speeches . . . before great big audiences that take up great BIG collections. Practically all the colored lecturers and readers use my poems (of which I'm glad) but none before you ever dreamed of sending a penny. With me, Fred, you have made *history*."[8] With his poetic powers of suggestion, is Hughes hinting at a concealed truth when he activates the metaphor of "dreaming" near the end of this response? By offering soft rhymes in the key of "e" between "penny," "dreamed," and "history," is Hughes reminding O'Neal that King's central metaphor of dreaming had made history by raising untold sums of money for the civil rights movement? This exchange reveals an underappreciated tension between King's speeches and Hughes's poems. In mentioning King's name, Hughes indicates that he has been listening from a distance as King took on the role of the star performer of some of Hughes's greatest scripts.

Hughes's cultural status within the African American community, his documentation of the black experience in America, and the accessibility of his ideas made him the perfect poet for King to rewrite. In fact, the accessibility of Hughes's everyday language invited revision, as Hughes made writing poetry look simple. Moreover, the simplicity of his style has often relegated him to being discussed in high school English classes while being ignored in many universities. Given the inklings expressed in his letter to O'Neal, Hughes understood the frequent appearances his poetry made in King's speeches. The depth of this engagement is finely documented here.

This study has major implications for King, Hughes, the civil rights movement, and poetry itself. Hughes fueled King's auditory imagination so that his congregation heard echoes of familiar tropes and rhythms when King spoke. King's ability to reawaken Hughes's metaphors calls for a dramatic reassessment of some of King's most significant principles. If the subject of the dream is always the dreamer, then every text is but a dream waiting to be interpreted. The interconnectedness of dream imagery in these two sources initiates moments of deep interpretive reflection. Psychologically, historically, and sociologically, what is the significance of King's use of poetry to motivate, clarify, and build consensus? What does it mean that King used poetry to effect social change? How does an understanding of King's poetic sensibilities provide a deeper understanding of him as a man? What fortitude and determination is reflected in the fact that, rather than bowing to its political pressures, King rhetorically outwitted accusations of Communist subversiveness? Answers to these and other questions can only come by integrating King's personae to acknowledge that he was simultaneously a preacher and a leader, a prophet and a poet.

The repeated appearances of Hughes's poetry in King's rhetoric reminds us that Hughes made lasting contributions to the century's two most significant African American initiatives. In very different ways, Hughes's poetry is just as important to the civil rights movement as it is to the Harlem Renaissance. Oftentimes we have ignored the later years of Hughes's life. The late civil rights movement depended on the coalescence of a variety of factors, including the use of poetry. By transforming Hughes's poetry, King was able to inspire, unify, and organize people to work toward making lasting changes in American society. Such motivations do not stem solely from logic or anger. King's visions are so invigorating because they are poetic. From the mouth of King, Hughes's reinvigorated metaphors gave voice to black demands on stages all across America. Rather than fading into history, Hughes's poems returned as echoes that were used to move America. King validated Hughes's words more than any other poet's, because both of them wanted America to achieve what it claimed to believe.

This study reminds us of the role poetry played in the passing of civil rights legislation. Above all else, the sacrifices, abuses, and determination of those who marched and fought for civil rights have rightly earned our attention. This study adds further insight into the role of poetry in King's ability to inspire, motivate, and unify the people charged with trying to achieve its goals. Such inspiration "fortified activists to face police dogs, fire hoses, beatings, jail, and even death" (K. Miller, *Voice of Deliverance* 84). Given what he attempted to achieve, the literal poetry of King's dream serves as the ultimate defense of poetry.

Critical Framework

This study discusses King's ability to revitalize Hughes's poetry through several critical lenses. Because King and Hughes spoke with and wrote letters to each other, biographical information is critical to reconstructing this relationship. To make comparisons between their ideas as accessible as possible, the connections between these two men's words are discussed in terms of similarities between diction, theme, and structure. King's engagement with Hughes's poetry becomes most evident in the analysis of how King's textual revisions of addresses develop over the trajectory of his career. This applies to both his spoken words and the written texts of these speeches that he carefully prepared from 1956 to 1968. Because audience is so central to King's addresses, several of the rhetorical strategies he engages are of paramount importance. These strategies include wordplays that sound like mispronunciations, parallel constructions that mirror biblical poetry, and repetitions of epistrophe and anaphora that unveil the deep structures of his speeches. In his addresses, King also displayed intentional flourishes of his ability to mirror the poetic style and grammatical features of the poems he was re-creating. The cultural and political contexts of King's words reveal why King simultaneously exalted and submerged Hughes's words within his own voice. This subversiveness can be seen most clearly in the metaphors King embeds within his dreams of a new world.

A Brief Biographical Overview

Although their lives as public figures overlapped for twelve years, from 1956 to 1967, personal meetings between King and Hughes were limited. Combined with living lives in two very different professions, Hughes's subversive reputation forced both men to avoid such intersections. The red-baiting of the early 1950s had damaged Hughes's reputation to the point that their visible presence together would have brought serious threats and lasting accusations of subversiveness to King. This can be understood through one simple fact: no photograph of the two men together was ever taken. Thus, their contact was both limited and clandestine as they fought similar battles on different fronts. Unlike the younger King, the early 1960s found Hughes devoting his energies to writing rather than marching. While the chapters that follow detail the links between these two iconic figures in African American history, a brief biographical overview creates a useful frame for understanding their relationship.

Along with the rest of the world, Langston Hughes became aware of Martin Luther King in 1956. Hughes published a long article in the *Chicago Defender* on King in June 1956 ("Simple Produces a Film") and then followed two months later with a poem that directly addressed King's role in the Montgomery Bus Boycott. King had begun reciting, alluding to, and rewriting some of Hughes's poems in May of that year. Based on their correspondence, it is clear that the two met in person sometime before December 1959. In January 1960 they exchanged personal letters, and Hughes sent an unpublished poem specifically requested by King as well as two additional unsolicited poems. In November 1960 they discreetly joined a number of other prominent African Americans on a trip to Nigeria.

Around this time, Hughes's reputation became of great concern to King. In fact, from early 1960 through the end of 1965, King was careful to remove all overt references to Hughes and his poems from his speeches. Publicly distancing himself and the SCLC from people and organizations that could be labeled as subversive, King had no direct contact with Hughes until King invited Hughes to join him for the march from Selma to Montgomery in 1965. For various reasons, Hughes declined the invitation. With the FBI's wiretaps removed and the immediate effects of the red scare past, King challenged America's involvement in the Vietnam War, and Hughes's poetry suddenly resurfaced in King's speeches, making numerous overt appearances in 1967. King received one of the last letters ever written by Hughes immediately before the poet's death in May 1967. Less than a year later, King was assassinated.

Chapter Previews

The chapters in this book trace King's varying engagements with Hughes's poetry. Chapter 1 charts King's use of Hughes's poem "Mother to Son" to show how changes in the political climate over the course of his lifetime required King to shift between overt references and covert allusions to Hughes's poetry. Chapter 2 establishes the cultural and historical climate that forced each man to be careful about his personal and professional associations. Hughes's poem "Brotherly Love" and King's larger engagement with poetry are examined in chapter 3, as the poems he quotes and the others he receives unsolicited through the mail establish the cultural context for how poetry was written and received in this era. Chapter 4 connects King's first sermon on dreams to the cultural phenomenon of the play *A Raisin in the*

Sun, where Hughes's poem "Dream Deferred" becomes a source of inspiration for both the playwright and the preacher. King's request for and receipt of a poem written by Hughes is the subject of chapter 5. Chapter 6 reveals how King rewrote lines from Hughes's poem "Youth" and documents the origins of King's ability to visualize integration through his ability to rewrite Hughes's poetry. Chapter 7 documents King's use of Hughes's poem "I Dream a World" as a verbal echo in his first enunciation of the beloved community. Chapter 8 traces how King's first documented use of the phrase "I have a dream" emerged from his rewriting of Hughes's "I Dream a World." Chapter 9's explication of the dream King presented in Detroit in June 1963 offers insight into King's fully matured poetic sensibilities. In light of the new insights offered throughout this study, chapter 10 offers different possibilities for rereading King's most famous speech. The conclusion investigates King's "Beyond Vietnam" address in 1967 as well as how Hughes responded to the civil rights movement in a play inspired by one of King's most famous addresses. What we all remember most about King's speech is its metaphor of the dream. It was poetry, not prophecy, that made this moment memorable.

Because the dream metaphor has become a touchstone for all King stood for, tracing its origins to the poems of Langston Hughes is especially significant. Scholarship has already established that, in its final enunciations, King's dream sought equal access to the American dream, and that the power of this inevitability could only be measured against the visions recorded in Old Testament prophecy. Here, for the first time, we can see that the dream's signature refrain and its deep structure originated in Hughes's poetry. The chapters that follow locate the origins of the dream as a means to chart the development of King's poetic sensibilities.

1

"Mother to Son"

The Rise, Removal, and Return of Hughes

While the degree to which Martin Luther King used Langston Hughes's poetry has long been the subject of speculation, a speech King prepared for an address on June 27, 1956, serves as one of the many moments when King invoked Hughes's poetry. Writing by hand on paper torn from a yellow legal pad, King composed a twenty-one-page draft of his remarks. He planned to share these remarks in San Francisco before the forty-seventh annual NAACP convention, where he was expected to speak about the current state of the Montgomery Bus Boycott. King built toward the conclusion of a speech he titled "The Montgomery Story" by extending a metaphor from Philippians 3.13–14: "straining toward what is ahead, I press on toward the goal to win the prize for which God has called me heavenward in Christ Jesus." King's four uses of the phrase "we must press on" in this speech allude to this passage. King braided this phrase together with a well-known metaphor of Walter White, one of the NAACP's past champions, as he wrote about a football player moving the ball toward the goal line. He concluded his written remarks as follows:

> This is our profound challenge and lasting responsibility. We must continue to move on in the face of every obstacle. This is expressed quite meaningfully in Langston Hughes's memorable poem "Mother to Son":
>
> Well, son, I'll tell you:
> Life for me ain't been no crystal stair.
> It's had tacks in it, and splinters,

And boards torn up,
And places with no carpet on the floor—
Bare.
But all the time
I'se been a climbin' on,
And reachin' landings,
And turnin' corners,
And sometimes goin' in the dark
Where there ain't been no light.
So, boy, don't you stop now.
Don't you sit down on the steps.
'Cause you finds it's kinder hard.
Don't you fall back—
For I'se still goin' boy
I'm still climbin'
And life for me ain't been no crystal stair.

Well, life for none of us has been a crystal stair. But we must keep moving. If you can't fly, run; if you can't run, walk; if you can't walk, crawl, but by all means keep moving![1]

Having successfully linked the passage from Philippians, the metaphor from Walter White, and the poetry of Hughes, King then had the speech typed, word for word, and packed it with him as he flew to San Francisco. When it came time to speak, King extemporaneously riffed on many sections of his prepared text. At the end, he omitted the quotation of Hughes's poem and closed with his own version of Hughes's theme: "Let us keep moving on. . . . Let nothing stop us, let us keep moving, let no obstacle stand in our way" (Carson 3: 309). Two weeks later, King's typed version of this speech, featuring Hughes's complete poem at the end, was published in *U.S. News and World Report*. King's extemporaneous comments were only heard by the thousand or so listeners at the convention. King had learned a valuable lesson: under the pressure of the spotlight, he could easily substitute his own words in place of Hughes's poetry. It was a practice he would continue for the rest of his life.

King had quoted "Mother to Son" for the first time the previous month in his May 13, 1956, Mother's Day sermon at Dexter Avenue Baptist Church in Montgomery.[2] In this sermon, King highlighted the "practical problems" mothers face in raising their children (Carson 3: 264). As means of encouragement, King delivered Hughes's poem at the end of his sermon that Sunday as he "recited [it] with a rhapsodic lilt to his voice" (3: 267). In the years that followed, the phrase "keep moving" became King's means of echoing Hughes's poem "Mother to Son."

It is hard to exaggerate the effect this poem had when it was recited by King from memory. In 1960, Clarence Jones's life was changed by King's recitation of this poem during a sermon. As he helped King and others prepare for the March on Washington, Jones enjoyed a moment of deep reflection:

> As I moved through the train station, I thought of that Sunday in February 1960 in the Baldwin Hills Baptist Church outside of Los Angeles. I thought of Martin's sermon, the one that changed my life. Because when Martin Luther King, Jr. preached about you personally, that is a life-changing event. He didn't mention me by name, of course, but he used bits of my past he had picked up in our conversation at my home two nights earlier—my parents' struggle as poor domestics, my legal abilities put to work chasing after recording royalties instead of justice, my lack of compassion for my downtrodden brothers—and read me the riot act. With his arsenal of powerful words, Dr. King poignantly painted a picture of my mother scrubbing floors and hoping for better things for her son while he recited Langston Hughes' "Mother to Son." I sat in the pew with tears streaming down my face. As he quoted from memory, "Life for me ain't been no crystal stair," I felt like I had been pierced in the heart with an arrow. Was I the son my mother deserved? And from that point on, I was a Martin Luther King, Jr. disciple. I joined him in Alabama. I gleefully helped Judge Delany and his superb team of defense lawyers destroy the obviously trumped-up tax evasion charge. I had gone from the willfully blind comfort of my living room in Southern California to the sticky air of the District of Columbia's Union Station and the March on Washington in only three short years. I couldn't help picturing my mother again, smiling at me this time and saying, "Clarence, you've come a long way, baby!" (qtd. in Jones and Connelly 43–44)

Jones's decision to become a disciple turns King into Christ and elevates Hughes's poem to the status of gospel. This powerful combination of

Hughes's words and King's rhetorical prowess would have similar effects on many of King's listeners who were called to march, protest, and engage other equally important roles in the fight for civil rights. When put to use by King, Hughes's poem was far more than a point of connection for listeners; it became a mantra to "keep going" as this mother figure motivated ordinary citizens to accomplish extraordinary things throughout America. King's various engagements with Hughes's poetry are critical to understanding how and why so many of King's listeners were able to walk, march, protest, and organize on behalf of civil rights.

King consistently allotted "Mother to Son" a significant place in his public speeches and sermons from 1956 to 1967. This fact has been overlooked. In fact, a clear allusion to this poem even appears in King's "I Have a Dream" speech delivered on August 28, 1963. As figure 3 shows, this use began in 1956, disappeared in early 1960, and then reemerged as a staple of King's speeches in 1967. This chapter traces the long trajectory of Hughes's "Mother to Son" within King's speeches from 1956 to 1967. In doing so, it also charts how political tensions persuaded King to alternate between referencing Hughes's poem overtly and submerging his words quietly through allusion—shifts that resulted from accusations of Communist influence against both Hughes and King. This chapter reveals how challenging it was for Hughes's poetry to become a measurable inflection in King's voice.

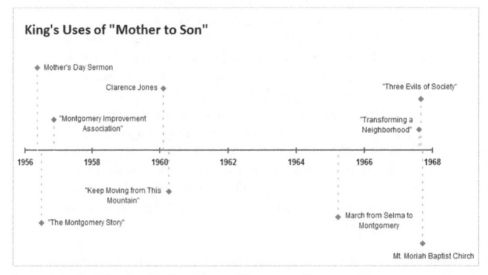

Figure 3. A timeline of King's uses of Hughes's poem "Mother to Son" in his speeches.

Mother Figure

As R. Baxter Miller has shown, Hughes's maternal grandmother, Mary Langston, was the inspiration for the mother Hughes portrayed in this poem. She is "Madam as much as Madonna," and given the long line of female figures in poetic history, her literary success ends "the myth of the transcendent woman" who serves as either muse or image of incomparable love (66–67). In fact, she becomes "the figure of American possibility" (59). This mother would appear over and over again to inspire real people to adopt her attitude as they prepared to engage racism with vigor and endurance. Or, as in Clarence Jones's case, it offered conviction to young men who wanted to make their mothers' efforts worthwhile.

King had at least three motivations to invoke "Mother to Son" for the first time on Mother's Day of 1956. First, Martin and Coretta's first child, Yolanda, was born a mere six months earlier, making this the first Mother's Day that Coretta had enjoyed. Second, "Mother to Son" was one of Coretta's favorite poems and one that she herself recited on multiple public occasions. Third, King was still leading the residents of Montgomery through what would become an eleven-month boycott of the city's segregated buses. Rosa Parks's famous refusal to give up her seat and her subsequent arrest had elevated King to a leadership role as the head of the boycott. Parks was regarded as a mother figure by King (Brinkley 143). In addition to Parks, the seventy-year-old "Mother Pollard," a revered member of King's congregation, had also joined the boycott. When asked if walking across town rather than riding the bus did not leave her tired, she responded, "My feets is tired but my soul is rested" (Washington 227).

Gender was at the very center of the boycott. Because of their need to travel across town to the white neighborhoods in which they worked, "Montgomery's working class women . . . made the greatest sacrifices during the yearlong protest" (Wilson 309). With JoAnn Robinson of the Women's Political Council first calling for the boycott, E. D. Nixon challenging the male ministers of the community to finally stand up and do something for the exploited black women of the community, and the continuous abuses from bus drivers aimed most consistently at black female riders, women had been the inspirational center of the entire movement (Wilson 302–10). Many of these factors contribute to understanding King's invocations of Hughes's poem. The degree to which these invocations slowly shaped individual response and communal memory is revealing.

As the voice of the boycott, King seemingly spoke for all of black Montgomery. Just as King began using Hughes's poem, he also became particularly fond of citing Sister Pollard's response. Over time, these coalesced in the reactions from community members. It was commonly remembered that "if a day laborer's feet got so tired that he thought of riding the bus, all he had to do was mutter, 'Rosa Parks,' and the temptation was gone" (Brinkley 142–43). Over time, Parks's and Pollard's stories came together in King's retelling of events so that Hughes's "Mother," Parks, and Pollard became indistinguishable. When King referred to Pollard in his "Letter from a Birmingham Jail" (1963) and his speech on the steps of the Alabama capitol in 1965, he spoke of her "ungrammatical profundity." Listening closely, we can hear how King subtly began conflating Pollard, Parks, and Hughes's "Mother." Speaking not of Pollard but of Hughes's "Mother to Son" on a later occasion, King said, "Her grammar wasn't quite right but she uttered words of great symbolic profundity."[3] The coalescence of these three figures eventually became apparent to Parks herself, who later explained: "It is funny to me how people came to believe that the reason I did not move from my seat was that my feet were tired. . . . My feet were not tired" (Parks and Reed 25). What accounts for this? Because King mixed these symbols in so many of his addresses, the residents of Birmingham and even those beyond Alabama had slowly begun to conflate Parks with comments by Sister Pollard and the repeated exhortations from the speaker in Hughes's "Mother to Son."[4]

When King struck upon Hughes's poem, he could not have selected a more appropriate image of inspiration, as Parks and Pollard came to represent all the unknown mothers in the community who had been most affected by the boycott. Just as in the poem, women were leading the way by modeling how the men should follow. Although the reality was present from the first day of the boycott on December 5, 1955, it took King until Mother's Day to give new validity to Hughes's old poem. It was not the trope of the Madonna figure who led poets through armed passages and into dark bowers that served to galvanize the significant contributions of Montgomery's heroic women; rather, it was the everyday realism of the type of women Hughes himself had long ago realized had unforgettable inspirational powers. With gender at the center of the original issue, King's invocation of Hughes's poem was the perfect source of inspiration.

In his prepared remarks for the June 27, 1956, NAACP convention, King both overtly referenced and intentionally riffed on Hughes's original poem.

In his own prepared rendition of "Mother to Son," King ended with slight but significant changes to Hughes's lines:

> Don't you fall back
> For I'se still goin' boy (Carson 3: 310)

King altered the original text of Hughes's poem in significant ways. In the first line quoted above, Hughes's final word in his original poem is "now," not "back"; in the next line, Hughes's "honey" becomes King's "boy"; earlier in the passage, King turned Hughes's "So boy, don't you turn back" into "So, boy, don't you stop now" (Carson 3: 310). King is not being sloppy with Hughes's verse. Rather, even in his drafts, he is riffing on these lines of "Mother to Son" to emphasize his own points. These points of emphasis change from one context to another, and Hughes's words change as a means to reinforce the larger goals of King's sermons and speeches.

King used another memorable epistrophe, "Keep going," at the end of a pair of speeches delivered on November 14, 1956. Minutes earlier, at the Hutchinson Street Church, King had addressed the citizens of Montgomery about important events affecting their boycott; now he was delivering the same speech again at the Holt Street Baptist Church. Two important legal decisions had been handed down the day before. Locally, the city had temporarily ordered citizens to end their car pools; however, the U.S. Supreme Court had ruled that segregated busing was illegal. More than four thousand citizens congregated at each of the two official meetings in these churches to learn how soon they would be riding desegregated buses in Montgomery. King had the difficult task of simultaneously celebrating the Supreme Court ruling, letting listeners know the car-pool ban must be obeyed, and informing them to wait to ride the buses until the Supreme Court's decision had been fully put into effect in Montgomery. He ended both of these speeches with lines from "Mother to Son." After overtly paraphrasing the whole poem, King drove home his point: "Well, life for none of us has been a crystal stair, but we've got to keep going. We'll keep going through the sunshine and the rain. Some days will be dark and dreary, but we will keep going. Prodigious hilltops of opposition will rise before us, but we will keep going. Mountains of evil will stand in our path, but we will keep going" (Carson 3: 433).

The variations between the June and November speeches are noteworthy. In particular, June's "keep moving" becomes "keep going" in November. The immediate context of these events, that is, the immediate need to continue the boycott, directly informs this change in diction. The mother in Hughes's poem who testifies to her son that "I'se still goin'" is turned by King into the imperative command to "keep going" with the boycott as it is spoken by the fatherly preacher to God's children. Hughes's original word "dark" is linked with King's addition of "dreary," and King extends Hughes's metaphors to include the daily hindrances of "rain" and the spiritual and cultural obstacles suggested by "hilltops" and "mountains," which are not mentioned in Hughes's poem.

King's choices worked. The citizens kept going by foot until December 20, 1956, when King informed them they could begin riding city buses the next day. When King delivered his brief celebratory remarks that day, he first spoke of "tired feet." Soon after, he alluded to Hughes's "Mother to Son" as he declared that they had "kept going" (Carson 3: 486). Hughes's poem was a critical component of King's rhetoric throughout the Montgomery Bus Boycott. The success of this boycott both introduced and immediately solidified King as a national leader on the issue of civil rights.

As the years passed and his leadership role grew, King successfully masked connections to "Mother to Son" during the highly charged political climate of the early 1960s. His phrasing continued to vary slightly from speech to speech, but the overt references to Hughes himself were reduced to key phrases. Eventually, King dropped Hughes's name but kept the words of his poem's inspirational mother as he varied his imperatives among "don't fall back," "cannot turn back," "keep going," and "keep moving." For example, on September 2, 1957, King told his audience at Highlander Folk School in Tennessee: "We must not slow up. Let us keep moving" (Honey 17). Speaking in Albany, Georgia, on December 16, 1961, at the very start of his involvement in the heated voter-rights drive, King proclaimed to a mass meeting at Shiloh Baptist Church: "Don't stop now. Keep moving" (Lewis 148). From 1960 to 1965, persistent accusations of Communist influence followed King. He had to drop Hughes's name from his speeches because of this political climate. In order to avoid this connection during this time, King would simply activate the skills he demonstrated in San Francisco.

King's Subversive Strategy

King's relationship with Hughes's poetry reveals how accusations of Communist influence affected King's rhetoric. Despite these tensions, King continued to invoke ideas from "Mother to Son" in his speeches between 1960 and 1965. On November 13, 1960, King preached on "The Dimensions of a

Complete Life" in the Sage Chapel at Cornell University. Because this was an academic setting, he referenced the names of painters Raphael and Michelangelo, luminaries like Saint Augustine and Plato, and writers such as John Keats, John Donne, Thomas Carlyle, Shakespeare, William Cullen Bryant, and James Russell Lowell. But he did not mention Langston Hughes. More telling is that King used the phrase "this is the faith that can keep us going" immediately after naming Carlyle, Bryant, and Lowell.[5] The text reads as if King would have quoted "Mother to Son" if he only could. Near its customary place at the end of his sermon, Hughes's idea was heard while its controversial author remained invisible.

As King continued masking Hughes, his words resulted in even wider variations. King riffed on old ideas in new ways, always being sure to refrain from mentioning Hughes by name. On November 1, 1961, King spoke in Savannah, Georgia. Referencing his early work in Montgomery, he exhorted his listeners with a single statement: "So, don't give up, but keep going." Later, he employed much of this same strategy: "Now, if you keep on following that. . . . And if we keep on moving at the rate that we are moving now, it will take 94 more years to get there. I submit that we don't have that long. I submit at this hour that we must get on the move now."[6] Such language did not just activate Hughes's poem; as an allusion, it simultaneously revived the declarations sung in the spirituals known by many of King's listeners. These songs extended King's reach as he redeemed Hughes's metaphor. In this way, Hughes's poem may have continued to appeal to King because it brought together common themes in the African American freedom struggle. King's subversive strategy continued right on into the "I Have a Dream" speech on August 28, 1963. The changes that King made to Hughes's poem in these speeches do not indicate carelessness on King's part; rather, they demonstrate a larger and more significant approach he took as he rewrote the lines of others.

Voice Merging/Submerging

Rather than discussing the relationship between King's speech and his sources through the lens of allusion or even plagiarism, Keith Miller has developed and applied the concept of *voice merging* to analyze some of these relationships. According to Miller, "a black Baptist clergyman creates a self as his identity converges with those of others." By quoting anything from song lyrics to preachers from the near or distant past, "ministers create their own identities not through original language but through identifying themselves with a hallowed tradition" ("Voice Merging" 24). For Miller, King's speeches don't allude to other's texts or steal from them; rather, King's words fuse with these sources. I extend Miller's ideas in this discussion to the reading of King's invocations of Hughes's poetry.

If voice merging allows such ministers to identify with this tradition in the pulpit during Sunday sermons, what happens when that minister faces a political gathering and speaks before an integrated audience that includes members who might revile one of these sources? The speaker either submits to this constraint or finds a way to creatively resist. King's ability to continue to use Hughes's poetry is an act of subversion. King's references to Hughes's poetry are simultaneously intended to invoke and to mask. The added tension surrounding such sources results in what can be termed an act of *submerging*. *Submerging* occurs when a speaker simultaneously invokes a source *and* seeks to make that source invisible to a particular audience. It is a subversive extension of voice merging bound in a political context.

For the speaker, such submerging is a rhetorical and symbolic act of defiance. It is no small thing to speak truth to power through a voice that power has tried to silence. When these powers fail to see this irony, they are duped. The suppressed voice speaks against their wishes. If members of the audience who identify with the voice that's being suppressed recognize this act of defiance, resisting the oppressor's unjust systems of verbal and political control is seen as a testimony that models and thus encourages their own desire to protest. When such acts of subversion are finally recognized by the members in power, submerging holds the potential to embarrass and undress the levels of power the oppressor thought it had the capacity to successfully enforce. King's use of Hughes's poem "Mother to Son" exemplifies the practice of submerging at work.

"I Have a Dream"

The most recognizable enunciation of King's "I Have a Dream" speech was delivered on August 28, 1963, in Washington, D.C., before a crowd estimated at 250,000 or more. Many of King's allusions in this speech are difficult to connect to their original source. In other instances, they are easily recognizable. For example, King does not mention Lincoln's name, but only the man who "signed the Emancipation Proclamation," that "great American, in whose symbolic shadow we stand today" (Washington 217). King used the space of the National Mall and its proximity to the Lincoln Memorial to signal listeners to think of Lincoln.

It is important to recognize that King was very liberal in his use of literary sources during this speech. Shakespeare's opening lines from the first act of *Richard III*, "Now is the winter of our discontent / Made glorious summer by this son of York," merge with King's own rhetoric to become so bent and twisted that they become nearly unrecognizable. King says, "This sweltering summer of the Negro's legitimate discontent will not pass until there is an invigorating autumn of freedom and equality" (Washington 218). Shakespeare's "winter" morphs into King's "summer"; "summer" becomes "autumn"; what the "son of York" brings by way of his entrance is extended to be equaled by the appearance of "freedom and equality." In short, King transposes, extends, blurs, and so recasts original sources in this speech that those sources become almost unrecognizable. This absorption and reinvention fulfills the speech's desire to model integration and at the same time makes pinpointing the traces of Hughes's poem so difficult.

The process by which King prepared his remarks for this event reveals a great deal about Hughes's cultural status in 1963. This status is one reason why Hughes's poetry is especially hard to unpack from King's speech. While writing the final version of his speech, King had the unique burden of trying to "meet the expectations on the part of multiple audiences" (Patton 114). Despite this burden, King's speech submerges Hughes's "Mother to Son" in each of its drafts as well as the publically delivered speech. In the second draft, originally titled "Normalcy—Never Again," King ended the sixth paragraph with the transition "We cannot walk alone." He then began his seventh paragraph, "And, as we walk, we must make the pledge that we shall always march ahead. We cannot turn back."[7] Though not naming Hughes, King returned to the language in "Mother to Son" where Hughes wrote: "So boy, don't you turn back" (14). The placement of this idea is significant. This paragraph introduces the speech's main idea, the idea of "normalcy," for the first time. This sequence also survives into the third draft, though it is moved one paragraph closer to the end of the text.[8]

King was playing a high-stakes game when he invoked even the most subtle inflections of Hughes's poetry. He negotiated this danger by submerging Hughes's ideas so deep that power itself could not hear them. The speech King delivered on August 28, 1963, offers a clear and direct trace of Hughes's "Mother to Son." King submerges Hughes within his own voice with only one slight variation from the previous two drafts. Within the context of walking, he omitted the word "always" to say: "We cannot walk alone. As we walk, we must make the pledge that we shall march ahead. We cannot turn back" (Washington 218). As he did with the Shakespeare allusion, King alters Hughes's climb upward into a march forward. Just as Hughes's "mother" led her son by example, King extends the community to include everyone. The preacher is now imploring his children as if he were their father. No longer bound by any racial dimension, King's "we" replaces Hughes's "I" to highlight his theme of integration. King committed to using this in his speech from first draft to final delivery. Even on this large stage, and after countless reflections on his speech, this muted riff on Hughes's poetry passed unnoticed.

It appears that King may have inadvertently returned to the exact language used by Hughes. King had become so use to his own phrase "stop now" that he must have thought this was the original fourteenth line of Hughes's poem. As such, he tries to vary his text so as not to give Hughes or his source away. However, in this process he actually uses the exact language used by Hughes in his poem: "turn back."

Within the long trajectory of King's use of this poem, this example of King blurring his voice with Hughes's finally resonates with meaning. King's use of "Mother to Son" was unknown to nearly everyone in his immediate audience. Only those such as Clarence Jones, who had heard King speak repeatedly over the course of the previous several years, might have heard this echo of Hughes's poetry.

Caught in this cultural context as he prepared for his most important public performance, King again relied on his creative ability to submerge this idea during this key moment to simultaneously invoke and distance himself from Hughes's poetry. King's ability to submerge Hughes's metaphor displays the depths of his subversive imagination. King risked embracing Hughes in the most significant speech of the entire civil rights movement. It worked. Neither Hoover, nor his surveillance teams, nor anyone else could decode this covert rhetorical strategy. In fact, it may have been Hughes's vulnerable political image combined with King's penchant for giving new validity to old forms that motivated King to include this remnant from Hughes's poem.

The fact that King deliberately submerged Hughes's poem within his speeches between 1960 and 1965 can be seen most clearly by the fact that the poem reemerges so overtly in the years after 1965. There seems to be a specific reason why Hughes reemerges by name in March 1965.

President Johnson, March 15, 1965: "We Shall Overcome"

In late March 1965, Hughes suddenly reappeared as an amplified voice within King's campaign for civil rights. What had changed to allow King to align himself with Hughes? Significant changes had occurred earlier in 1965. Hoover was no longer manipulating the now assassinated President Kennedy. Most importantly, Lyndon Johnson was now president, and he formally linked the institution of the presidency with King and the civil rights cause when on March 15, 1965, he delivered the speech of his life on national television. With this address, King saw immediately that Hoover's smear tactics had fallen flat. Now the originators of such propaganda were reduced to throwing sand at a man wearing armor.

Johnson's speech was a specific response to the murder of Jimmie Lee Jackson in Selma, Alabama. The president assured his audience that "it is not just Negroes, but really it's all of us, who must overcome the crippling legacy of bigotry and injustice. And—we—shall—overcome."[9] Johnson's rhetoric unequivocally linked the goals of dominant culture with the civil rights cause. The rhetoric King himself had inherited had now fully merged with dominant culture. In the wake of this speech, suddenly many things had changed. Johnson, who was opposed to wiretapping, put through an order to Hoover to cease all such existing modes of surveillance (Branch, *Canaan's Edge* 186–88). In the wake of surviving accusations of King's Communist influence, Stanley Levison himself recommenced communication with King via a letter in late March 1965. This is why it again became safe to use Hughes's poem publicly a mere ten days after Johnson's speech. It is difficult to ignore the fact that overt references to Hughes's poetry appear in King's speeches both immediately before and after the accusation of Communist influence was used against the civil rights leader. Hughes's name reemerged as soon as it was safe for King to mention Hughes in his speeches.

Johnson's speech was a turning point. Six days before the president's speech, King was still submerging Hughes's "Mother to Son": "We have no alternative but to keep moving with determination. We have gone too far to turn back now, and in a real sense we are moving and we cannot afford to stop because Alabama and because our nation has a date with destiny. We must let them know that nothing will stop us."[10] King understood his prerogative to bend, riff, and rewrite ideas based on context. While the imperative he most commonly took from Hughes's poem was "keep going," on this day he declares to his listeners that they should not "turn back." Here, "turn back" is linked with a declaration that "nothing will stop us." This context reveals something extraordinary: because of the literal and physical context of the Montgomery Bus Boycott, King consistently encouraged citizens to "keep going." They literally had to keep walking to boycott segregated buses. Here, the day before "Turnaround Tuesday," King extends this idea because these protesters have set their benchmark for Tuesday's march as the act of defiantly crossing the Edmund Pettus Bridge to pray on the opposite side. King triumphantly declares that they will not have been stopped from reaching their goal so long as they are not literally "turned back" before crossing to the other side of the bridge. In this way, line fourteen of "Mother to Son" became a source of inspiration that King invoked and altered to fit each historical moment he encountered.

Six days after King spoke these words of defiance, there was no longer any need to reference Hughes so elusively. Immediately after Johnson's speech on March 15, King confided to Clarence Jones: "In his address to the joint session of Congress last night, President Johnson made one of the most eloquent, unequivocal, and passionate pleas for human rights ever made by a President of the United States. . . . His power of persuasion has been nowhere more forcefully set forth. We are happy to know that our struggle in Selma has brought the whole issue of the right to vote to the attention of the nation. . . . [W]e have the support of a President in calling for immediate relief of the problem of the oppressed and disinherited people of our nation."[11] King was literally moved to tears as he listened to this speech.

Although King had had no direct communication with Hughes since January 1960, he felt so assured that the toxic atmosphere had changed because of Johnson's speech that he personally invited Hughes to participate in the upcoming march from Selma to Montgomery. (Not coincidentally, the last entry in Hughes's official FBI file dates from 1965 as well.) In a March 18, 1965, telegram to Hughes, King wrote: "The President and Judiciary have spoken affirmatively of the cause for which we struggle. I therefore invite you to join me in a march to Alabama's capitol beginning at Brown's chapel in Selma, Sunday, March 21, at 1:00 pm."[12] King knew that this era of red-baiting could no longer harm him or the Southern Christian Leadership Conference. One of the first people he thought of in this new era was Langston Hughes.[13]

Rather than submerge Hughes's poetic ideas, the program on the eve of March 25, 1965, once again included Hughes's poem in its entirety. After a five-day march from Selma to Montgomery, Coretta Scott King read "Mother to Son" to the crowd after having taken the stage at the request of Harry Belafonte (Wofford 196).[14] On that night, Martin Luther King joined various performers at "the athletic field at the St. Jude center, a forty-acre Catholic complex" located less than three miles from the state capitol where "ten thousand citizens of Montgomery and early arrivals for the final march" had gathered (Lewis 289). For Harris Wofford, this was one of the most memorable events from a night that featured such stars as Leonard Bernstein, Sammy Davis Jr., Nina Simone, James Baldwin, Anthony Perkins, Odetta, Pete Seeger, and Dick Gregory.[15] "Mother to Son" reveals both the intensification and later the waning of anti-Communist propaganda against King. Bearing in mind that Hughes and King had to maintain this distance in their relationship between 1960 and 1965, these two men might have become even closer if not for the powerful effects of Cold War politics.

The Reappearance of "Mother to Son"

Another tantalizing gap exists in the correspondence between Hughes and King. On May 12, 1967, Hughes was preparing for an operation that would relieve his symptoms of what appeared to be prostate cancer. Now sixty-five, he hurried to "set his affairs in order . . . he gave Raoul Abdul [his secretary] a long list of tasks, including banking transactions" (Rampersad 2: 422). At this time, Hughes sent King a letter. Although we have no record of this letter in either of the two men's papers, we do have a postcard reply dated May 17 that acknowledges receipt of Hughes's letter: "Your letter came during Dr. King's absence from the city. He is scheduled to return to the Atlanta office in about ten days, at which time your correspondence will be brought to his attention for reply."[16] What did Hughes say? Why is the letter missing from King's files? On May 22, Hughes died from complications after his surgery.

After Hughes's death, and with the period of red-baiting coming to an end, King overtly returned to Hughes's "Mother to Son" on several occasions. In Atlanta on August 11, Hughes's poem was once again the final flourish of King's speech. King honored Hughes as best he could by quoting him in his speeches. Whereas Hughes was once submerged while King rattled off quotes from writers Thomas Carlyle, William Cullen Bryant, and James Russell Lowell, Hughes was once again the final crescendo: "Let us keep moving. Let us keep climbing and let us not allow anything to stop us as we move toward the goal of peace and the goal of brotherhood. A great noble black bard who left us a few days ago, but who will go down in history for his eloquent pen, Langston Hughes, has a mother to utter some words to her son." King then recited "Mother to Son." His penchant for riffing well ingrained, King made line fourteen his own by saying "don't you stop now" rather than using Hughes's original "don't turn back." Then he ended this speech as he had so many others before: "Well life for none of us has been a crystal stair but we must keep moving. If you can't fly—run. If you can't run, walk. If you can't walk—crawl. But by all means keep moving."[17]

Ten days later, at the Palmer House in Chicago, King ended his speech "The Three Evils of Society" virtually the same way. About three weeks later, on September 18, he used the same ending again in Atlanta. In both speeches, King used the phrase "stop now" instead of Hughes's original "turn back."[18] The poem was also included in its entirety in King's book *Where Do We Go from Here: Chaos or Community?* In this book, published in June 1967, the line was presented accurately as Hughes's original "turn back." King's renewed willingness to include the poem in this era serves as a remarkable bookend, as King's first major publication in 1956 in *U.S. News and World Report* also quoted Hughes's poem in its entirety. Eventually, the imperative to "keep moving" became so linked with King that it was used in a newspaper description of the way King's mule-drawn carriage carried his casket on the day of his funeral: "Every now and then, the wheels groaned in protest and the mules laid back their ears. But the cart—bearing Dr. King's body in a polished mahogany coffin—kept moving" (Gale).

As further evidence of the impact and longevity of red-baiting, the establishment of a national holiday honoring King was undermined as late as 1979 when a congressman proclaimed that if Congress passed such a measure to recognize King, then the American flag flying above the Capitol might just as well be replaced with a red one. Even when the measure passed four years later, Senator Jesse Helms passed out documents that chronicled King's supposed Communist ties (Hansen 215). Such accusations still held a measure of power in the minds of some legislators in the early 1980s. But much earlier, when the tensions were much higher, King eluded such accusations by submerging Hughes's poetry within his addresses. For twelve years, King had outwitted and outplayed his adversaries.

King's ever-changing and elusive incorporation of "Mother to Son" reminds us that Hughes's poetry included powerful metaphors capable of inspiring listeners. King's first uses of the poem captured the reality of the working women most affected by the Montgomery Bus Boycott. Its absence and then sharp return to King's repertoire highlight the distance King and Hughes maintained throughout the first half of the 1960s. But King's use of Hughes's "Mother to Son" incites three further questions: What had Hughes and King done to earn their subversive reputations? How did King incorporate other poets' writings in his public addresses? What other traces of Hughes's poetry can be found in King's rhetoric?

2

Black *and* Red

Accusations of Subversiveness

In addition to celebrating the everyday folk of African American culture, Langston Hughes embraced a socialist ideology that is impossible to miss in his poems. A significant part of this ideology was reinforced by the lack of racism he witnessed firsthand during his extended time in Russia during 1932 and 1933. Also, the fact that Hughes was on "friendly terms with known Hispanic American Communists—notably the Cuban Nicolás Guillén, whose poems he would translate in the late 1940s, but also the Chilean poet Pablo Neruda and the Argentine Raúl González Tuñón—no doubt made him a politically appealing figure for many members of the Hispanic Americas' intellectual elite" (Kutzinski 69). His connection with international socialism allows Hughes to still be regarded as "the most important 'Negro Poet' of the twentieth century in many parts of the Hispanic world, including Spain" (Kutzinski 57).

Even earlier, Hughes's leftist politics were motivated by the fact that the American Communist Party had defended the Scottsboro Boys in 1931. While "Scottsboro made Communism a household word in African-American clubs, beauty shops, and churches" in Harlem, Hughes was far from alone in his leftist attitudes. In fact, "during the second half of the 1930s . . . over two thousand black Harlemites spent time as party members" (Naison 279). However, while Hughes's attitudes were solidified during this era, they were not born here. From the beginning of his career he submitted poems to the most liberal magazines and journals. This attraction to the left resulted in several poems that earned him the label "Communist." While in the USSR in 1932, Hughes wrote and published the poem "Good Morning, Revolution," which imagines a world where the "tools of production" (line 42) will no longer be in the hands of bosses and capitalists. Instead, the revolution will "turn 'em over to the people who work / Rule and run 'em for us people who work" (lines 45–46). Hughes ends the poem by urging the revolution to start the process as soon as possible.

In a poem that can be read as less anti-capitalist and more anti-religious, "Goodbye Christ," Hughes suggests that Judeo-Christianity has been exhausted as a means for building and sustaining businesses that hide under the mask of religion. The poem asserts that religious leaders of the world have made all the money they can off Christ and the Bible. The poem imagines that once this profiteering has been exhausted, a new economy will replace it, one in which evangelists, churches, and even newsprint agencies will have to "Make way for a new guy with no religion at all—/ A real guy named / Marx Communist Lenin Peasant Stalin Worker Me" (lines 20–22).

Curiously, one of Hughes's most alarming statements against capitalism received no attention whatsoever from reactionary groups, the government, talk-show hosts, magazines, or the FBI. First published in 1934, "Revolution" collapses the distance between Communist revolution and the uniquely American practice of lynching. It isn't surprising that Hughes would find a way to turn the tables on America, as he wrote nearly three dozen poems during his lifetime decrying its lynching culture (W. Miller, *Langston Hughes* 1). In the poem, the mob is not out to hang, burn, and torture a lynch victim but rather out to slaughter a capitalist "pig" that has been strung up and ready to have his "golden throat" slit from "ear to ear" (lines 13–14). But Hughes makes it clear this has all the overtones of a lynching as he asks the fearless mob to "tear him limb from limb" (line 12).

Hughes makes his desire for America clear in "One More 'S' in the U.S.A.," which calls for a socialist revolution within the continental United States. Believing that then and only then would the farmers and factory workers truly have control, the poem asserts that "The U.S.A. when we take control / Will be the U.S.S.A. then" (lines 7–8). Regarding this takeover as one that would unite American citizens through the common bonds of poverty and exploitation rather than divide them through race, Hughes argues that "Black and white can all be red" (line 31).

When pressed, Hughes asserted that his radical period dated mainly to the decade of the 1930s; however, the literary record suggests otherwise. As late as 1946 he published "Lenin," a poem that clearly empathizes with Communist ideals. According to David Roessel, "Hughes really did want to play his part with the Left.... [F]or as long as he could, he did try to write poems in the accepted revolutionary and proletarian manner" (188–89).

Hughes approved the reading of his poems at official Communist Party rallies. Along with other black cultural ambassadors, he headlined a "thirteen-city tour" for the International Workers Order in the 1930s (Dawson 193). His poetry was read and sung at the ninth-anniversary celebration of the *Daily Worker* on New Year's Eve in 1933. The Communist-affiliated paper secured Hughes's mother, Carrie Langston, to read one of his poems about lynching and then featured this poem sung, with musical accompaniment, by Soviet singer Sergei Radamsky ("Langston Hughes's Mother" 2).[1]

Hughes's leftist record can be traced to political writings that extended into the realm of journalism as well as poetry. Understanding the connection between satirical humor and activism better than many of his contemporaries, Hughes wrote articles that were published in the *Daily Worker* throughout the 1930s. One of these, "The Negro," praises the political cartoons of Jacob Burck, who contributed to the *Daily Worker* on a regular basis and won a Pulitzer Prize in 1941 for his cartoon "If I Should Die before I Wake."

"The Negro" demonstrates how easily Hughes could invoke Marxist rhetoric to undercut capitalist values and beliefs. After listing a series of illegal arrests, reciting excessively high bonds for union members, and then listing repeated reminders about the vigilante retribution being exacted by revivals of the Ku Klux Klan, Hughes repeatedly denounces the acts of unprosecuted lynchings that are occurring "Almost weekly" (141). His focus on lynching highlights one of the Communist Party's focal points during the 1930s. Hughes's language is ripe with metaphors of class warfare. While citing two socialist martyrs, he alludes to Lincoln's Gettysburg Address by stating that Ralph Graves "did not die in vain" and declaring that Tom Mooney "does not lie in jail in vain" (141).

Hughes saves his most powerful visual imagery and seething anger to reverse the tables on American lynching culture. Using the language of Marxism, he gives his audience this unforgettable sentence: "Burck's powerful drawings, with their crooked judges peering out from behind the pillars of justice and their fat sheriffs carrying the ropes of the lynchers they whitewash, portray the America of today with a laughter that chokes the proletarian throat and makes the blood run to fists that must be increasingly, militantly clinched to fight the brazen terror that spreads and grows from Alabama to the Pacific, from New York to Texas" ("The Negro" 141). Hughes suggests that Burck's cartoons, which capture a country that allows such lynchings to go unpunished, are helping to galvanize a bloody resistance that is growing quickly from coast to coast. He envisions this as merely a part of an inevitable revolution as he closes: "the black and white masses slowly but surely will put their two strengths together, realizing they face a common foe" (141). This foe, capitalism, is so commonly understood by readers that it goes unnamed by Hughes. Hughes's writings earned him a reputation as a Communist subversive in the mid-1930s. Roessel writes that "Hughes was aesthetically more supportive of the communists than not for most of the 1930s. It is also noteworthy that in both the published and unpublished versions of his reasons for not joining the Communist Party, he makes no objection on political grounds" (Roessel 189).

To create a critical frame for the rest of the intersections I investigate between Hughes and King, I will use this chapter to address how Hughes earned his subversive reputation and document how King had to deal with accusations of Communist influence during his time as a public figure. This context is essential to understanding the choices these men made in their interactions with each other. Most significantly, understanding Hughes's reputation reveals why King had to be so careful in redeeming the ideas he encountered in Hughes's poetry. Important mileposts mentioned here will serve as key reference points for the close readings that follow in the chapters ahead. I address Hughes's reputation first before moving on to consider how King faced his own accusations of subversiveness.

Hughes and the FBI

In 1944 the FBI increased its surveillance of Hughes, which had begun as early as 1940 after an appearance by Hughes in Los Angeles was picketed and subsequently canceled. Most of the FBI's evidence and the questions asked of Hughes when he later testified before Congress in 1953 centered around two publicity flyers.[2] Aimee Semple McPherson, the leading evangelist of the Foursquare Church, used her uncommon popularity and media expertise to prepare leaflets condemning Hughes as a Communist and distributed them before Hughes's appearance at the Vista Del Arroyo Hotel on November 15, 1940. Her key evidence was Hughes's 1932 poem "Goodbye Christ," in which McPherson's name appears on a list of people whom Hughes sarcastically labels "saints." McPherson's choice of poem and anger were personal on both fronts. She reprinted the poem in its entirety after stating that Hughes was a "member of the American Section of Moscow's 'International Union of Revolutionary Writers.'" Because he was scheduled to speak during a luncheon, McPherson suggested that the poem was so repulsive that guests should "eat, if you can." This flyer is noteworthy because it appeared in the December 12, 1941, edition of the *Saturday Evening Post* and became the first entry in Hughes's official FBI file. Although Theodore Graebner had named Hughes a "Communist Poet" in his testimony before the House Un-American Activities Committee in December 1938, it was the publication of Hughes's poem in the *Post* that first brought Hughes to the attention of the FBI.[3]

In 1943, FBI surveillance noted that tickets were sold at the "Communist Party headquarters on West Boardman Street for an appearance in Youngstown, Ohio," by Hughes. The poet was observed so closely that a filed report indicated which local Communists he had been invited to speak with after the reading. It noted that his previous commitments kept him with six other "intellectuals" (all identified by name) until 1:00 a.m.[4] J. Edgar Hoover himself began reviewing Hughes's file, and a thirteen-page report was entered in Hughes's official FBI file on October 4, 1944. At this time, agents made calls to Hughes's friends trying to document his movements and verify his residence.[5] G-men from the New York divisions collected handwriting samples.[6] When Hughes traveled to visit Noel Sullivan in Carmel, California, people in the area were questioned.[7]

Although Hughes's name was removed from the bureau's "Key Figure List" on November 26, 1945, a second round of circulars garnered Hughes even more intense scrutiny. This new period of interest began when Hoover received two handbills from Minnesota senator Joseph H. Ball in May 1947. Produced and circulated by Detroit's Gerald K. Smith, a white supremacist, minister, and political organizer, the handbills featured a large photograph of Hughes, the poem "Goodbye Christ," and an image of the southern United States that presumably mapped how the Communist Party had envisioned a separate "Negro state." Remarkably detailed, this new state extended north to Virginia, south to Florida, and west to Texas.[8]

Though armed only with citizen accusations, Hoover placed Hughes squarely in his crosshairs. Hughes was in the terrible position of being both black *and* red. Because he was red, he was an object of suspicion, and because he was black, he was vulnerable. Hoover was invited to speak at a November 1947 conference of Methodist ministers in Evanston, Illinois (Rampersad 2: 140). Hoover's speech, "Secularism—A Breeder of Crime," made use of

Smith's handbills by directly naming and quoting from "Goodbye Christ." Because Hoover could not attend the conference to deliver his speech in person, Louis B. Nichols read it on his behalf.[9]

Two days after the conference in Evanston, the New York–based *Journal-American*'s front-page story identified Hughes as a Communist Party member (Rampersad 2: 140). With an article titled "Leftist Poet Opens Education Parley," it appears that Hoover had intentionally opened a campaign against Hughes in the wake of Hughes's appearance on Thanksgiving Day in Chicago before the American Education Fellowship. Ever since Hughes had begun to write for the *Chicago Defender*, the Chicago branch of the FBI had followed him closely. Hoover seems to have sensed a chance to discredit Hughes and progressive educators simultaneously by speaking on the heels of this engagement and by using the Chicago branch's influence to flood key media outlets. Two weeks later, Henry J. Taylor used his radio show *Your Land and Mine* to demonize Hughes.

A close analysis of Taylor's broadcast reveals how Hughes's name became sullied. Taylor began with these words: "I'm going to read you a brutal, blasphemous poem over the air tonight." He said he was responding to the "infiltration of communist doctrine into our schools and colleges." Taylor denounced the recent meeting of the American Education Fellowship. In fact, this event was the focus of Taylor's show. After first berating Dr. Harold Rugg of Columbia University for his textbooks, which "have now been thrown out of over 1,400 schools," Taylor turned his attention to Rose Russell, leader of the New York teachers union, claiming that it was a Communist organization.[10]

Several inaccuracies regarding Hughes can be found in the FBI file and Taylor's commentary. As the FBI had listed Hughes four inches taller than he was, and invented both a wife (June Croll) and son he never had, so too, Taylor and his staff could not even spell Hughes's name correctly in its transcripts, repeatedly referring to him as "Langsdon." Mirroring the FBI's own files, Taylor identifies Hughes as a contributor to *New Masses* and the *Daily Worker*. Taylor then introduces the menace he yearns to expose: "Oh, my friends, please listen to this poem. Certainly no long, hazy, theoretical arguments that you and I might present against communism or its morals could possibly be so revealing, so convincing to anybody and everybody in our country, as this poem itself. It says more in a few words than a dozen books could say to reveal communism in the raw."

Taylor then quotes the first five lines of "Goodbye Christ," thinking that these lines constituted the entire thirty-seven-line poem. He then emphatically adds, "No, my friends, your ears didn't deceive you. Let me read those words again." His ire raised, he implores listeners to "Get a copy of this poem. Write the radio station to which you are listening. . . . Help expose the communist cult in the raw. Give this poem to the editor of your local newspaper. Distribute copies of the poem yourself. Put this poem in the hands of any misguided, innocent man or woman, boy or girl, school leader or student, who is confused, uncertain about the real nature of the communist ideology in Your Land and Mine."

Taylor and Hoover did not merely label Hughes a Communist; they used him as an exemplar, the very embodiment of communism in America. With a coordinated campaign between Hoover, the FBI, and radio outlets, Hughes was nearly helpless to combat such forces. His name was tainted red nearly everywhere he or his poems went, and the force of such a coordinated campaign would soon achieve its desired effects.

Abingdon Cokesbury Press

Publication and copyright issues were at the heart of the conflict between Hughes and Hoover. Aimee McPherson's and Gerald Smith's unauthorized circulars, most notably the ad in the *Saturday Evening Post* featuring "Goodbye Christ," violated copyright law, as they published the poem without Hughes's permission. Hughes vented his frustration over these copyright violations on several occasions. Unauthorized circulation of the poem led to cancellations of his public readings, financial losses on the lecture circuit, and permanent damage to his public persona. Hughes responded to the one outlet that obeyed copyright laws during this period. When Abingdon Cokesbury Press requested permission to reprint "Goodbye Christ," Hughes answered in May 1948, "I do *not grant permission.*" He continued: "The Gerald K. Smith forces, the Klan, and other anti-Negro groups have, in recent years, usually on unsigned mimeographic sheets and entirely without permission distributed this poem."[11]

As a result, Hughes's poem was pulled from publication in the forthcoming volume *The Christian Faith and Secularism*. The volume was to include Hoover's well-circulated speech "Secularism—A Breeder of Crime," which featured Hughes's poem to dramatize Hoover's claims. Louis Nichols was irate. Nichols, who had delivered Hoover's speech in Evanston to coincide with Hughes's appearance in nearby Chicago, fired off a scathing response to the publishers. In his first letter, he threatened to pull Hoover's entire speech from the volume if the matter wasn't resolved to his liking.[12]

After receiving from the press a lengthy explanation of how copyright and permission laws work in America, Nichols responded in a second letter: "The handling of Mr. Hoover's lecture exceeds anything I have ever heard of and if ever a public official was insulted it was Mr. Hoover by the action which was taken by you people in questioning a statement in his speech and then communicating with a character like Langston Hughes with a view of securing permission for Mr. Hoover to quote his poem." Frustrated that the volume was already in press, he explains to "you people" with self-incriminating language: "the thing that infuriates me is the thought that . . . you would communicate with an individual like Langston Hughes without at least giving Mr. Hoover the courtesy of saying whether he would agree to having his lecture edited in this manner. Were it not too late I would urge the Director most vigorously to withdraw the lecture." In regards to Hughes, Nichols explains, "I cannot stomach his mouthings. While we are on the subject, it likewise seems to me the Methodist Church has no right to be giving a forum to officials of the Communist Party to spread their hateful lies and deceitful propaganda when they are anti-Christ, anti-god, anti-church, and anti-religion." Nichols concluded by stating that this whole business would discredit the editors.[13] Hughes was unaware of the exchange. Worse, he had no idea that he had insulted the FBI by defending his intellectual property.

While Nichols's stance, anger, and sense that Hoover and the FBI were exempt from obeying copyright laws are disturbing, even more disturbing in this exchange is the fact that this timeline of events points to collusion between the FBI and the press in attacking Hughes. Nichols responded to the first letter about this issue on June 16, 1948. Less than three weeks later, on July 4, *Reader's Digest* ran part of the transcript from Henry Taylor's latest broadcast concerning Hughes. Since that broadcast had originally aired on March 8, this was hardly timely. However, Nichols's second letter to Abingdon, dated July 9, suggests how close either he or his agency was to the publicity in *Reader's Digest*. Nichols writes: "I am enclosing a photo static copy of page 124 of the July issue of *Reader's Digest* which you may have missed. It quotes a few lines from Hughes's poem and I am informed by one of the Senior Editors of *Reader's Digest* that they did not get permission to quote his poem in *Reader's Digest*."[14]

Why would Nichols be communicating directly with a senior editor of

Reader's Digest? It is even more revealing that the article itself comes from Taylor's broadcast, as he timed his broadcast of December 1947 to coincide with both Hoover's and Hughes's Illinois speeches. It seems Nichols spoke with the senior editor of *Reader's Digest* before its publication of Hughes's poem. Perhaps he even coaxed him to publish Hughes's poem. This would explain the timing as well as Nichols's fury. Why would a small Methodist press refuse to do what *Reader's Digest* would? It also helps to explain how the FBI acted out of vengeance. It appears that Nichols might have gotten Hughes's poem published with much larger fanfare and readership in *Reader's Digest* than if Hughes or Abingdon would have simply allowed it to be in Hoover's published speech.

Although the evidence in the FBI file draws our attention to Nichols, it is clear that an equal if not greater anger was felt by Hoover himself. Given his power, it is not hard to imagine the lengths he might go to exact revenge or the real or false premises he might create if needed. One comment from Hoover reveals how he saw his enemies as well as his preparations for a future battle. He writes to Nichols after this event: "Make certain we furnish this outfit no more material for publication. They are too squeamish about offending the commies."[15] Because he believed that Hughes was a "commie," Hoover placed no restraints on investigating his activities.

It does not seem coincidental that the FBI's most intense period of investigation on Hughes followed these events. What is so unsettling is that circumstances surrounding Hughes intensified not because of actual evidence, admissions, or legitimate national-security threats, but merely out of personal revenge. Less than two weeks after Nichols's response to Abingdon, Hoover himself reviewed Hughes's file in detail. In a rather lengthy letter, he then ordered that the bureau seek out J. B. Matthews to try, for the first time in its investigative history, to find out if Hughes ever ran on the "Communist Party Ticket."[16] Matthews, a disillusioned former Communist organizer, was being paid as a government consultant to offer insight into Communist activities and to identify past and present members. Throughout the remainder of 1948, Matthews is found unreliable by Hoover's foot soldiers, but Hoover prods them to question him anyway. By December 3, an agent comes close to something more convincing than even he might realize. A source reports that Hughes did not run for office because "HUGHES was more valuable to the party interests in his capacity as a writer and lecturer."[17]

This rings truer than any other statement in Hughes's FBI file. Four days later, Hoover asks the agent for a full report. A six-page report reveals that Hughes had unknowingly been contacted by the FBI on his private and unlisted phone line in New York under the pretext of seeing if he was available to give a reading.[18] Countless hours of surveillance and taxpayer money were exhausted until another call followed in July 1949 while Hughes was in Chicago.

An agent even visited Hughes at his home on Halloween of 1950. It's hard to measure how shaken or angry Hughes may have felt during the interview that followed. Unknotting the strings in this eleven-page report reveals that the agent, "T-1," knew that Hughes had just published *Simple Speaks His Mind*.[19] With a title that must have caught their attention, and the character's title (Simple) that is reminiscent of Aimee McPherson's middle name, Hughes's book had reached bookstore shelves in April 1950. With his character of Jess B. Simple ("just be simple"), Hughes's works had literally continued to perpetuate "the illusion of simplicity—a slight of hand that hides the depth of complex uses of language, psychology, sociology, and history" (Harper, *Simple* 1).

Despite such red-baiting, the book sold more than thirty thousand copies. What makes this feat all the more remarkable is the mystery surrounding it. When the book was on the verge of becoming a certified best-seller, a Simon and Schuster internal memo noted: "Curious errors in delivery plagued the sale. . . . [T]ime and time again, copies were imperfect, failed to arrive on time, 'or at all'; in fact, the page proofs had disappeared after leaving the printer. By November, the problem had become so serious that a 'terribly disturbed' [Maria] Leiper insisted that all orders for *Simple Speaks His Mind* be delivered to her desk to be personally handled by the head of the shipping department. The mystery, and the question of sabotage, was never resolved" (Rampersad 2: 179). The first suspects for interview in this case would have been members of the FBI. With the issue of publication itself the clear battleground on which to attack Hughes, the motive is clear. The relationship between Hughes and Hoover points less and less to hysteria or paranoia and more toward personal vendetta. If this is true, the only evidence that remains is textual. It appears something important may be concealed under five redacted lines of an FBI report filed at this time. Perhaps disappointed that Hughes's book wasn't more overtly subversive, the bureau appears to have engaged in a multilayered campaign to keep American citizens from having to stomach Hughes's art. This campaign soon intensified on a more public front.

McCarthyism

Hughes testified publicly in Washington, D.C., before a Senate subcommittee on March 26, 1953. After his public appearance, the entire nation knew that the U.S. government feared that Langston Hughes was a Communist. Subpoenaed just five days before he was called to testify, Hughes was understandably concerned and nervous. His testimony was broadcast on both radio and television. For many, he was guilty by appearance. Knowing what we now know about the collusion between the FBI and the media, it is not surprising that the questions the committee asked were based exclusively on letters and evidence collected by the FBI from the fliers produced by McPherson and Smith. In an executive session two days earlier, attorney and chief counsel Roy Cohn peppered Hughes with questions about the poems in the FBI files and demanded that Hughes answer in plain language, once and for all, if he was ever a member of the Communist Party. Hughes denied party membership, just as he had on the radio and in print throughout his career.

Despite acquitting himself well, Hughes was shaken by the experience and feared what it might mean to his career and reputation. Three days after his appearance, Hughes wrote to his legal counsel, Frank Reeves: "No words—and certainly no money (even if it were a million dollars) could in any sense express to you my gratitude or from me repay you for what you have done for me in a time of emergency. Without your able help . . . I would have been . . . a dead duck among the cherry blossoms." Promising full payment for all services, including phone calls from Reeves's residence, Hughes included a check as partial thanks for now as he declared again: "There is no way for me to repay you."[20]

Hughes contacted Reeves again on April 8. In this letter, he reveals how little he has understood the FBI's activities prior to his testimony. Hughes says that he has decided not to contact the FBI himself and that "since the FBI has interviewed me on two or three occasions concerning folks who work for me or given my name in reference in applying for government jobs (which they got), if the FBI wish to interview me, they would come send for me." Accepting the FBI's pretext for its personal interviews with him, Hughes is still unaware that the bureau's main focus was actually on him and not these candidates for employment. Further indicating how poorly Hughes understood the intensity of Hoover's campaign against him, he writes that "Cohn told us Hoover once used 'Goodbye Christ' in a speech."[21] As we have seen, this poem had been the occasion of anger and embarrassment and the motivation for future retribution.[22] Hence Hughes was unaware of how the FBI's varied tactics had spawned the media slander against him.

A Review for *Stride toward Freedom*

In this era, the country was divided along lines that separated many things, including politics and culture. While Hughes was considered a political radical, he was also a cultural icon, particularly in the African American community. Hughes was simultaneously prestigious and subversive in 1958. One way this can be expressed is through a vignette of what happened when King sought reviewers for his book about the Montgomery Bus Boycott. King sat down to list the top five people he would most like to see review *Stride toward Freedom* and listed the first five who came to mind. The list seems to take into account several factors: those who had a personal interest in civil rights issues, influential outlets to publicly announce their endorsement of the book, and those King personally admired or read himself. In the following order, these five individuals were contacted owing to their "interest in solving the moral and social crisis that confronts us":

Chester Bowles—Washington Post
E. Roosevelt—Louisville Courier Journal
Lag. Hughes—
George Meany
Harry Emerson Fosdick—[23]

It is certainly no small matter to be placed third on a list that includes former First Lady Eleanor Roosevelt; George Meaney, the current president of the AFL-CIO; Chester Bowles, a noted author and politician who would eventually serve in John F. Kennedy's cabinet; and Harry Emerson Fosdick, one of the nation's most revered preachers. This was the company Hughes kept in King's mind. Eventually, a form letter was drawn up (likely by Stanley Levison), and King also sent requests for formal reviews to Benjamin Mays, Ralph Bunche, Norman Cousins of the *Saturday Review*, Ralph McGill at the *Atlanta Constitution*, Rev. John Lafarge, and Harry Golden. Hughes was considered a more desirable option than Bunche, winner of the Nobel Peace Prize in 1950.

What happened next provides further confirmation of Hughes's public status as a subversive. Bayard Rustin, another member of King's inner circle who worked closely with Levison in New York, wrote a three-page memo in

July 1958 in which he, too, suggested potential reviewers. Hughes tops his list. After Hughes, he mentions Eleanor Roosevelt of the *Louisville Courier-Journal*, Fanny Hurst of the *Birmingham News*, and Lillian Smith of the *Los Angeles Times*.[24] By mid-November, about a month after its release, about 38,500 copies had been sold.[25] However, when King later forwarded reviews he had received to demonstrate how well the book had been received, Hughes's review was nowhere to be found. What happened with King's and Rustin's desire to have Hughes review *Stride toward Freedom*?

A November 28 letter from Hughes's secretary, Raoul Abdul, suggests that someone involved in the publisher's promotion of the book felt that linking Hughes's name with the book would do more harm than good. Hughes's secretary responded directly to King: "I remember that Mr. Hughes wrote the publishing company and told them how much he enjoyed the book."[26] Because this letter simply confirms that Hughes received a new, autographed copy of *Stride toward Freedom* sent directly from King, it is clear that Hughes had already read a review copy delivered earlier from the press. Moreover, Hughes wrote a formal review and passed it on to the publisher.[27] With Hughes high on King's list of potential reviewers, Rustin suggesting him as the first man he would pick to review the book, and Hughes having written a positive review and then sending it in a timely manner to the publisher, only one conclusion remains: the publishers did not want Hughes's name associated with the book for fear that his Communist reputation and leftist sympathies would hinder the sale and promotion of the book.

This vignette illustrates the contrasting prestige of Langston Hughes. He was revered by public figures such as Rustin and King, yet he was off-limits to the dominant establishment. Hughes occupied "contradictory positions *at the same time*" (Kutzinski 178). It is worth noting that the editors at Henry Holt were fired in 1952 when word got back to Texas ownership that they had allowed Hughes to publish at their press (Rampersad 2: 230). It is also possible that that information had become well known inside the publishing community and carefully weighed by those at Harper's several years later. Most publishers with knowledge of Hughes's reputation at this time would have steered clear of associating themselves with his politics. They would not have wanted to lose their jobs or have FBI agents potentially snooping through proof sheets and affecting sales.

Hughes was still being loudly accused of being a Communist throughout the early 1960s. The *New York Times* and *New York Post* ran articles on September 27, 1960, claiming that Hughes had dined with Cuba's Fidel Castro during Castro's visit to Harlem. As a result, Hughes was forced to answer over "two dozen" phone calls the next day from stunned friends (Rampersad 2: 323). Less than ten days later, *Time* magazine said that the "Left-Wing Poet" had just visited with Castro as well (2: 323). Who had informed them of this imagined lunch? Although both of these prestigious media outlets soon corrected their stories, the damage had been done. The climate even affected Hughes's role as editor as he revised the anthology *New Negro Poets*. Hughes was directed by the publisher to exclude poems that might appear too radical or angry (2: 323). Nothing had changed by September 1963, when a Chicago production of one of his plays fell victim to "an anti-communist smear campaign" and a television station in Nashville refused to air an outdated interview of Hughes, stating that touting Hughes as a "celebrity" would be nothing less than "an affront to decency" (2: 368).

An April 1965 appearance in Kansas was marked by Hughes's receipt of telegrams from several ministers calling him a Communist, and in Oakland, California, lawsuits were promised if Hughes's *Pictorial History of the Negro* was not taken off the shelves of school libraries (Rampersad 2: 387). The desire to paint Hughes red in 1953 shaped much of the public perception of the poet for the next twelve years. Hughes's reputation was so negative during this time that Jonathan Kozol, a high school English teacher in Boston's public school system, was fired for teaching one of Hughes's poems to his students.

Although the red scare eventually ended, its effects continued to define Hughes's political reputation. In 2001, the highly influential author and blogger Andrew Sullivan responded angrily when President George W. Bush mentioned Hughes's name in a speech given to celebrate Black History Month. In 2004, the title of one of Hughes's poems, "Let America Be America Again," was used as the slogan of John Kerry's presidential campaign. Kerry received the same criticism as George W. Bush. Referencing "Let America Be America Again," this political commentary describes Hughes as follows: "After bashing America silly, the poet says he will still strive to make this nation a nicer place. By nicer place, he meant a Communist place."[28] In 2011, Republican presidential hopeful Rick Santorum initially chose "Fighting to Make America America Again" as his campaign slogan. Once the attacks began to link the slogan with Hughes, Santorum dropped the slogan and distanced himself from it.[29]

Mirroring the fallout that resulted when Hughes refused to allow "Goodbye Christ" to be included in Hoover's published speech, the intensity of Communist accusations rose against King when he publically embarrassed the FBI's hierarchy. As historian David Garrow notes in *The FBI and Martin Luther King, Jr.*, on November 18, 1962, King answered reporters' questions about how FBI agents had been conducting their work in Albany, Georgia. King suggested that these agents were white southerners who had developed and maintained close friendships with the local police. In short, he stated that their personal desire to prolong segregation informed their actions and reports. The next day, headlines in the *New York Times* and *Atlanta Constitution* read: "Dr. King Says F.B.I. in Albany, Ga., Favors Segregationists." By the end of the week, two calls from FBI representatives to King's office had gone unreturned. Although it was common for King to be remiss about returning calls, the FBI took this as a rebuke. "Little did King know that his comments about the Albany agents, and his supposed slights . . . would affect the events of the next three years" (Garrow, *FBI* 56). More than twenty years later, William C. Sullivan, who had played a central role in the FBI's investigation and harassment of King, wrote that "Hoover greatly resented King's criticism of the FBI and never forgave him for it" (qtd. in Garrow, *FBI* 82).[30] In each case, vindictiveness, not evidence, initiated the FBI's accusations of Communist sympathies against both Hughes and King.

To be sure, King leaned further to the left than is often acknowledged. More than ten years before such accusations of subversion came his way, King made it clear on numerous occasions that he had found American capitalism wanting from both a personal and a philosophical standpoint. While King was at Crozer Theological Seminary in the early 1950s, one of his professors noted that King was "becoming increasingly hostile towards capitalism. . . . [King] believed that Marx had analyzed the economic side of capitalism right" (Honey 43). When writing about his own religious development, King said that seeing people stand in bread lines during the Depression had an effect on his "present anti-capitalist feelings" (Carson 1: 359). King's rejection of the status quo can be seen clearly in notes he made for himself during one of the classes he was taking at this time: "I am convinced that capitalism has seen its best days in America, and not only in America, but in the entire world. . . . It has failed to meet the needs of the masses." He noted that the rise of labor would bring its own "president to the White House" and that this "will be the end of capitalism" (Carson 1: 436). His future wife, Coretta, noted that nothing had changed in the years after she met him at Boston University: "I remember him talking about his concern for the masses. He talked about the unequal distribution of wealth before asserting that 'I don't believe in capitalism as it is practiced in the United States'" (Honey 45–46).

By May 1958, King understood that he needed to choose his words carefully. In response to King's drafts for *Stride toward Freedom*, editor Melvin Arnold informed King of the need to "see that not even a single sentence can be lifted out of context and quoted against the book and the author" (Carson 4: 404). Arnold had learned this lesson the hard way during his days as head of Beacon Press, where he had helped anti-McCarthy books get into print.[31] Arnold suggested six careful revisions to King's statements regarding communism. Fearful that one King sentence could be "distorted" to read that only his "*initial* response to communism was negative," one of these revisions became "my response to communism was and is negative" (4: 404–5). King accepted all of Arnold's detailed revisions that included substituting "collectivism" with "social cooperation" (4: 405). These changes reveal two things. First, King was gaining an awareness of the danger of being labeled subversive. Second, making such revisions amid this climate reminds us that King appears to have been much more open to socialist ideology than we generally assume. If the original drafts here were more pro-Communist than the published text, how much of King's deepest influences and Marxist sympathies have been lost to us by way of self-reflexive editing done in the anticipation of political backlash? It is clear here that King is less anti-Communist than his final text would make it appear.

King: Communism and the Southern Christian Leadership Conference

By early 1960, King and his fellow leaders in the SCLC had to take steps to avoid accusations of Communist infiltration. Although this might seem surprising, given that this is the early 1960s rather than the height of the red scare of the mid-1950s, King's relationship with Bayard Rustin is highly revealing. Early in 1960, King advised Robert Moses behind closed doors "against any more demonstrations with the SCEF [Southern Conference Education Fund] people. Some people think it's communist, and that's what matters. We have to be careful" (Branch, *Parting* 328). Despite trying to laugh off the Communist allegations against some of the people he knew, King could not afford to ignore public perception. As a result, he was eventually forced to sever ties with Bayard Rustin, Jack O'Dell, and his longtime friend Stanley Levison.

King cut off contact with Rustin in March 1960. Rustin had served King in several capacities, including raising funds as executive director of the Committee to Defend Martin Luther King Jr. Rustin's association with King had two drawbacks. Rustin's role as the SCLC coordinator had been steadily resulting in "internal resistance" among those on the board who were "put off by Rustin's homosexuality and communist past" (Branch, *Parting* 329). As a result of this potent combination, Rustin's relationship with King had drawn a blackmail threat against King. Though the accusations were unfounded, the New York congressman from Harlem, Adam Clayton Powell, made it known that "if King did not call off his plans to picket the Democratic Convention in Los Angeles, Powell would tell the press that King was having a homosexual affair with Bayard Rustin" (Branch, *Parting* 314). The implication was that even when the accusation was disproved, King's working relationship with a former Communist like Rustin would be damaging enough.

Since 1957, Rustin had been of inestimable help to King. Rustin was intimately involved in every aspect of planning King's tour of India and Russia in the spring of 1959. In February 1958 he had drafted the letter King sent to the Reynolds Foundation to request funding for the trip, and he also acquired the applications for visas to travel to Russia.[32] Letters exchanged between King and one of the sponsors from December 1958, the American Friends Service Committee, mention Rustin no less than three times. Rustin is copied on every letter and is far more involved than King's own secretary. King's intention to see Russia was well known. Edith Lovejoy Pierce wrote to King on January 18, 1959, "I am delighted to see in 'Fellowship' that you are about to embark for India and the Soviet Union."[33] She enclosed a copy of her review of *Doctor Zhivago* and asked King to mail it to Boris Pasternak when he visited Moscow. A month earlier, L. D. Reddick's formal request for leave to Alabama State University president H. C. Trenholm argued, "Our friend Martin Luther King is being sponsored by the Quakers to India and the Baptists to Russia," and Reddick hoped "also to keep the record of the journey and . . . afterwards to write up the whole experience."[34] Reddick turned this opportunity into the first full-length biography on King.

Less than a month before King planned to leave for Russia, he signed a contract with the *Amsterdam News*. For a payment of $1,500, King agreed to write "ten (10) articles concerning my trip to India and the Soviet Union," promised not to submit any articles anywhere else, and confirmed that Reddick would not sell his articles to any outlet during the period of the trip.[35] So, with the well-traveled Rustin in control of the scheduling, King's own desire to see the country, and clear and repeated announcements that Russia was a destination on this journey, why did King cancel his visit to Russia in the spring of 1959?

At first, a very practical matter seemed to dampen the chances of seeing the Soviet Union. In December 1958, King's secretary wrote to the travel agency that the Kings' "Passports expire on February 12, 1959. We are not sure whether or not they should be renewed before leaving or just what action should be taken regarding them before leaving."[36] In the end, though, passport renewals were not what kept King from visiting the USSR. With Rustin and Levison working so closely with King that they even earned invitations to a formal lunch sponsored by the American Friends Service Committee in Philadelphia a mere week before the trip, the matter of public perception became insurmountable: a trip to Russia would make King look like a Communist sympathizer. It could be used against him for years to undermine his cause. By only going to India, the focus could be shifted to King's commitment to Gandhi's principles of nonviolence.

Instead of revealing any of this tension, King issued a formal statement filled with a very different explanation. Four days before he left for India, the *Los Angeles Tribune* reported:

> Dr. Martin Luther King, Jr. announced from here before leaving the country last week that he will not visit the Soviet Union following his visit to India as he had earlier announced. Dr. King said that although he has made excellent progress since he was stabbed, the state of his health and the urgency of the racial conflict in the South "indicated that the trip to the Soviet Union must be reluctantly postponed at this time."... Dr. King said that he had planned to spend several weeks consulting with Christian leaders in the Soviet Union following his stay in India. Money for the trip was donated last December by the American Baptist Convention in keeping with a resolution passed at the denomination's 1956 meeting calling for the establishment of Christian Fellowship across National boundaries as a step towards understanding and peace.[37]

This rationale distracts attention from the political implications of visiting a Communist country during the Cold War, when taking a glance behind the

Iron Curtain could be seen as an affront to American patriotism. With red-baiting as intense as ever, King's announcement anticipated these threats and hid behind an obscure and outdated initiative established more than three years earlier at a Baptist convention. There was no better way for King to protect himself from accusations of subversion than to appear to be kneeling in prayer.

The Communist Label

Even after King canceled the trip to the Soviet Union, accusations that he was a Communist sympathizer continued to mount against him. On October 5, 1961, Dr. Billy James Hargis published a brochure titled "Unmasking the Deceiver: Martin Luther King, Jr." The brochure was reprinted from an article that appeared in the Christian Crusade's *The Weekly Crusader*. Its eight pages documented many of King's alleged Communist associations and subversive activities. The brochure aimed for large-scale exposure, as five hundred copies could be purchased for ten dollars. A copy of the brochure came into King's hands after it was given to his father with this handwritten verdict: "Your son can't be much of a Christian with such a record as shown here—I doubt God's approval of such hypocrisy."[38] The brochure asked: "Why does this man, who has selected known Communists as his closest associates and advisers, have access to top offices in our government and personal audiences with our policy making leaders?" It summarized its position as follows: "It is time Martin Luther King was unmasked before the American public. Only a full-scale investigation will serve the best interests of both the Negroes and whites of our nation." Ironically, King wrote "file. Advise" across the top of the brochure and likely sought Levison's advice on how to handle such accusations.

In mid-December 1961, King found himself defending an answer he had given on a television show in Cleveland. During a taping of *Open Circuit*, King was asked if he thought black Americans would turn to communism or the Muslim movement if their freedoms continued to be ignored. As a result of suggesting that this would likely be the case if the situation was not solved in the "distant future," afterward he was compelled to compose a two-page press release in response to a newspaper article in the *Nashville Tennessean* that highlighted this stance. King's press release declared: "Suffice it to say that I can see no greater tragedy befalling the Negro than a turn to Communism or Black Nationalism as a way out of the present dilemma." Then, adding a sentence he would have opportunity to use in many similar instances in the future, the press release said: "It is my firm conviction that Communism is based on an ethical relativism, a metaphysical materialism, a crippling totalitarianism, and a denial of freedom which I could never accept."[39]

The Rose Garden

King's flight arrangements changed as he prepared to travel to Detroit on June 23, 1963. Instead of following his original itinerary, he found himself in Washington, D.C., the day before. President Kennedy invited King and 250 other religious leaders to the East Room (Branch, *Parting* 833). King was scheduled to speak with the president himself, but before he could, Attorney General Burke Marshall informed King and members of King's inner circle that the president was prepared to fully back the civil rights bill so long as no charges of communism could be made against it. Then Marshall told King that Levison was a "paid agent of the Soviet Communist apparatus" and that Levison himself had deliberately embedded Jack O'Dell within the SCLC (835). King was told to immediately drop all association and personal contact with Levison and O'Dell. When King asked for proof of such allegations to warrant the separation, Marshall brought in Robert Kennedy, who repeated J. Edgar Hoover's claim that the highest levels of U.S. intelligence had hard evidence to support these claims. After King casually dismissed these two men's directives to part ways with Levison and O'Dell, President Kennedy took King for a private walk through the Rose Garden. Placing his hand on King's shoulder, Kennedy whispered that King had to "get rid of" Levison and O'Dell because "they're Communists" (837). According to Kennedy, O'Dell was classified as the "number five Communist in the United States (833).

The requested dismissal of these two men brought the Communist allegations against King's camp to new heights. In March 1960, King's own people had urged him to let Rustin go. Releasing O'Dell and Levison would be difficult.

Jack O'Dell

Born in Detroit as Hunter Pitts O'Dell, Jack O'Dell had taken his father's first name to distance himself from his own Communist Party membership during the 1950s. O'Dell had first come to the SCLC after he worked with Bayard Rustin and A. Philip Randolph to organize the 1959 Youth March on Washington. Building off his assistance with voting campaigns to aid Kennedy's election in the Bronx in 1960, he had assumed a similar role within the SCLC by March 1960. Levison likely placed him in this role as a replacement for Rustin, who left that same month. By March 22, 1962, King had been specifically referring many requests to O'Dell, whom he listed as the acting director of voter registration. An October 26, 1962, article in the *New Orleans Times-Picayune* brought O'Dell's Communist past into the news. In January 1963, Joseph Alsop's editorial in the *New York Herald Tribune* named O'Dell as a known Communist working with King and the SCLC. This prompted King's team to respond regarding its relationship with O'Dell. As a result of these articles, on January 18, 1963, King asked for O'Dell's temporary resignation. He also asked O'Dell for formal statements regarding his stance on democracy and communism. Less than a week after King's meeting with Marshall and the Kennedys in the Rose Garden, O'Dell was officially let go. In a July 3, 1963, statement from King, it was inaccurately concluded that O'Dell did not have any known past or present associations with the Communist Party. However, the letter states—with implications that apply as much to Hughes's poetry as it does to O'Dell himself—that "any allusion to the left brings forth an emotional response which would seem to indicate that SCLC and the Southern Freedom Movement are Communist inspired. In these critical times we cannot afford to risk any such impressions."[40]

By July 25, 1963, King knew these threats were very real. That day, Bill Shipp of the *Atlanta Constitution* wrote an article spotlighting O'Dell's Communist past based on information he received from the FBI (Branch, *Parting* 857). King had to move quickly. Articles had appeared before, but reading about this in his hometown newspaper took on a different flavor. That same day he communicated with Marshall's office to reach what came to be known as "the treaty." President Kennedy would sign a secret order allowing Hoover to wiretap King if Hoover agreed to stop sending newspapers information that would allow them to paint King's organization as a Communist front (858).

Stanley Levison

It was more difficult for King to part with Levison. The request to dismiss Levison at this time was no small matter. Although Levison was a longtime friend of King's, "the treaty" motivated him to step aside and forgo all direct interaction and conversation with King of his own volition. This would free

Kennedy and King from having to endure public accusations of subversion (Branch, *Parting* 859). Levison stepped aside before King asked that they part ways. They decided it was not even safe to exchange letters.

A successful attorney, Levison (along with Rustin) had begun offering advice when they volunteered their services to King during the Montgomery Bus Boycott in 1956. His formal relationship with King began to solidify in 1957. On January 17, 1958, Levison came to King's aid when the preacher had come under scrutiny from the IRS, which claimed that King was receiving more money than he was reporting. Levison filed King's original tax forms that year and also made the arrangements for an extension later in March.

Levison's assistance went well beyond the realm of filing tax returns. His support for the civil rights movement included raising money for King and the organizations he represented. On June 3, 1958, Levison wrote that his organization In Friendship had raised $500 and was set to send along another $1,500 to the SCLC.[41] Eventually, Levison forwarded a donation for $3,450 he had gathered from the Roslyn, Long Island, Committee for Civil Rights.[42] The financial leadership he and Rustin provided the SCLC was even more important than the money Levison generated. By December 1958, Rustin and Levison were working together to develop a new financial model for the SCLC. Rather than merely marking letters "Read and file," King read Levison's letters carefully: "While on the subject of Funds, Bayard and I have been discussing the subject of the SCLC and Finances. . . . [T]he organization is now burning the furnace to keep the house warm."[43] Such ideas responded to directives that King gave these men, as Levison refers in this letter to conversations he had with King when the two met recently in Brooklyn. Often, when checks were written by Harry Belafonte, they were mailed by Levison.[44]

Levison became so trusted that he even provided King with signature cards for a bank account he had created in New York. Before King arrived, Levison told him that the bank he sought, Manufacturer's Trust Company, was located at Fifty-Seventh Street and Fifth Avenue.[45] Part secretary, part financial adviser, Levison soon became King's personal friend. A letter from February 28, 1958, indicates how close they had become: "I was in Atlanta yesterday for the Consultative Conference on desegregation and saw your dad. He took me home and your mother fed me chicken and home-made lemon pie which was presented as a favorite dish of yours. They were lovely hosts." Seeing each other so often left the two trading small condolences two years later, as Levison consoled King about another personal meeting by writing that "I was sorry you were ill while I was in Atlanta."[46] Levison played a vital role as he worked behind the scenes on nearly every aspect of King's life. The two men spent countless hours plotting strategy together. Many letters from Levison include statements such as "I expect to talk to you on the telephone, so I will not extend this letter."[47]

Although Levison became a lawyer, promoter, speech writer, and trusted consultant to King, one of his most enduring monikers is that of Communist sympathizer. During 1953 and 1954, Levison reportedly "directed some $50,000 a year into Communist Party coffers" (Garrow, *FBI* 41). He apparently "decided to reduce or perhaps terminate his involvement in the communist party's secret financial dealings" in November 1955 (Garrow, *FBI* 41). It was this recent past that likely kept Levison from wanting to be named in the acknowledgments for *Stride toward Freedom* three years later (Pearson 13). Levison brought his socialist philosophy to bear on what he said and did for King, and it would have been impossible for King to have been completely unaware of Levison's background. Levison himself became undeniably aware of the heightened interest in subversive activities in early 1960. On February 9, 1960, Levison was personally approached by the FBI about becoming a double agent (Garrow, *FBI* 42).

This cultural background is essential for understanding the constraints placed on King as he sought to invoke images and ideas from Langston Hughes's poetry. Hughes's last overt appearance in King's speeches between 1956 and 1960 was on April 10, 1960, only a month after Rustin's firing.[48] Because of continuous accusations and the removal of former Communists like Levison, a tension developed in King as he wavered between wanting to invoke Hughes's powerful metaphors and having to avoid his tainted public image. As a result, Hughes's name and direct quotations are completely absent in all contexts during the years he was most visible in the public's eye. Despite King's consistent engagements with poetry, Hughes's poetry had to be submerged between 1960 and 1965.

3

King and Poetry

Quotations, Revisions, and Unsolicited Poems

A handwritten draft of the first known copy of "Remaining Awake through a Great Revolution" captures how King prepared for a June 2, 1959, address at Morehouse College, his alma mater. He began writing in blue ink on unlined paper, then switched to a color he rarely used, green, and proceeded to write pages 17–27. When King came to the point in this address where he is about to quote lines of poetry, he did something strange. Just before he wrote "no man is an island," he wrote the name "John Donne" in large letters.[1] No other words on the page are as large or as elegant, as King reveals his respect for Donne by introducing the poet's name with unusual flourishes. In a visual effect that is lost when we read the typed version of the speech, King's own hand speaks to us about the prestige that certain figures held in his eyes.

King ends his address by quoting a poem by Douglas Malloch. King's handwritten version ends on two significant notes. First, King writes, "In the words of Douglas Malloch."[2] Without so much as spelling out a single word of Malloch's 1926 poem "Be the Best of Whatever You Are," King reminds himself to recite the lines from memory. Memorization of these lines reveals not only King's receptivity to the poem but also a deep investment of time and energy. By memorizing these lines, King is able to recite them at will. King's investment in memorization reminds us that the best performers always internalize their scripts. King ended his address with a nod to his first mentor, Benjamin Mays, from whom King first heard Malloch's lines and who, as college president, was likely in attendance that day.

Second, King adds an even greater flourish in his handwriting of this poet's name than he did to Donne's. The large initial "D" in "Douglas" is wrapped softly around the first stroke with a large half moon that then folds back on itself like the end of a ribboned bow. Moreover, the "M" in "Malloch" has a full three humps written in overly dramatic script. This letter is so large that the parallel "l"s command only half the size of the "M."

Further examination of this penmanship reveals that similar esteem is not bestowed on other authors. In this same draft, King writes Ralph Waldo Emerson's name simply. The "E" in "Emerson" is absolutely pedestrian. Even more telling, King writes a quote from Henry David Thoreau in the same green ink he used to write Donne's and Malloch's names: "How much of our modern life can be summarized in the shrewd diction of the poet thoreau, Improved means to an unimproved end." The lowercase "t" in "thoreau" is startling. King physically downgrades the lyrical prestige of Thoreau's ideas with his use of a lowercase "t."

Equally interesting is that King has taken Thoreau's words from a work of prose yet described him as "the poet Thoreau." King used this quotation as early as 1949 (Carson 6: 87). Thoreau wrote in *Walden*: "Our inventions are wont to be petty toys, which distract our attention from serious things. They are but improved means to an unimproved end, an end which is already too easy to arrive at; as railroads lead to Boston or New York" (58). Why has King called Thoreau a "poet"? One explanation is that King came to this quotation through a secondary source and did not realize the quote was from a work of prose. However, a more interesting possibility is that Thoreau's overall status is being downgraded to lowercase letters. Is King suggesting that Thoreau is a second-rate poet?

King's speeches are filled with poetry quotations. To understand King's engagement with Langston Hughes's poems, we first have to understand how King engaged with poetry in general. It is an intricate engagement that assumes many different forms. King often gleaned material for his own oratory directly from the sermons of other preachers. King did not merely incorporate ideas from other preachers in his sermons, though; what he often took from these other speakers were quotations of poetry. Most interesting, King rewrote small sections of these quoted poems in his own words. This execution was so subtle and deft that listeners often had no idea where the poet's ideas ended and King's own words began.

King compiled a large catalog of poetic quotations during his time at

Boston University. Moreover, the cultural climate during King's lifetime was rife with poetry. We will examine the poetry featured in a journal to which King contributed as well as representative samples from the dozens of unsolicited poems King received from around the world (including a few from one of King's earliest fans, Langston Hughes). The end of this chapter braids these ideas together by considering one of Hughes's poetic tributes to King, lines from which King incorporated into several of his public addresses.

While it is hard to know with certainty how much King was exposed to the world of poetry, several things are known. At the age of ten, he joined his siblings, mother, and grandmother to compose an eight-line poem commemorating the life of King's maternal grandfather, who had died eight years earlier. King's language skills were consistently impressive. During his years in high school, David Garrow notes, "If anything distinguished him from the others, it was his ability to use words" (*Bearing* 35). Perhaps most remarkable of all (and largely ignored) are King's formal scores in regard to his aptitude as a reader of literature. To prepare for his pursuit of a doctorate, King completed his GRE exam in March 1951. The breakdown of his scores is startling. In areas such as physics, chemistry, biology, social studies, and fine arts, King placed in the bottom 25 percent. He managed only a little better in philosophy, where his score put him in the bottom 33 percent. However, King's score in literature placed him in the top 25 percent, that is, nearly 50 percent higher than in nearly all the other areas (Carson 1: 407).

The poems King used in his speeches often surfaced years after he was introduced to them. For example, one evaluator summarized King's performance at Crozer Theological Seminary by writing that King was "fertile minded" and someone who "rarely misses anything he can subsequently use," as "All is grist that comes to his mill" (Carson 1: 354). This trait was observed when King was only twenty-one years old. Remembered for being especially attentive during the days that followed at Morehouse when Dr. Benjamin Mays spoke every Tuesday, King later rearranged one of Mays's poems and quoted it at the very end of one of his addresses more than ten years later: "a tiny little minute, just sixty seconds in it. I didn't choose it, I can't refuse it" (Honey 63). Over the years, King not only retained the poetry that came his way but also sought out poetry much more than has been acknowledged.

Index Cards

King owned Mark Twain's *Tom Sawyer*, Irving Stone's biography of Vincent van Gogh titled *Lust for Life*, Ralph Ellison's *Invisible Man*, and Jane Austen's *Pride and Prejudice*. Of poetry, he owned Paul Lawrence Dunbar's *Complete Poems*, Kahlil Gibran's *Tears and Laughter*, Milton's *Paradise Lost*, the *New Pocket Anthology of American Verse*, and Charles Reznikoff's *Testimony* (Carson 6: 629–55). King was given a copy of the 1955 edition of Bartlett's *Famous Quotations*, which he kept in his personal library.[3] King's penchant for collecting aphorisms and quotations is indicated by the large number of index cards he began amassing during his time at Boston University. Alongside the cards he assembled specifically for his dissertation, King amassed a large collection of indexed quotations. The process by which he worked and prepared reveals a man who saw the collection of other people's words as one of the primary acts of learning.[4] This process of seeking and collecting is key to understanding King's approach to literary sources. One of King's primary objectives in preparing to motivate and teach his congregation was to inform himself through the accumulation of a varied and extensive body of quotations he could invoke, alter, or appropriate as needed.

This vast file indicates how enamored King was with poetry. His largest section of biblical entries comes from Psalms. These 148 items reveal that King engaged much more deeply with the poetry of the Old Testament than with the letters of Paul. It is also noteworthy that King created entry after entry tracing a long list of British romantic poets. He made multiple entries on Wordsworth, noting that "Wordsworth felt among the great mountains the power of an unseen and eternal presence." King handwrites the words of Percy Shelley: "Poetry is not like reasoning, a power to be exerted according to the determination of the will. A man cannot say, 'I will compose poetry.' The greatest poet even cannot say it; for the mind in creation is as a fading coal, which some invisible influence, like an inconstant wind, awakens to transitory brightness." He even defined romanticism on another entry and made a special note to himself to see the poems "The Lamb" and "The Tyger" in William Blake's *Songs of Innocence and Experience*.[5]

In addition, entries abound on literary figures such as Matthew Arnold, Herman Melville, and John Milton. He reacts to lines from the poet Charles Swinburne, writing: "Must we sing with Swinburne, 'Praise be to man in the highest, for man is the master of all things'?" With multiple entries on Alfred Lord Tennyson, King quotes lines from Tennyson's poem "Sea Dreams" and then another entry from "The Higher Pantheism": "Speak to him, then, for he hears, and spirit with spirit can meet—closer is he than breathing, and nerves than hands and feet."[6]

Prose entries are far outnumbered by those of poetry. An entry named "Truth" includes six lines from Robert Browning's poem "Paracelsus." King also wrote out lines from Browning's poem "A Death in the Desert." But King's tastes were not confined to the acknowledged masters of verse. King created an index card listing thirteen lines of poetry by the lesser-known George Santayana. Ever eager to cull from every source, King filed lines from Mary Baker Eddy's poem "Teach Me to Love." Why did King collect all of these poetry samples? Would they be sampled during speeches? Some items suggest that he simply loved to read and refer to the beauty, power, truth, and goodness captured in verse. What was King responding to when he wrote this entry under the subject heading "Life"?

"As Mr. Noel Coward put it in his "Twentieth Century Blues":

In this strange illusion
chaos or confusion
People seem to lose their way.
Nothing left to strive for,
Save or keep alive for.[7]

King may have envisioned a moment when depressing days would need to be addressed from the pulpit, but when he sought to connect with his listeners' woes he went more often to poetry than to the epistles.

King's index, though exhaustive, does not contain all the lines of poetry he included in his speeches. As invested as he was in this collection, it was not designed to be a single storehouse for everything he ever read. The vast majority of the lines King quotes throughout his career do not come from this index. For example, there are no cards for John Keats, but King quotes Keats in several speeches he delivered between 1955 and 1960.[8]

No quotation from Langston Hughes appears in these index cards. Either King encountered most of Hughes's poems after his time in Boston or he already knew them so well that they did not need to be handwritten.

Poetry in *The Pulpit*

Quoting poetry was as common in sermons of the 1960s as hearing an amateur sing someone else's songs on television is today. This connection between preaching and poetry can be made clear by considering a publication of the era. *The Pulpit: A Journal of Contemporary Preaching* was one of the preacher's most useful resources. Appearing monthly, it included four to six exemplary sermons, advertised religious books intended to guide the practice of writing and delivering effective sermons, and showcased opportunities for the country's most innovative and best-known pastors. Poetry and preaching overlap throughout *The Pulpit*. The July 1963 issue featured King's sermon "A Tough Mind and a Tender Heart," and another sermon he delivered on January 29, 1961, had been published in the June 1961 issue.[9]

King's typical references to poets and poetry appear in "A Tough Mind and a Tender Heart." The content of the journal helps us see that such references are commonplace. On the page that immediately precedes King's sermon, Creighton Lacy's poem "Whose Church" appears. This poem comprises two sonnets and stands on its own. In fact, this edition of *The Pulpit* published three poems by men who appear to be members of the clergy. These men were clearly invested in writing poems, and many subscribers must have hoped to have their own verses published. Such poems were listed in the table of contents and appear in every issue of this journal.

After reading Lacy's poem, readers who flipped the page to King's sermon confronted the following words: "They would rather bear those ills they have, as Shakespeare pointed out, than flee to others that they know not of" ("Tough Mind" 10). King's references were not out of place in a discussion of spiritual matters: "If God were only tough minded, he would be a cold, passionless despot sitting in some far-off heaven 'contemplating all' as Tennyson puts it in 'The Palace of Art'" (10). King wasn't the only man of the cloth to incorporate poetry in his sermon. David A. MacLennan's sermon "Forever Yours" follows immediately after King's in the journal. MacLennan had authored *Preaching Week by Week*, which was aimed at the type of reader who subscribed to *The Pulpit*. On the second page of his sermon, MacLennan quotes all three stanzas of Robert Burns's "My Love Is Like a Red, Red Rose." Later in the journal, Robert N. Zearfoss's poem "Reconciliation," composed of thirty-four lines of free verse, appears, as does Stanten A. Coblentz's "Materialist," whose four lines, rhyming ABBA, follow a more traditional structure.

The poems quoted in the sermons in this issue of *The Pulpit* were all written by white men. This makes the quotations indicators of the speaker's formal education. Even King's quotations from Shakespeare and Tennyson follow this pattern. When King quoted, appropriated, or alluded to the works of Langston Hughes and other black poets, such as Paul Lawrence Dunbar and James Weldon Johnson, as he would in other contexts, he was embracing poets who were admired within the African American community. King was always sharing poetry with the world, but when he chose to share the works of black authors, he was also transmitting works that had been largely ignored or were completely unknown to most white listeners—and wholly unknown to the majority of *The Pulpit*'s readers. While King did not reference Hughes in "A Tough Mind and a Tender Heart," this context reveals the extent to which King was incorporating a genre common to his profession while simultaneously readying listeners for the ways in which he would eventually integrate such sources and introduce new poets in ways that no other preacher of his time had ever attempted.

Other Poetry

Various studies have documented King's use of poetry from Douglas Malloch, William Cowper, Isaac Watts, James Russell Lowell, and William Cullen Bryant, among others.[10] For example, a set piece of quotations featuring Bryant and Lowell are so common in King's rhetoric that they appear in both the earliest surviving sermon we have from King in 1954 and in one he delivered five days before his death in 1968 (Luker 43).[11] As we have seen, unlike these examples, the use of Langston Hughes's poetry had overt political implications. What I want to emphasize here is not how King came to know these texts but the fact that the texts he borrows are poems. It is not nearly so important here to show where they came from as it is to note what they are and how they are altered. King consistently engaged in two critical practices that have not been explored. As such, the following pages briefly document the ways in which King presented prose sources as poetry as well as the significant ways in which he intentionally rewrote the poems he presented.

Turning Prose into Poetry

King was always looking for material to recycle. What makes him unique is that this material sometimes shifts mediums. With his ear attuned to prosody, King turned a line from Thomas Carlyle's prose work *Sartor Resartos* into a line of poetry. Carlyle had written: "Is there no God, then; but at least an absentee God, sitting idle?" (Carson 4: 108). On January 15, 1957, parishioners heard King say something very different: "In our moments of despair, some of us find ourselves crying out with the earnest belief of Carlyle that 'It seems that God sits in His Heaven and does nothing'" (4: 108). Though he credits the source, King gave little thought to altering Carlyle's words. At first glance, he seems to be merely revising the language of an outdated source to make it more accessible to his congregation. This is indeed a good reason to drop the elevated "absentee." However, the end result is something much more than paraphrase.[12]

Carlyle's prose becomes more poetic in King's presentation. The line "God sits in His Heaven and does nothing" scans as perfect iambic pentameter. "His" is entirely unnecessary, as God is already the subject of the statement, and this "His" appears nowhere in Carlyle's original. King takes Carlyle's prose and imposes a poetic rhythm and cadence to make it more memorable. Similarly, "Heaven" and "nothing" begin with a stress and end unstressed. These trochaic words are muted but repeated so as to create tension and irony. The God who sits in repose rises sonically in these words to remind listeners that such action is wanted from Heaven. Perhaps King is also suggesting that, despite appearances, God is always active.

King had complete control over what he referenced or ignored in regard to where his materials were sourced. This complex amalgam results in some fantastic combinations of allusions and words that are, all at once, from the pages of other writers and simultaneously shaped by the mind of King. Figuring out where one idea stops and another begins is sometimes difficult. While the exact dividing line is unclear, one thing is almost always true: some element of every quotation comes from King, and another comes from his source. One comes from King and another from history. Poetry is often the round molecule that binds the two.

Emerson

One of the more accomplished American poets is identified in King's December 3, 1956, speech as an essayist rather than a poet. King calls on a quotation from Ralph Waldo Emerson that appears to come from Emerson's 1855 journal. Thoreau, most often associated with *Walden*, is classed a poet, and Emerson, a transcendentalist who wrote numerous poems, is an essayist to King. As he would on so many other occasions, King encourages listeners to achieve greatness in whatever endeavors they pursue: "Emerson said in an essay back in 1871, 'If a man can write a better book, or preach a better sermon, or make a better mouse trap than his neighbor, even if he builds his house in the woods the world will make a beaten path to his door'" (Carson 3: 457). Comparing this direct quotation with the original reveals that King is being rather loose with Emerson's actual words. Emerson wrote: "If a man has good corn, or wood, or boards, or pigs to sell, or can make better chairs or knives, crucibles or church organs, than anybody else, you will find a broad hard-beaten road to his house, though it be in the woods" (Carson 3: 266). Should we think King simply heard these lines wrong and then extemporized on what he heard? Or has King once again revised a statement to make it more lyrical?

Rhyme and rhythm are essential elements of poetry. Here, King incorporates each in his revision. He has created an off rhyme between "neighbor" and "door." "Neighbor" does not appear in Emerson's quotation. King then keeps the rhythms of anapests repeated in Emerson's original phrases "in the woods" and "to his door." Though Emerson's line features the consecutive stresses of "hard-beaten road" to mimic the force of so many feet on the broad path, King retains the softer anapests to communicate this private retreat.[13]

Now we can make an important observation: King's quotations do not differ substantially from their original sources simply because King learned the quotations secondhand. Nor does mere carelessness account for why so many of his statements differ so sharply from the original sources; rather, in many cases, King's poetic sensibilities moved him to turn the prose he inherited into the poetry he delivered.

King literally wanted the ideas to leave his tongue sounding better than they sounded originally. As Richard Lischer has noted, "Like a poet, King took pleasure in the purely labial quality of language. He did not look *through* words or *behind* them. . . . He enjoyed their surfaces and gloried in pronouncing them" (*Preacher King* 120).[14] Many of King's addresses feature moments where he inserted his own lines of poetry. For example, King summarized Poe's "Annabel Lee" by saying, "I would imagine Edgar Allan Poe was talking about Eros when he talked about his beautiful Annabelle Lee with a love surrounded by a halo of eternity" (Carson 5: 417). Although he consistently misspelled her first name, King also wrote his own highly creative summary of Poe's poetic tribute to his wife by rhyming "Lee" with "eternity." The line "a love surrounded by a halo of eternity" is not in the original poem.[15] If these were the liberties of pleasure and poetic license King invoked with these quotations, imagine how hard it can be to decipher a King allusion when an author such as Langston Hughes goes unnamed.

The Hidden Poetry

King's engagements with Josiah Holland's 1872 poem "Wanted" in his December 3, 1956, speech reveal the way King went far beyond mere paraphrasing when it came to using another writer's poetry to meet the specific needs of a speech. In this instance, he personalizes Holland's poem to highlight his own focus on the need for leadership. King deliberately replaces Holland's word "men" with his own "leaders" throughout this poem:

> To paraphrase Holland's words:
> God give us leaders!
> A time like this demands strong minds, great hearts,
> true faith and ready hands;
> Leaders whom the lust of office does not kill;
> Leaders whom the spoils of life cannot buy;
> Leaders who possess opinions and a will;
> Leaders who have honor; leaders who will not lie;
> Leaders who can stand before a demagogue and damn his
> treacherous flatteries without winking!
> Tall leaders, sun crowned, who live above the fog
> in public duty and private thinking. (Carson 3: 461)

But it is King's introductory remarks that reveal his deepest engagements with Holland's poem. These remarks reflect his ability to rewrite Holland's poem. King was not merely preparing the way for Holland's poem; he was tacitly revealing that he himself was a poet. Although King's words are often reprinted as prose, King was actually delivering his own poem. Immediately before Holland's poem, King says:

> The urgency of the hour calls for leaders
> with wise judgment and sound integrity—
> leaders not in love with money
> but in love with justice;
> leaders not in love with publicity,
> but in love with humanity;
> leaders who can subject their particular egos
> to the greatness of the cause. (3: 461)

The prosodic elements in this passage include the repeated trochaic feet found in the mirror phrases that end with "money" and "justice" and the consecutive anapests in "to the greatness of the cause" that echo as softly as nonviolence. Most apparent, King follows his own unique rhyme scheme in these eight verses. While Holland's poem is a sonnet, King truncates it into an eight-line structure. This poem follows the rhyme scheme ABBABBAA with the sibilant "s" and "c" sounds repeated in lines 1, 4, 7, and 8 and the "y" and "e" sounds paired in between. King went far beyond paraphrase, allusion, and voice merging. Because he memorized poetry and understood it so well, King was able to present his own poems as the occasion required. What is highly unusual is that King has presented not just a poem but a "rewritten" poem. He has taken Holland's basic ideas and created his own poem to mirror "Wanted." On this stage, in successful mimicry, the lines above emerged entirely from King's own mind. Rather than submitting them to journals like *The Pulpit*, King's poems were embedded in his addresses, masquerading as prose.

Typescript Confusion: King or Oxenham?

If King preempted his quotation of Holland on December 3, 1956, with his own poetry, he was also bold enough to add his own lines of poetry after quoting another poet three years later. King's March 22, 1959, sermon again highlights the difficulty of determining where King's words end and another's start while simultaneously revealing King's penchant for poetry. One of the clearest ways to document the confusion about where King's own ideas start and end is to examine the choices a careful listener makes when trying to formally represent lines from one of King's sermons. A typed transcript of this speech re-creates the confusion listeners would have had when listening to King speak. King ends this sermon with a version of John Oxenham's poem "The Ways" (1916). To better understand the confusion about which words belong to King and which are Oxenham's, let's begin with the original poem:

> To every man there openeth
> A Way, and Ways, and a Way,
> And the High Soul climbs the High Way,
> And the Low Soul gropes the Low,
> And in between, on the misty flats,
> The rest drift to and fro.
> But to every man there openeth

A High Way, and a Low.
And every man decideth
The Way his soul shall go.[16]

Here is how a listener transcribed the end of King's sermon:

> I close my quoting the words of John Austungham (?) "Whoever man thou openth the way and ways and away. The high soul climbs the highway and the low soul gropes the low. And In-between on the mystic flat, the rest drift to and fro, but to every man, to every nation, to every civilization, there opens a high and a low way. Every soul decideth which way it shall go. God grant us that we shall choose the high way even if it will mean assassination, even if it will mean crucifixion. For by going this way, you will discover that death will be only the beginning of our infinite." I have others, he said, Jesus, which are not of this fold. If you will believe in me and follow my way, you will be even, you will be able to do even greater works, than I did in my lifetime.[17]

The typographical slips are obvious, as "by" is mistyped as "my" in the first line, and the poet's name is spelled phonetically. It becomes more difficult to know if King actually said "misty flats," as he had on some earlier occasions, or if he altered these words for this sermon to be what is captured here as "mystic flat." What is clear, though, is that King has taken too much liberty with the source to permit the label of "quotation." He has inserted an entire riff that includes not only "every man" but also "every nation" and "every civilization."

The most telling aspects of this transcription, however, involve points where the transcription extends the poem to include King's own words. Unable to tell where the poem proper ends and King's words begin, two full sentences sound "poetic" enough to the typist that they are placed within quotation marks. Looking again at the last two sentences that are captured within what appears to be Oxenham's poem, King says:

> God grant us that we shall choose the high way
> even if it will mean assassination,
> even if it will mean crucifixion.
> For by going this way,
> you will discover that death
> will be only the beginning of our infinite.

The listener's decision to include these words as part of Oxenham's poem reflects confusion that arises because these lines sound like poetry. "Assassination" creates an internal rhyme with "crucifixion," and to say "death will be but a beginning of our infinite" sounds like poetic language. However, neither of these ideas has any connection with the original poem. Their placement here reveals that King both believed and demonstrated that he could versify as well as any poet. Moreover, here his lines could come last and outshine the ones he recited before them.

On two very different occasions, with Holland and Oxenham, King's own poetry literally comes before and after other poets.' In what other ways did King incorporate poetry this subtly? Here, King was able to rewrite both Holland's and Oxenham's lines as his own. Eventually, many of the most memorable lines King rewrote resulted from similar engagements with the poetry of Langston Hughes.

Unsolicited Poetry

Throughout his life, King received letters on a variety of topics. Among the submissions, requests, and donations he received, some of the most surprising and revealing documents were unsolicited poems. Poems started arriving on King's desk immediately after he came to prominence in 1955. And once they started coming, they never stopped. One day, King's secretary would open a poem that Edna Brody Christian had published in 1955 titled "Tomorrow's Light." Next, an amateur poet would be introducing lines he composed in honor of Jackie Robinson. W. B. Douglas described what he called a "keen feeling of relationship" to Robinson, though the two had never met. The twelve-stanza poem's title, "Keep Punching," becomes the poem's refrain. Though light on artistry, the first quatrain captures some of the tension of the times:

> There's those that say, "let's speed it up."
> And others say, "go slow."
> And then there's some that will not say
> Which way we ought to go.

The poet provided the following handwritten comments: "I am W. B. Douglas of 276 Origabla Ave., San Francisco, California. I am 39 years old, a 6 foot 2 inch, 210 pounder. I am employed by United Airlines in San Francisco. I would appreciate your using this poem in any way that you see fit.

If you care to add to, or delete, any part of it, you have my consent, however, I would like to be informed prior to your changes."[18] This request was typical. A surprising number of authors imagined that King might quote their poem during one of his speeches. They were aware that he frequently quoted poetry in his speeches, and they hoped he might use one of their very own creations.[19] Behind these submissions lay the writers' understanding of King as a man who uses, quotes, and admires poetry. They were in tune with King's poetic persona, and they understood King's affection for poetry.[20]

Odell Wilson of Wilmington, Delaware, made his intentions plain. His poem "There Were Twenty Slaves for Jamestown" arrived in 1961 with this cover letter: "I wrote the enclosed poem in 1959. Three editors have refused to publish it. You, no doubt, can give this message to the world at this time of crisis when decisions of far-reaching consequences must be made."[21] Wilson articulates his desire to have King personally read his poem to the world, whereas others folded their hands in prayer hoping that this would be a divine result of their literary enterprise. What, if not the repeated appearances of poetry in King's addresses, led Wilson to believe that King might share his poem with an audience?

The "Prayers" of Wright and Hughes

On March 22, 1957, Eva Darwin Wright mailed King a copy of her poem "A Prayer." Its eight quatrains offer a traditional rhyme between the second and fourth lines of each stanza. Sent from her apartment on Sixtieth Street in Chicago, Wright's poem was accompanied by a cover letter that ended by explaining that two murders had brought her to these thoughts: "The attached poem entitled 'A Prayer,' is an outpouring of my heart over the many vicious crimes perpetrated against a helpless people. It began building up with the murder of Emmett Till, and overflowed with the hammer slaying here in Chicago, of Alvin Palmer, high school victim of a teen-age mob 'out to get a Negro.'" Wright's submission captures the grassroots attitude that connects the brutal murder of Till to her current desire for civil rights.

Wright's letter also leads into one of the final thoughts of the poem. In her letter she writes: "May God, Who certainly inspired you to lead your people, preserve you and bless you, and permit you to bring to a righteous end the great work you have so bravely and nobly begun." These sentiments are captured in her last stanza:

Dear God, please preserve our country,
Give it leaders, brave and true;
Who'll defend the rights of all men,
'Neath the Red, the White and Blue.[22]

Wright speaks on the topic of leaders, a subject King wrote his own verses about before quoting from Josiah Holland.

Hughes's works reveal a tension between approachability and mediocrity that has long existed in American academic circles. Though Hughes is revered within the African American community, his verse has been ignored by professional scholars during periods when abstraction and confession have been overprivileged. Hughes has achieved some of his greatest successes overseas. In 1960, a Venezuelan newspaper article, not an American one, recommended Hughes be considered for the Nobel Prize in Literature (Mullen 1400). One of Hughes's poems, "I, Too," has been translated into Spanish over one hundred times, twenty-one times in the year 1925 alone. Some of his works have been translated into Russian, and during the 1930s the interest in the Harlem Renaissance was so high in Germany that many of Hughes's poems were published there without his knowledge or permission. Because of America's racist heritage, Hughes has often received less praise in the United States than in countries throughout Africa and the Caribbean.

By comparing Hughes's unsolicited submissions to King with Wright's, we can see the contrast between Hughes's best poetic accomplishments and his flat efforts. On January 18, 1960, Hughes sent two items to King. The two men had already been in correspondence regarding Hughes's attendance at an event to honor A. Philip Randolph that was only six days away. Although King initiated the correspondence and asked Hughes for a poem just for the occasion (addressed at length in chapter 5), Hughes sent two unsolicited works to King as well. Upon receipt of one of King's written requests for a poem, Hughes took a pencil and wrote "ans. by 'mantle piece'" in the lower right-hand corner.[23] This poem resembles many of the unsolicited poems that had been sent to King from all over the world.

Hughes sent King a song intended to be sung in an opera he was working on. As with so many of Hughes's projects, in another context this arietta would easily pass for poetry. In fact, Hughes himself may have set the piece to music less than two weeks after he sent it to King.[24] The complete title of the song/poem Hughes abbreviated in the bottom corner of his letter from King was "Prayer for the Mantle-Piece," which begins as follows:

Oh, Holy One Who Maketh
In The Morn The Sun To Rise,
Who Maketh All The Earth So Bright
And Blorifies The Skies.[25]

Capitalization of every word parallels the typographical errors found in so many other missives, and the intended word "Glorifies" is replaced by "Blorifies." Hughes's metaphors are unimaginative clichés:

Who Sendeth Gentle Rain To Fall
Upon Each Dusty Place,
Oh, Thou Who Maketh Flowers Bloom,
Help Me To Grow in Grace.

Bordering on parody, this work only earns attention because it is accompanied by Hughes's signature. Its uninspired lines continue:

Most Humbly Do I Bow My Head
And Humbly I Do Pray
For All The Sins I Know Are Bad
That Daily Block My Way.

Hughes's diction betrays any hope for this work to achieve redemption, as he calls his sins "bad" to complete a simple rhyme with "head." Mailing this piece too quickly, without allowing time for revision or a disinterested evaluation, or simply trying to express a state of prayer that was neither genuine nor real, this work stands as a reminder that even famous writers could fall prey to testing their spiritual eloquence out on the Reverend King.

However, when he was at his best, speaking social commentary in verses plain and imaginative, Hughes earned the title King assigned to him: a "great noble black bard."[26] The second item Hughes sent, "Merry-Go-Round," must have had a very different effect on King:

Colored child at carnival:

Where is the Jim Crow section
On this merry-go-round,
Mister, cause I want to ride?
Down South where I come from
White and colored
Can't sit side by side.

Down South on the train
There's a Jim Crow car.
On the bus we're put in the back—
But there ain't no back
To a merry-go-round!
Where's the horse
For a kid that's black?[27]

With neither a ranting word nor an angry tone, the illogic of segregation is exposed by the deft hand of a poet whose simplicity dramatizes this child's honest confusion. Hughes's verse captures the emotions of a reader through the voice of a child speaker who is inadvertently teaching a white man the rules of segregation. The poem ends without a response, as if no sound logic for segregation's principles have been or can be offered. Worse, readers are moved by a child who has been so conditioned by segregation that he or she expresses confusion that its principles have not been extended further and deeper into society.

King apparently never referenced or quoted either of these works by Hughes. There was, however, an earlier offering by Hughes that King did use. On one occasion, the audience response was so overwhelming that King simply ended his remarks, leaving the rest of his prepared script undelivered.

The Windy City Press Club: "Brotherly Love"

On January 10, 1957, King was invited to accept an award in Chicago at an event sponsored by the Windy City Press Club. Unfortunately, King was unable to attend the awards banquet that evening, and he accepted the award in absentia.[28] As a result of the unparalleled success of the Montgomery Bus Boycott, which began on December 5, 1955, and ended just over a year later, King had received no fewer than sixty national awards for his leadership role during the crisis. The keynote speaker for the event was Langston Hughes. That evening, Hughes, a longtime contributor to the black press, expressed his interest in and affection for publications written especially for black audiences: "My favorite reading is the Negro press. Perhaps it should be *The Iliad*, *The Odyssey*, Shakespeare, or Tolstoy, but it isn't. It is the Negro press. Every week the Lord sends, if possible, in Harlem I buy the *Afro*, the *Courier*, the *Amsterdam News*, the *Age*, and of course, the *Defender* for which I write—so I can read myself."[29] It is not surprising that Hughes's subject that night was

"Humor and the Negro Press." Modeling his topic, Hughes found humor in a number of places: "Easterners have not yet forgotten an Afro-American news headline some years ago: GROOM HONEYMOONS WITH BEST MAN." Declaring that "Humor is a weapon," Hughes demonstrated how its bullets could be fired: "Since we have not been able to moralize our enemies out of existence with indignant editorials, maybe we could laugh them to death with well-aimed ridicule."

Expecting the award winner to be in attendance, Hughes put extra effort into connecting his speech with King. His first draft seeks a level of formality (or uncertainty), as he lists leading figures who are often found in the pages of the black press: "Adam Powell, Hagel Scott and Daddy Grace and the Rev. Martin King." By his second draft he has inserted the full "Rev. Martin Luther King," leaving off "Jr." Perhaps, having settled that important issue, Hughes then notes others who may have been in attendance, as he adds the names Harry Belafonte and Dorothy Dandridge in pencil to his final prepared script.

But Hughes has much more than a passing reference to King in mind when he delivers this speech. In fact, it is not hard to read the speech backwards. Beginning with the end and finishing with the start, Hughes may very well have thought about a poem he had already written about King and, wanting to share it in his presence, wrote the speech to justify the satire in its verses. Hughes ended his speech by transitioning from speaker to writer, introducing one of his best-known creations, Jesse B. Simple, who could be found exclusively in the black press's *Chicago Defender*. At the end of his speech, Hughes shares an imaginary conversation between himself and Simple, then reads a revised version of his poem "Brotherly Love." Like King, Hughes begins to model what he has preached. After declaring that humor can be a weapon, Hughes invokes the low-down, streetwise Simple:

> Simple, with his beer at the bar, helps me. The other day Simple said to me. "Listen, you know, with my wife's help—her name is Joyce—I have writ a poem."
>
> "I know you are determined to read it to me," I said, "so go ahead."
>
> "It is about that minister down in Montgomery who has committed a miracle," said Simple.
>
> "What miracle?" I asked.
>
> "Getting Negroes to stick together," said Simple.
>
> "I presume you are speaking of Rev. King," I said.

"I am," said Simple," and this is my poem. Listen fluently now! I have writ it like a letter. It is addressed to the White Citizens Councilors of Alabama. And here it goes."

Hughes, speaking as Simple, then delivers his previously published poem "Brotherly Love" at the Windy City Press Club, though with significant changes from the published version.

Before we consider the alterations Hughes made to his poem on this occasion and how they express his considerable admiration of King, it is important to understand the published version. While King often used Hughes's poetry in his addresses, it is also important to acknowledge the ways in which Hughes was also influenced by King.

On August 18, 1956, Hughes had published his poetic response to the Montgomery Bus Boycott, "Brotherly Love," in *The Nation*. It addressed the subject of Montgomery in its opening line and referenced "Reverend King" in its last sentence. While "Brotherly Love" demonstrated King's spiritual means for initiating change, Hughes's original subtitle was more aggressive: "A Little Letter to the White Citizens Councils of the South."[30] Because of Hughes's reputation, the editors carefully embedded the poem within an article by a former Communist deputy in the French parliament who had just resigned after soundly criticizing the Communist Party. Building on Hughes's own associations, the article was titled "Inside the French Left."

Hughes begins the poem with an allusion to one of his own poems, "Negro," where he had referenced the King Leopold of Belgium's practice between 1885 and 1908 of removing the right hands of African citizens if they could not pay their taxes (W. Miller, *Langston Hughes* 33). Here, in "Brotherly Love," Hughes writes, "When I reach out my hand, will *you* take it—/ cut it off and leave a nub above?" (lines 3–4). He then presents a covert reference to lynching, linking the large number of victims found dead in rivers to his audience's desire to see the speaker go under water until he has drowned. Next, Hughes captures the logic of King's own appeals in the cadence of the preacher: "So long, *so long* a time" (line 9). If this is no coincidence, Hughes's choice may point to King's own rhetoric. To consider this, we can compare it with one of King's addresses. Published in a source more accessible to Hughes than most, King's "The 'New Negro' of the South: Behind the Montgomery Story" appeared in the June 1956 New York edition of *Social Call* well before the publication of Hughes's poem. This printed version of a speech King had delivered in May 1956 repeatedly references this syntax and cadence. King reminds his listeners that "we have come a long way . . . but . . . we have a long long way to go" (Carson 3: 281). After two more uses of this phrase, King repeats it two more times (for a total of six times) in his address until it became a refrain.

The thrust of Hughes's poem is that the speaker has learned to love his audience despite the history of violence and continued hatred of his race. Hughes brings up the topic of "love" in the second stanza, then uses it as the centerpiece of a newfound logic. Replying to the idea of being forced to sit in the back of the bus, the speaker states: "'Anyhow, I'm gonna love you,' / Still" (lines 15–16). Throughout Hughes's many newspaper articles that address King, the word "love" is consistently used when depicting King.[31] Although not unexpected, King's references to "love" in his own speech highlight the depictions in the poem. The address claims that "the great instrument is the instrument of love." This love must be "at the forefront of our movement . . . and when we speak of love, we speak of a redemptive sort of love." We find that "love is a transforming power" because "love is our great instrument and weapon" (Carson 3: 278). More specific to Hughes's poem, King asserts, "We could not allow ourselves to retaliate with any type of violence, but that we were still to confront the problem with *love*." During the harshest moments of the boycott, King "urged the people to continue to manifest love" with his unshakable belief in "this primacy of love." Finally, after a relatively short address, King closes with "we will not retaliate with hate, but we will stand with love in our hearts" (Carson 3: 279).

Hughes ends "Brotherly Love" with a pun that demonstrates the speaker's ability to overcome adversity with passive resistance. As we have seen, humor was important to Hughes, who often asserted that he was laughing to keep from crying: "In line with Reverend King down in Montgomery—/ Also because the Bible says I must—/ I'm gonna love you—*yes, I will! Or BUST!* (lines 18–20). The hitchhiker's plea "Memphis or Bust," often scribbled by hand on a cardboard sign, is reinvigorated by Hughes's play on its homophone, "bused."

Was it possible that King knew Hughes's poem well enough to later incorporate its lines into his own speeches? Three examples suggest that he did. Four months after the publication of "Brotherly Love," King was reminiscing about the accomplishments of the Montgomery Bus Boycott. With many of the boycott's participants on hand at the location where much of the decision making, inspiration, and direction had occurred, King returned

to Montgomery's Holt Street Baptist Church on December 5, 1957, to cel-
ebrate the second anniversary of the boycott's start. His speech framed the
end of the first day of the four-day event, and it began with a tone of common
reminiscence. King uses Hughes's phrase "so long, *so long*" as he expresses
appreciation for "your loyalty across our long, the days of our long struggle
together" (Carson 4: 329). This is no coincidence. In fact, King is delivering
a parallel version of the speech published in *Socialist Call* that may have been
familiar to Hughes. Once again, further into his remarks, he twice reminds
listeners that they have "come a long, long way" (4: 339).

Most interesting of all, however, is the refrain King drives home through
epistrophe. Though it was completely absent in the original speech from
which he is working, one that was delivered before Hughes published "Broth-
erly Love," a significant element from Hughes's poem suddenly appears. Four
consecutive lines in this speech end with the phrase "we will still love you"
as King begins "Do to us what you want. Threaten our children, and we will
still love you" (4: 341). The final refrain is "Bomb our churches and go by our
churches early in the morning and bomb them if you please, and we will still
love you" (4: 342). "We will still love you" can be read as a riff on Hughes's
"'I'm gonna love you,' / Still."

In a speech that featured borrowed poetry or made references to John
Oxenham, Josiah Holland, Douglas Malloch, Shakespeare, William Cow-
per, and Isaac Watts, King was also quietly merging Hughes's poetic state-
ment on the boycott into the fabric of his elaborate tapestry.[32] King made
this a permanent addition to his addresses. In his February 11, 1958, address
before the NAACP in Greensboro, North Carolina, his voice can be heard
building as he emphasizes the word "still" to offer five consecutive lines
of epistrophe. Using this at the end of his lines further mirrors the use in
Hughes's poem. The word "still" slowly builds ever louder with each re-
peating.

On this occasion, the effects are stunning. King drew such a swell of ap-
plause after this passage that he stopped his speech short. Intending to quote
lines from Oxenham's "The Ways," King simply stepped away from the po-
dium immediately after invoking these lines from "Brotherly Love."[33] Did
King deliver these lines with even greater force and intensity because of
some added confidence he took in knowing they had come from a poem by
Hughes that acknowledged and revered him? What does it mean that the
voice of Simple was embedded in these refrains? Though his audience was
unaware of any connection to Hughes's poetry in this instance, it is not hard

to imagine what such audience response taught King. Even when the lines themselves were unknown to his listeners, with every invocation of lines he used or rewrote from Hughes, audience response continued to drive him to ever increase its use. Furthermore, having felt such thunderous applause after this section, what poem could follow Hughes in one of King's speeches? Or said another way, where else would Hughes's poems serve as a better fit than at the end of an address?

Even more convincing evidence of King's use of Hughes's line can be found in King's sermon on Christmas Eve of 1967. Here, King not only invokes this phrase on five consecutive occasions but preempts it by referencing the same group to whom Hughes's poem is addressed: "I've seen too much hate to want to hate, myself, and I've seen hate on the faces of too many sheriffs, too many white citizens' councilors. . . . Do to us what you will and we will still love you. . . . throw us in jail and we will still love you. Bomb our homes and threaten our children, and, as difficult as it is, we will still love you. . . . leave us half dead as you beat us, and we will still love you" (*Trumpet* 77). Again, this phrase and its context of "white citizens' councilors" appears in King's addresses only after the publication of "Brotherly Love." King always used these lines without crediting Hughes's poem.

To prepare for the public reading of this poem at the Windy City Press Club in 1957, Hughes made substantial changes to the published text. He evidently thought enough of "Brotherly Love" that he made four passes through this poem to revise it. Hughes's ability to assume the voice of Simple as the speaker of some of his other poems has been overlooked.[34] Here, Hughes makes the connection explicit as he simply calls "Brotherly Love" a "poem" that was "writ" in Simple's hand. To reinforce this connection, he shapes its verses in the form of an actual letter that simply begins: "Dear Citizens Councilors."

Framing the poem within a discussion of humor and then identifying the speaker of the poem as Simple himself offers both a different reading of the poem and, by the time Hughes has completed his fourth set of revisions, a different poem. The first two lines of "Brotherly Love" can now be reread: "In line of what my folks say in Montgomery, / In line of what they're teaching down there about love." Hughes, through the worldly wisdom of Simple, has turned the common phrase "in light of" into "in line of." "Line" simultaneously opens this poem with a pun that bookends the poem's final pun on "Bust" and roughly suggests that Simple is following the boycott's line of thought and that he is "in line with them" as he agrees with their points. This phrase turns up again in the final stanza to elicit yet another visual image: "In line with Reverend King in Montgomery" suggests the idea of marching and walking side by side in protest. Interestingly enough, offering an idea early in the text and then returning to it at the end mirrors organizational speaking strategies often invoked by King himself. Hughes may have been aware of this pattern. He had certainly heard King speak, and Hughes once declared: "I heard Rev. Martin Luther King say at a meeting not long ago that perhaps it was the Negro's destiny to save America for itself" (Bigsby 105).

To fit this occasion, Hughes took something old and made it new. Despite the fact that each man prepared for a different type of performance, there are similarities. Like King, Hughes shaped an old thought to fit into a new context, all the while enjoying the process of revision. Hughes made two improvements to the first stanza:

When I reach out my hand, white man,
Will you take it?
Or will you try to cut it off
and make a nub?

Now protecting himself behind the character of Simple, Hughes raises the level of anger against the members of the White Citizens Council by labeling them "white man," and he breaks what was once one full line into two parts to capture the idea that the hand offered in friendship could be "cut off."

Even after making his third set of revisions, Hughes returns in pencil to add a similar emphasis to the idea of waiting. The third "paragraph" of this letter is marked to set off "So long, / so long" into separate lines to use this empty space to highlight the feeling of waiting. These revisions suggest that Simple is much more begrudging the act of love than openly extending it, as it is portrayed in the published version. Simple now declares even more defiantly that he has not been drowned as Hughes underlines the intensity of "Well, I didn't!" While more "love" is added to the letter/poem in this version, with Simple now saying "I'm gonna love you" twice in the final stanza rather than just once, Hughes combines Simple's anger with his reluctance to accept the line of passive resistance. In the second revision, Hughes drafts an ending that is atypical of his approach to writing: "I say I'm gonna love you. / I'll be damned if I won't love you—/ Or BUST!" While the spiritual context allows us to read "damned" literally, Hughes was usually very reluctant to incorporate such strong language, even through an invented character.

Unsatisfied with this result, Hughes typed the third ending, which shifts the focus away from the original ending. The third ending reads, "But I won't put my change in your segregated bus / Even if your home office is here in Chicago!" Apparently tripping over the irony that the White Citizens Council had its headquarters in the city where he is scheduled to speak, Hughes seems momentarily inspired by the irony and imagined ending this performance of the poem in a completely different way. However, this wasn't the ending he read on the night of the banquet. Returning again, now for the fourth time, he crosses out "here" in the above line with a red pen, indicating that perhaps it was the final change he made before he left New York. In pencil, Hughes settles on this as his final line, removing the "damned" so that the act of paying to ride a segregated bus is one that Simple declares an impossibility: "Before I'll do that—I'll BUST!"

Returning to the pun on "Bust" that marked the first published version of the poem, Hughes now gives this word an entirely new meaning. Instead of highlighting the hitchhiker's travails or suggesting that the way to end this crisis is to let Montgomery's citizens be "bused," the revisions enable Simple to declare that he would rather gamble his money away and "go bust" than spend it on bus fare. It is a risk he is willing to take; it is a bet he will place. This final reading of this revised (and delivered) line also suggests victory. Simple may also be asserting that the boycott was a bet to see which side would fold. He puts his money on those who fall in line with Reverend King. Having now won, the boycott ended, he triumphantly and rebelliously asserts that even if he had lost by placing his money "on the line," that would still have been the right choice to make. What appeared to be biblical is now blurred into the logic that Simple lives with every day on the streets. If the gamble involves choosing between the White Citizens Council and Reverend King, Simple would rather bet on God than the devil.

As Simple's remarks implied, Hughes thought it was a miracle that the boycott was successful. He was shocked that such unity could be achieved among African Americans. News of Montgomery had spread all the way to Harlem, and even Jesse B. Simple begrudgingly fell in line with organized nonviolence. All of these were triumphs Hughes revisited, explored, and celebrated through a poem inspired directly by the Montgomery Bus Boycott led by King. Possibly pleased with the response it drew, or perhaps by direct prompting from his listeners, Hughes republished the poem two months after speaking at the press club, placing the poem in its entirety in the *Chicago Defender* on March 23, 1957, under the title "Simple Says Acting Right Is Better Than Writing Right." In this context, Hughes made additional changes. Line five became "Since God put it in my heart," and Hughes replaced line nine's "So long" with "Since slavery time." In addition, he removed a contraction in line thirteen's "you've," leaving just "you" to make the line sound even more as if it came from the mouth of Simple. As expected, he once again reserved the majority of his revisions for the end. This version ends:

> In line with Rev. King down in Montgomery—
> Also because the Bible tells me that I must—
> In spite of bombs and buses, I'm gonna love you.
> I say I'm gonna LOVE you—White folks, OR BUST![35] (10)

When Boyd, Simple's formally educated foil, challenges Simple, "You never wrote a poem that logical all by yourself in life," Simple removes the veil to momentarily reveal Hughes himself when he replies, "I know I didn't." After sharing another poem rich with dialect in the article (a poem that Hughes never published elsewhere), Simple's logic becomes clear. He cites the fact that he knows "plenty of Jim Crowers who speak fine grammar, but do very evil." Thus he concludes after citing his own lack of schooling and unique elocution, "I figure it is better to do right than to write right" (10).

Hughes's Articles in the *Chicago Defender*

Aside from their actual engagements, Hughes and King were quite often separated by the smallest degrees just as they were for this event at the Windy City Press Club. In late September 1957, Hughes met with one of the most aggressive attorneys in America. William M. Kunstler later recalled that "Langston forgot his tie and I wore it throughout the South as an attorney for Dr. Martin Luther King, Jr. I once wrote Langston and told him that one of the great ironies of life was that his tie had gone to places which were closed to him. He wrote back and said that it was a shame that ties had more rights than people!" (Rampersad 2: 276). However, Hughes quietly learned that his words could often go places where he could not. Writing weekly articles for the *Chicago Defender* for more than twenty-four years, Hughes mentioned King no fewer than forty times between 1956 and 1965. A survey of these mentions reveals Hughes's unwavering respect and admiration for a man he most often referred to as "Rev. King." While Hughes's support might seem inevitable, it is important to remember that the NAACP and other civil rights groups were far from unified during this turbulent era.

While Hughes was first and foremost an artist, he was also an accomplished journalist, and the articles he wrote for the *Defender* appeared nationally. They were aimed primarily at black audiences, who were sometimes divided over the best approaches to achieving civil rights. In his first article about King, Hughes activated his favorite prose character to address the Montgomery Bus Boycott.[36] Hughes used this famous (and humorous) character throughout his work to dramatize the feelings of what he called "the low-down" people in Harlem. He allowed the argument between passive resistance and brute force to play out between Simple and his more formally educated foil Boyd. Through these arguments, Boyd's more civilized approach drove Simple's instinctive hotheadedness to new heights of humor. The satirical point and counterpoint on the issue of nonviolence recurred on at least five other occasions, with the last coming in June 1963.[37]

In addition, using his own voice, Hughes called readers to donate to King's cause on more than one occasion (even providing mailing information).[38] Hughes recognized immediately that King was unique, noting twice in 1957 that King would become a permanent fixture of black history. Within the first year of King's ascendancy as a public figure, Hughes dedicated an entire article to Simple's brave recommendation of King for president of the United States. When informed by Boyd that King was below the minimum age requirement, Simple argued that "What Rev. King lacks in years . . . he makes up in guts. . . . That minister is a wise man" ("Let's Organize" 10).[39]

In May 1963, when Simple dreamed that he himself was president, one of his first orders of business was to deliver a declaration: "I hereby command the misusers to turn over all dogs, prod rods, and fire hoses to Rev. Martin Luther King" ("Simple as President" 8). While Hughes himself did not go to the march to Montgomery in the spring of 1965, he went figuratively by allowing Simple the opportunity to imagine what he would do if he had the money to go to Selma. Hughes's article "If Simple Went to Selma" was published in the *Chicago Defender* on April 24, 1965. After reminding readers of his respect for King, Simple worried that he would not have the poise to remain nonviolent given the circumstances. Boyd declares that he himself does not have the nerve to go. In an article that highlights the multiple acts of violence taking place in Alabama, Simple satirically cites the country's militancy in Vietnam before sympathizing with Annie Lee Cooper, a black woman who was beaten by police officers after she struck Sheriff Jim Clark. Observing the beating on a "TV in the bar in Harlem," Simple suggests that her suffering is worthy of King's Nobel Prize. Simple's empathy denotes his latent desire for fighting back and his lack of fitness for nonviolence. Thus, both he and Boyd are better off spending this Easter in Harlem, where Simple cannot retaliate and Boyd will not get his own "head beaten" (8).

Given his political status, it may be no coincidence that Hughes often imagined that Jesse Simple traveled places Hughes himself could not go. After the May 17, 1957, Prayer Pilgrimage to Washington, D.C., Hughes penned a column in which Simple describes the events of the day. The article makes it clear that Hughes carefully followed the event, even though he did not attend. After suggesting that King himself could run for president of the United States if a black political party ever emerged, Simple also suggests that King should have prayed the final prayer of the event, "because Rev. King would not have had to read no prayer off no paper" ("Let's Organize" 10). Ten days before the Prayer Pilgrimage, Hughes spoke about his stance on racial issues at a national assembly of the Authors League of America in Manhattan. Hughes addressed how he and other African Americans felt about censorship in America: "Censorship for blacks . . . begins at the color line." He declared that black writers lived abroad because "the stones thrown at Autherine Lucy at the University of Alabama are thrown at them, too. Because the shadow of Montgomery and the bombs under Rev. King's house, shadow them and shatter them, too. Because the body of little Emmett Till drowned in a Mississippi River and no one brought to justice, haunts them, too" (*Collected Works* 9: 358). Hughes sometimes said the words that Simple only imagined.

As we have seen above, King and the Montgomery Bus Boycott inspired Hughes to write poems and articles in the *Defender*. However, King's varying engagements with Hughes's poetry are a much longer story. Next, we will turn our attention to the ways in which Hughes's poetry inspired King. One of the most important poems to consider came in the form of a play.

4

"Dream Deferred"

King's Use of Hughes's Most Popular Poem

Martin Luther King took the podium at Ebenezer Baptist Church in Atlanta in a solemn mood on Christmas Eve in 1967. He used the occasion to connect his lived history of African American persecution in America with the Vietnam War. King's address, "A Christmas Sermon on Peace," was broadcast on radio by the Canadian Broadcast Company, and the audio recording allows us to experience the event. King's father encouraged Martin Jr. as he was advocating nonviolence. Through the spontaneous call-and-response common to all who attended Ebenezer, the elder King added his standard "Make it plain" in the background eight sentences into his son's sermon. These interjections continued as he encouraged his son to rise to the moment and to feel affirmation in the spaces where he paused. When his son told his listeners about the three types of love identified by the Greeks, eros, philos, and agape, King Sr. repeated "agape," and soon after he added a "Yes" and a "That's it."[1] King heard his father consent with "Yes, sir" at least five more times before the speech ended.

King himself rapped his knuckles on the podium to emphasize key points. Speaking of the world's poverty, the preacher asked: "Can we in America stand idly by and not be concerned?" (*Trumpet* 71). King's hand slowly gained force as two declarative raps arrived simultaneously with the words "Oh, no!" (71). Seconds later, King Sr. added another "Make it plain."

With respectful listeners unavoidably coughing in the pews, King punctuated another point to show that violent means could not lead to peaceful ends. He rapped his knuckles on the podium six times behind key words to reinforce that "the means represent the seed and the end represents the tree" (73). King then softened his emphasis as the sound from his clenched fingers gradually faded away behind the word "sacredness" (74). He spoke as if listeners would understand the force of his speech through the activity of his fingers. In full conversation now, it is hard to distinguish who is leading whom as King responds to his father's "Yes" five words later to strike the podium louder than he would all night to emphasize the word "respected" when he preached that "Man is a child of God, made in His image, and therefore must be respected as such" (74). From there, the podium strikes abated entirely.

At the end of his speech, King returns to ideas mentioned in his introduction. There, King had said that "peace and goodwill toward all men can no longer be dismissed as a kind of pious dream of some utopian hoper" (69). In the conclusion of this sermon, King reanimates these thoughts when he repeats the phrase "I still have a dream" (79). This is not the only idea mentioned early in the sermon that is echoed in the conclusion. At the end, King imagines that "nations will no longer rise up against nations, neither will they study war anymore." The line "study war no more" is from the well-known refrain in the spiritual "Down by the Riverside." Linking the words "study" and "nonviolence" in the conclusion reanimates what appeared to be only an innocuous statement in King's introduction: "I would like to suggest that modern man really go all out to study the meaning of nonviolence" (69–70).

As the sermon proceeds, the repetitions of key phrases slowly replace the raps on the podium. Beginning his thoughts by asserting that he could love his enemies through agape even when philos is lacking, he confesses, "I can't like anybody who would bomb my home" (75–76). He repeats "like" near the beginning of five consecutive sentences, energizing both himself and the audience with this invocation of anaphora. With perfect symmetry, King strikes a balance that is so subtle it is easy to overlook. He responds shortly thereafter with five consecutive examples of epistrophe as he ends these sentences with "we will still love you" (77). Using an allusion to Hughes's poem "Brotherly Love," he moves from an inability to "like" and arrives at a capacity to "love." The rhetorical combination of such a balanced use of anaphora and epistrophe to start and then conclude these sentences suggests that what began as an inability to "like" ends with the capacity to "love."

With a double force that can be measured literally by number, King builds off these earlier uses of the five invocations of anaphora and epistrophe as he uses another line exactly ten times. Each of these ten consecutive thoughts uses the refrain "I still have a dream" (79). Listeners are hard pressed to say with certainty if this phrase ends or begins King's statement, as King's delivery blurs the categories of epistrophe and anaphora. As if he realizes that he has gone beyond the pattern of five which he has been consistently invoking up to now in the sermon, King now begins to ring out with added zeal on his sixth pronouncement. The effect? King is ending where he began. Unlike the earlier progression from "like" to "love," his dream is unchanged. He began 1963 with a dream that he still has today. It is neither past nor future; it remains perpetually suspended in time present. By blurring the line between epistrophe and anaphora, his delivery reinforces the meaning he projects.

Just before this section of the speech, we find that poetry itself has brought King's speech to these climactic refrains. King once said, "It's terrible to be circling around up there without a place to land" (Lischer, "Music" 61). King now sights his "landing strip" and says something quite remarkable: "I am personally the victim of deferred dreams, of blasted hopes" (*Trumpet* 79). King is referencing Hughes's most famous poem, "Dream Deferred." It is not an idle reference. This is a poem King knew well. In fact, King used many of the images that first appeared in this poem to give new validity to an old form. As we will see, Hughes's poem is the origin of King's dream metaphor.

This chapter documents how the cultural popularity of Hughes's "Dream Deferred" creates the fullest resonance for reading King's first-ever sermon on dreams. King's various allusions to "Dream Deferred" and Hughes's earliest drafts of this poem will be used to establish a textual basis from which to better view these engagements.

Hughes's Most Popular Poem

To better understand how King reinvented the most memorable image from "Dream Deferred," it is necessary to first take a closer look at the poem itself. "Dream Deferred" is Hughes's best-known poem. In his unpublished first draft, written in the fall of 1948, it appeared within a longer sequence titled "Harlem."[2] Hughes knew immediately that he had written something special when he wrote the words that would become "Dream Deferred." The original, handwritten draft of the poem is written on paper with the word "MEMORANDUM" embossed at the top in black capital letters. Just above this, Hughes drew a star and then circled it, as if to denote its importance. Of all the poems Hughes drafted and then published in the collection *Montage of a Dream Deferred*, this is the only one that survives in a handwritten draft. Perhaps Hughes himself wanted a record of the moment he drafted these lines.

The tall, thin page yellows as this memo paper shows signs of having been stapled and restapled perhaps five different times in its upper-lefthand corner. In pencil, Hughes begins with the first simile that remains in the poem: "Does it dry up / like a raisin / in the sun?" These line breaks are required by the narrow width of the page. He originally writes "Or does it fester / like a sore / and run?" but then crosses out "Or" to begin the line with "Does." He also strikes through "and" and writes "then" above in its place. After asking "Does it stink / like rotten meat?" he compresses the next line by drawing a line through a repetitive "does it." Hughes then writes a line that will be significantly revised before publication:

Or does it atom-
like explode
and leave death in
its wake?[3]

Hughes's evocation of nuclear explosion reminds us that he is living and writing in the atomic age. Not only has Cold War politics left the world in fear of cataclysmic destruction, but the shadow of World War II has left it with the very real reminder of the devastation at Hiroshima and Nagasaki. Hughes's original image thus imagines a similar fate for his dream. This destruction comes not from without, by bombs dropped from the sky, but through the hegemony of a political paradigm that splits dreams like atoms until deferment becomes death.

Continuing with the image of nuclear explosion, Hughes imagines this blast doing to dreams what it does to humans. He then asks: "What happens to / a dream deferred?" The response is more questions:

Does it just
disappear in
air
as smoke might
somewhere?

Hughes revises the syntax with two loops indicating that he would transpose the position of "smoke" and "might." But most important, he is considering in this first draft the idea that Harlem's residents literally watch their aspirations and dreams go up in smoke. He ends the draft with the dream obliterated. It is important to note that, in its final form, "Dream Deferred" offers a series of six unanswered questions.

On August 7, 1948, Hughes revised the poem by marking changes on his now-typed draft. Envisioning a single four-page poem, Hughes removed the direct connotations of nuclear explosion by drawing a line through "atom-like," striking it from further consideration. This line would stand from here on simply as *"Or does it explode,"* losing its direct connections with smoke and bombs. However, this image received greater emphasis with this revision. Larger possibilities for different types of explosions result from the ambiguity of the word *"explode"* as it stands on its own. The word "explode" was italicized to stand apart from the other similes in the poem, as it became the only direct metaphor.

Just as important, Hughes added a new image to rhyme with "explode." Boxed in the right margin he wrote, "Maybe it just sags / like a heavy load." While it is possible that Hughes simply needed a new rhyme for "explode" and drafted a new line, it is more likely that he engaged in auto-citation as he alluded to a line that appears elsewhere in his own works. Given his typical creative process, it seems more than a coincidence that Hughes was simultaneously revising the libretto for the opera *Troubled Island,* which debuted on March 31, 1949. It was common for Hughes to switch between projects during a given evening. If this is the case, there are no fewer than three instances where one of this opera's characters speaks about a "heavy load." In two scenes, Haitian native Azelia is portrayed carrying fruit in a basket on her head; however, she is really smuggling weapons to rebels who hope to overthrow their French rulers. As the third character to appear onstage, she immediately announces, "Heavy this load I bear" (*Collected Works* 6: 18). Her whips, blades, knives, and pistols are hidden below a layer of what appear to be melons and mangoes. Hughes signals viewers to the Marxist theme of perpetual revolution when he ends the play with a violent uprising by the proletariat. In the final scene, Azelia, now apparently deranged and remembering the overthrow she aided, is reliving her act of courage. We see that she carries a "wicker tray of fruits" (6: 45). When she claims she has weapons, she says, "Heavy this load I bear" and finally, once again, "Too heavy this load I bear" (6: 46).

If Hughes was thinking of this image when he added the new line to "Dream Deferred," the connection amplifies the suggestion that this poem negotiates censorship by subtly masking emotional pain through the analogy of lynching. Hughes's ability to activate the single most potent image of lynching, that of strange fruit, comes through when he borrows a line from *Troubled Island* to suggest the images of fruit and violence.

Hughes's line is also reminiscent of two classic spirituals: "Down by the Riverside" and "Bye and Bye." "Down by the Riverside" begins:

I'm gonna lay down my heavy load
Down by the riverside
Down by the riverside
I'm gonna lay down my heavy load
Down by the riverside

"Bye and Bye" repeats this sentiment in every other line: "O Bye and bye, bye and bye / I'm goin' to lay down my heavy load."

King's Engagements with "Dream Deferred"

King engaged with Hughes's "Dream Deferred" throughout his speeches. Although the reference to Hughes's poem in King's Christmas Eve sermon in 1967 is obvious, King usually riffed on this poem in more subtle ways. King alluded to five of the six images used in Hughes's poem: dreams that dry up in the sun, a "heavy load," things that "explode," things that "stink," and a "festering sore." King's most overt use of Hughes's poem came in a February 12, 1966, article he wrote for his column in the *Chicago Defender, My Dream*. In this column, King explains why he is spending several days a week living in a slum apartment in Chicago. Two weeks earlier, on January 26, he, Coretta, and the three children had moved to "the third floor of a building at 1550 South Hamlin Avenue in Chicago's West side in an attempt to graphically illustrate existing slum conditions" (Kirk, *Civil Rights Movement* 104). In his article, King announces that he and the SCLC are "waging war on the big city ghetto" (10). King concludes by writing: "Langston Hughes asks, 'What happens to a dream deferred?' But these dreams were not deferred, they were denied and repudiated by vicious though subtle patterns of exploitation. So the dreams do not, 'Dry up like raisins in the sun.' They decay like sun-ripened oranges that are devoured by worms and birds until they fall to the ground, creating a rotten mess. . . . And so the social consequences of our repudiated dreams, denied opportunities and frustrated aspirations are very much present" (10).[4]

King had first alluded to "Dream Deferred" ten years earlier, on August 11, 1956, when he invoked three different poems by Hughes. He alludes to "Dream Deferred" by stating, "The festering sore of segregation debilitates the white man as well as the Negro" (Carson 3: 337). King used the same line on November 4 and December 15 of that year, when he offered a similar allusion: "But not only that, segregation is evil because it scars the soul of both the segregated and the segregator. . . . The festering sore of segregation debilitates the segregated as well as the segregator" (3: 476). Over time, King's source becomes easier to spot as he locates it with another of Hughes's images. Speaking at the White Rock Baptist Church in Durham, North Carolina, on February 16, 1960, King said: "The festering sore of segregation debilitates the white man as well as the Negro. So long as America is burdened down with the ugly weight of segregation, she cannot expect to have the respect of the people of the world" (5: 369). Hughes's "heavy load" is transformed into King's "ugly weight" as the sore that once applied to deferred dreams is applied to segregation.

King subtly invoked "weight" and "deferred" in September 1963 when he imagined a future where the "weight of centuries" would be removed and the "long-deferred issue of second-class citizenship" would be resolved before a "seething humanity" became so despondent that it chose a "desperation it tried, asked, and hoped to avoid" (Washington 168). King is referencing rioting or outright revolution in his final phrases, two things also suggested by "explode" in Hughes's poem. King invoked the same imagery two years later in response to the outbreak of violence in Watts, California: "Ten years ago in Montgomery, Alabama, seething resentment caused a total Negro community to unite" but now the "flames of Watts illuminated . . . in the explosive ghettos" (Washington 189).

King's most important use of "Dream Deferred" comes in his reference to "shattered dreams." Although this phrase could have come from any number of sources, a comparison between the syntax of King's 1967 "A Christmas Sermon on Peace" and his earlier uses indicates a connection to Hughes's poem. The idea of "shattered dreams" became a critical component of King's rhetoric from 1959 to 1968. It repeatedly appeared as a key phrase, and even became the subject of one of his most personal sermons.[5]

April 5, 1959: Shattered Dreams

King delivered his first-ever address on dreams on Sunday, April 5, 1959, at Dexter Avenue Church in Montgomery, Alabama. This sermon reveals the origins of King's engagement with the dream metaphor. Of course, he had referred to dreams before on a few occasions, but these were as brief as a sentence or single thought, never developed into focal points large enough to stand as titles of his speeches. For example, on August 31, 1952, King suggested that Jesus's teachings are not "the pious injunction of a utopian dreamer" (Carson 6: 127). In January 1955 he used the term to introduce what he portrayed as humanity's earliest desires for pleasure: "It is an old dream, as old as the Garden of Eden with its luscious forbidden fruit so pleasing to the eye. It was a fascinating dream of the hedonist" (6: 205). King borrowed an idea from Henry Fosdick when he mentioned in July 1957 that some people deal with their inferiority complex by "fleeing to a world of fantasy and day-dreaming" (6: 305).

King's most common single-line refrain was to speak of those who were bold enough that they "dared to dream." For example, on May 17, 1957, King suggested that the *Brown v. Board* decision of 1954 was a "great beacon light of hope to millions of disinherited people throughout the world who had dared only to dream of freedom" (Carson 4: 210). Before 1959, King's most often used "dream" phrase came near the end of a speech in which he called upon listeners to be as maladjusted as Amos, Lincoln, and Jefferson before asserting that Jesus had "dared to dream a dream of the fatherhood of God and the brotherhood of man."[6] For King, dreaming was a bold, ambitious activity.

Before examining the cultural context of April 1959 in detail, we should note that the text of King's original outline for his April 5, 1959, sermon offers important links to many of the speeches and sermons that culminate in his 1967 Christmas testimony that "I am personally the victim of deferred dreams, of blasted hopes" (Washington 79). King wrote the following sentences in his outline for this sermon in red pencil under a roman numeral I: "Our sermon today brings us face to face with one of the most persistent realities in human experience. Very few people are privileged to live life with all their dreams realized and all of their hopes fulfilled. Who has not had to face the agony of blasted hopes and shattered dreams?" (Carson 6: 357). Later in this outline, King used Romans 15 to illustrate Paul's desire to go to Spain: "The story of Paul's life was the tragic story of blasted hopes and shattered dreams" (6: 358). King's outline suggests three ways people can respond when their dreams are shattered. First, they can become bitter and frustrated. Second, they can withdraw into themselves (6: 359). Either short on time or needing to reflect further, King initially ended his outline here in red pencil. The final two sentences that would eventually appear under roman numeral III are written with a different stylus: "The final alternative is creative. It involves the exercise of a great and creative will" (6: 359).

As written, King's sermon follows his outline closely. What we notice first is that King's original title in both his outline and sermon is not "Shattered Dreams" but "Unfulfilled Hopes." Immediately, in the second sentence of his sermon, King introduces his topic, and it reads as if he is simply restating the theme of deferred dreams when he says: "Very few people are privileged to live life with all of their dreams realized and all of their hopes fulfilled. Who here this morning has not had to face the agony of blasted hopes and shattered dreams?" (Carson 6: 359). King concludes this introductory section with a question that is both thematically similar to the end of Hughes's poem and syntactically reminiscent of Hughes's strategy of asking questions. Equally important, King presents his ideas in a definite pattern. In the first sentence, dreams and hopes begin as things we want to have "realized" and "fulfilled," but they end as items that are "blasted" and "shattered." Is King following the sequential logic of "Dream Deferred," which begins with dreams that are delayed and ends with ones that explode?

King had frequently been giving imaginative revisions of Hughes's well-known phrase. In many of King's addresses from this period we hear of "blasted hopes and shattered dreams"; in others, he speaks of "unfulfilled hopes and shattered dreams," and on Christmas Day of 1967 he says "deferred dreams, of blasted hopes." These three phrases are virtually interchangeable. "Deferred" finds a synonym in "unfulfilled," and "dreams" finds its parallel in "hopes." And "shattered" and "blasted" echo the notion of bombing and rioting suggested in the final image Hughes offered in "Dream Deferred," "*explode*." Obviously, things that "explode" are both "blasted" and "shattered."

The sermon passes swiftly through the negative responses of bitterness and withdrawal as King declares that listeners should respond creatively to unfulfilled hopes and shattered dreams. He expands on this last idea to suggest that the person who does this "discovers the power and the creativity of the human will, and he faces any circumstance with the power and force of his will" (Carson 6: 362). More than half of the sermon concerns this creative response.

King's decision to use Paul's aspirations to see Spain as this morning's scripture comes directly from Frederick Meek.[7] Furthermore, King first encountered the idea he presents as his alternative to the dilemma of unfulfilled hopes—namely, exhibiting one's creative will—in Howard Thurman's *Deep River*. Thurman writes: "The final alternative is creative. . . . It involves the exercise of a great and dynamic will" (38). If King uses Meek's and Thurman's ideas without acknowledgment, why would we expect him to name the poet whose ideas he was rewriting? There are likely two factors. First, Meek's and Thurman's ideas were likely unknown to King's listeners and hence could be repeated verbatim. Second, it was common for preachers to use each other's ideas without acknowledgment. Direct references to Hughes's poem, on the other hand, would have been recognized by some members of this audience.

Hughes is mentioned by name in this sermon with a complexity that requires some extended consideration. To better understand this, we need to look at King's elaborate use of echoing. He uses this technique in the middle of his sermon when he says that we ask questions where "the only answer that we get is a fading echo of our desperate cry, of our lonely cry" (Carson 6: 361). The repetition of "cry" becomes a literal echo in this line, but it is the framework around which King invokes the image of an echo that is most revealing. King echoes the word "cry" within a section that is devoted to asking questions. Moreover, these questions arise where King is addressing the disappointing aspect of unfulfilled dreams. This is the moment in the sermon when the theme most resembles Hughes's poem. Near the end of this section, King asks two questions addressing the philosophical implications of human existence. He then immediately addresses the idea of questioning itself: "These are the questions we ask, and we ask them because there is an element of tragedy in life" (6: 361).

Next, King restates and echoes the question he used earlier to create focus for the sermon. For the second time, parishioners hear: "Now, the question I want to try to grapple with you is this, with this morning is: 'What do you do when you find your dreams unrealized, your hopes unfulfilled?'" (Carson 6: 361). Is King's verbal stumble here a slip as he loses his place in the text, or is he drawing attention to how difficult it is to wrestle with this question? Or does he want listeners to notice that he is asking a question that echoes the one he asked in the introduction? Only the most attentive listeners would note these parallels. Nonetheless, many things in this sermon come in pairs that echo each other. These echoes are not coincidental. As we have just seen, King restates "unfulfilled hopes" as "shattered dreams"; he begins the sermon with one focus question, then restates it here in the middle of his address; he says "cry" twice; he asks twin questions in the section directly above; and he repeats the phrase "we ask."

King's use of echoing illuminates the idea of persistence that he introduced in the first sentence of the sermon. Nothing is more persistent than an echo that keeps returning. It is illuminating that the ideas of persistence and echoing center on King's direct reference to Hughes. As if to remind listeners of the poet who has dealt specifically with the subject he is busy addressing, King states near the end of this sermon that it takes writers such as "Langston Hughes to write poetry so that we can identify ourselves with reality through poetry" (Carson 6: 366). Once again, the word "poetry" is echoed through its repetition in this sentence. Given the topic of his sermon and the evidence surrounding King's appreciation for him, we should not be surprised that Hughes is named specifically at this time in a sermon that amplifies the most memorable image from "Dream Deferred."

King's rhetorical prowess is on full display here. Look again at how this reference to Hughes and its focus on "reality" echoes the first line of King's sermon: "Our sermon brings us face to face with one of the most persistent realities of human existence" (Carson 6: 359). Like the earlier repetition of the word "poetry," here the rhyme between "persistent" and "existence" creates verbal echoes as well. Also, King's synonyms "unfulfilled" and "shattered" can be read as verbal echoes of Hughes's words "deferred" and "explode." King is literally echoing the first idea from the title of the poem and the final image in "Dream Deferred."

In "Dream Deferred," Hughes's six questions echo one another. In King's eyes, Hughes was not merely a man who wrote of idealized dreams; he was the poet who kept asking questions about unfulfilled hopes in such a way that the questions themselves communicated the persistent nature of life's disillusionments. King's sermon, with its synonyms for "deferred" and "explode" and its rhetorical ability to echo and question these realities in the way "Dream Deferred" itself functions, was bringing listeners face to face with a message that gave new rhetorical validity to an old poetic form. This use of echoing provides a glimpse into how closely King was reading Hughes's poem as a series of questions that were restating the same basic problem. Like those of his listeners, King's reality was the lived experience of bombings.

Bombed Churches and Homes: January 1957

The terrorism that the citizens of Montgomery faced in 1957 provides a clue as to why King responded to the final metaphor of "Dream Deferred" on such a personal level. It is impossible to overstate the fact that exploding bombs were not metaphors; they were words used to describe the memories of real experiences. It is at this time—the early months of 1957—that King first used the words "shattered" and "blasted" when he spoke of what can happen to "hopes" and "dreams." Although bombs had previously intimidated those striving for integration, this criminal behavior reached new levels of intensity in January 1957. With King and Ralph Abernathy following a suggestion by Bayard Rustin to meet with other leaders in Atlanta for the first meeting that would lead to the formation of the Southern Christian Leadership Conference on January 10, "King learned that bombs had exploded at four black churches in Montgomery and at the parsonages of MIA [Montgomery Improvement Association] leaders Ralph Abernathy and Robert Graetz" (Carson 4: 3). When describing these events in *Stride toward Freedom*, King wrote: "The front of his [Graetz's] house lay in ruins, and shattered glass throughout the interior showed the violence of the explosion" (Washington 464). "Shattered glass" resulted from this "explosion." Three days later, King's address was "marred by the discovery of a fake bomb on the sidewalk of the church where he appeared" (Carson 4: 5). Two weeks later, "police spotted and disengaged twelve sticks of dynamite smoldering on the porch of King's Dexter parsonage. . . . [T]he office of the city's black taxi service had been bombed, sending three drivers to the hospital. Another bomb damaged the home of a sixty-year-old black hospital worker" (4: 6). In March an MIA flyer announced that "Segregation Hasn't Been Licked." Its evidence centered on four pictures of recent bombings. In his first sermon after the bombings of January 10, King addressed the fears of his congregation as he asked what so many must have all been thinking: "Where is God in the midst of falling bombs?" (4: 108).

In February 1957, the SCLC sent a telegram to President Eisenhower requesting action because "DYNOMITE BOMBS HAVE BEEN EXOPLODED IN OUR CHURCHES AND IN THE HOMES OF OUR MINISTERS AND CITIZENS" (Carson 4: 132). King added his name as president of the SCLC when April brought a declaration cosigned with Roy Wilkins and A. Philip Randolph at the Conference on Prayer Pilgrimage for Freedom reminding listeners that "Churches and homes have been bombed" (4: 152). On April 7, King declared from the pulpit that "the house of God is being bombed" (4: 172). The following Sunday, April 14, he briefly revisited this same theme when, near the very end of his sermon, he said: "Tired sometimes, disappointing experiences all around, sickness, facing the death of loved ones, facing disappointment, highest dreams often shattered, highest hopes often blasted" (4: 283). This was the first time he had used a phrase that linked the ideas that resurfaced in his April 5, 1959, sermon. King realized that his parishioners would make the connection between exploding bombs and shattered dreams when he delivered this sermon.

The structure of King's phrases suggests two things. First, the decision to state the same idea twice emphasizes the connection to actual bombs. When King spoke in response to the bombings in Montgomery on January 10, 1957, he linked the idea of echoing with these explosions when he said: "It is a question that rings and echoes across the hills from the oppressed. Where is God in the midst of falling bombs?" (Carter 4: 108). Second, the sound of a bomb literally echoes when the bomb detonates. King uses this auditory reality to shape the verbal means in which he presents this subject when he restates the idea with "blasted" and "shattered," allowing it to literally echo and repeat. For King, echoing bombs shape his later association with this metaphor.

Ends of Poems

King's reading habits suggest that the final image of "Dream Deferred" would have been the one he was most likely to admire. To examine another possible motivation for why King would have rewritten Hughes's "dream deferred" as "shattered dreams," it is important to acknowledge a pattern in the way King responded to the poetry he read. His personal copy of the 1961 edition of the *New Pocket Anthology of American Verse: From Colonial Days to the Present* includes annotations in King's hand, and it shows several signs that it was read in its entirety. Despite the fact that King faced more and more demands on his time, we can imagine him reading poetry during a cross-country flight, or perhaps late at night, or even on Tuesday afternoons alone in his study. While the edition did not include any Hughes poems, King marked the inside cover "Property of Dr. Martin King, 334 Auburn Ave. NE, Atlanta, GA."[8] He also wrote eight page numbers on the inside of the front cover. Written in blue ink, these page numbers corresponded to poems King liked and marked inside the book. His habits here reveal another reason why he responded to the final image of "Dream Deferred." In the margin of the last stanza of William Cullen Bryant's poem "Thanatopsis," King made a long mark resembling an opening parenthesis the length of the final stanza. The poem implores listeners to face their deaths "By an unfaltering trust, approach thy grave, / Like one who wraps the drapery of his couch / About him, and lies down to pleasant dreams" (lines 49–51). He made the same mark in the right margin of Emily Dickinson's "In lands I never saw, they say." Once again, he drew a closing parenthesis next to her final stanza. With language suggesting the majestic Alps and the "meek" worship of daisies playing at their feet, Dickinson's stanza ends, like Hughes's poem, with a question about who is being worshipped and who is doing the worshipping: "Which, Sir, are you and which am I / Upon an August Day?" (lines 7–8).

Ralph Waldo Emerson's "Concord Hymn" was marked in the same fashion. King must have identified with the speaker of Robert Frost's "Stopping by Woods on a Snowy Evening," because he marked the last stanza: "The woods are lovely, dark and deep. / But I have promises to keep, / And miles to go before I sleep" (lines 13–15). With its theme that the completion of duties supersedes the need for rest, the poem may have come to King as a thought he was just about to say himself. Intrigued by the final stanza of "The Star-Spangled Banner," King marked the final stanza of the song, lines that are rarely sung. The endings of poems were particularly interesting to King. This continued with Edna St. Vincent Millay's "Renaissance," where, in a poem of more than two hundred lines, King marked only the final stanza. King responded to Robinson Jeffers's "Shine, Perishing Republic" by bracketing the entire poem. He wrote himself a reminder to "Note at beginning of poem why [sic] it was written at" to better understand the headnote's relationship to the final stanza in William Vaughn Moody's "An Ode in Time of Hesitation." As he would often demonstrate, King realized that places created important contexts for interpretation. King responded to the opening of a poem only once, when he marked the first three lines of Ogden Nash's "The Terrible People," perhaps imagining the people whose attitudes he was trying to change: "People who have what they want are very fond of telling people who / haven't what they want that they really don't want it, / And I wish I could afford to gather all such people into a gloomy castle" (lines 1–3). Nash's lines resonated with King.

King's interaction with the poetry he was reading suggests that of all the lines in Hughes's "Dream Deferred," the final one, "*Or does it explode,*" was the one he would have admired most.

James Wallace Hamilton

Regarding King as only a preacher leads to a reductive assessment of the origins of King's dream metaphors. In this regard, J. Wallace Hamilton is unduly cited and overprivileged. Hamilton was a preacher whom King studied and borrowed ideas from as he prepared his own sermons. In 1954 Hamilton published *Horns and Halos in Human Nature*. King filled his copy of this book with annotations ranging from underlined sentences to whole sermon outlines.

Hamilton titled one of his chapters "Shattered Dreams." In blue pen, above this chapter title in his personal copy of Hamilton's book, King wrote, "A Dream that did not come True" (Carson 6: 524). However, despite the phrase "shattered dreams" and King's awareness of it, Hamilton is not the source for King's sermon "Unfulfilled Dreams." This becomes clear when we examine how and when King borrowed extensively from Hamilton's ideas for a series of sermons he presented in October 1956.[9] In this regard, it is important to examine King's process. A handwritten sermon outline appears on the blank page across from the chapter title. King titled his outline "The Meaning of a Dream" and underneath it wrote "Behind all great inventions was a dream." These lines are followed by "When a dream becomes an illusion" and its subpoint: "The prodigal illusion" (6: 524). King's outline directly correlates with a sermon King delivered in 1956 titled "The Prodigal Son."[10]

"The Prodigal Son" was the first in a series of sermons King delivered on the parable of the prodigal son at Dexter Avenue Baptist Church in October 1956. No audio or printed transcript of King's sermon survives, but a detailed outline remains that introduces the topic by suggesting that it was "the most familiar of all the parables of Jesus" (Carson 6: 271). King's sermon shows six unmistakable similarities to his original outline in Hamilton's book. First, each points out the errors of imagining that "pleasure is the end of life." Second, both use "The Hedonist" as an example. Third, King's sermon outline lists "Epicurus" as a major point (the fact that this follows "The Hedonist" clarifies King's abbreviation "Epic" in the first outline). Fourth, Hamilton's references in this chapter to Ecclesiastes are cited. Fifth, two poems from *The Rubaiyat of Omar Khayyam* (nos. 71 and 12) are quoted by King and mentioned specifically in Hamilton's chapter. Finally, King's first draft uses the term "illusion" on two occasions: "The prodigal illusion" and "When a dream becomes an illusion" (6: 524).

It is noteworthy that King's finished outline uses the term "illusion" exactly six times but does not use the word "dream" even once. Given the fact that this sermon makes use of Hamilton's ideas in the chapter "Shattered Dreams," the omission of the word "dream" here suggests that King did not immediately gravitate toward the image of a "shattered dream" after reading or preaching from Hamilton's book. It also reveals that the original sermon outline in *Horns and Halos* did not inspire King to use the dream metaphor in his April 5, 1959, sermon, as only the phrase "shattered dreams" occurs in King's actual sermon. It would be unprecedented for King to reference an earlier outline without borrowing even a single idea from it to revise, develop, and improve his ideas before delivering them in person. Something else accounts for King's use of the dream metaphor in April 1959. We know this because of the fact that he had already used Hamilton's chapter on the prodigal son without including even one mention of dreams. Others have also concluded that "there is little else from Hamilton in the sermon" besides the title (Lischer, *Preacher King* 106). If the sermon and chapter were related, King would not have hesitated to take sentences from Hamilton, just as he had from Meek's sermon and Thurman's book. The fact is, not even Hamilton's chapter title is relevant. That title merely seems to solve a mystery before an earnest investigation gets started. If Hamilton's title doesn't add resonance to this phrase, what does? Why would King wait until April 1959 to turn the topic of unfulfilled dreams into a sermon for the first time? Did something else in April 1959 motivate King to use the dream metaphor for the first time? It is clear that King knew and rewrote highly allusive lines from "Dream Deferred," but why did he echo its imagery of unfulfilled hopes and shattered dreams *now*?

A Raisin in the Sun

I would submit that the most likely reason King delivered "Unfulfilled Hopes" for the first time in April 1959 was that Hughes's poem had just returned in the form of a play. Lorraine Hansberry's play *A Raisin in the Sun* enjoyed immediate success when it debuted only weeks before King's first-ever sermon based on dreams. More than anything else, this play brought the metaphor of dreams to King's attention. According to Jordan Miller, "*A Raisin in the Sun* is the first play by a Negro of which one is tempted to say, 'everyone knows it.' Thousands of Americans have seen it on the stage in New York, in other large cities, on college campuses, and in community theatres. Many more thousands have seen it on the screen. And, finally, millions of Americans who might not seek it out have seen the movie on their television screens" (959). As Hughes himself wrote after attending the debut, "*Everybody* was at the *Raisin* opening" (Bontemps and Hughes 380).[11] The play debuted in 1959 and ran for 538 consecutive performances. Nominated for four Tony Awards, it won the New York Drama Critics Circle Award as the year's best drama.

The effect the play had on the black community is especially important and deserves attention. Jordan Miller notes that "members of the Negro community supported this Broadway production of a Negro play as they had supported no other; there were nights, even in New York, when the audience was almost half Negro. This particular Broadway play, then, was not performed for the usual white middle-class audience" (958). A columnist for the *New York Times* wrote: "I saw Lorraine Hansberry's play, *A Raisin in the Sun*, the other weekday and noted with great satisfaction that it played to a full house. Perhaps the popular misconception that non-musical plays by and about Negros cannot 'succeed' on Broadway can now be laid to rest" (Pitt). According to Elizabeth Brown-Guillory, "never in theater history had such large numbers of blacks supported a Broadway show. James Baldwin noted that 'he had never in his life seen so many black people in the theater'" (34).

Hansberry had discovered a way to encode and subvert her indignation at the dominant culture's political motives. In 1951, when she was twenty, "Hansberry took a position as a journalist and researcher at *Freedom* newspaper, a radical news organ founded by Paul Robeson and Du Bois in 1950." The monthly paper "became one of the leading left-wing newspapers in the United States during the high tide of McCarthyism" (Wilkins 195). *Freedom* was "a catalyst for Black American political growth" and soon became "a voice of, and political weapon for, the masses of Blacks and all progressive Americans" (Effiong 32).

Although it was often hailed for its universal themes, *A Raisin in the Sun* is a political play. The plot centers around the Younger family as they await the arrival of a $10,000 check from a life insurance company as a settlement for the death of their father. The mother, son, and daughter imagine how cashing that check will help them fulfill their dreams. Eventually, part of the money is put toward a new home in a predominantly white neighborhood. Bombs in this neighborhood and an attempted buy-out by a representative of the white community try to deter the Youngers from moving, but they take the risk and move into the Chicago suburb where current tenants have had their homes burned and bombed. The play was inspired by Hansberry's own life. Her family had faced white mobs "surrounding their home, screaming . . . and hurling bricks," and the family was "initially evicted by Illinois courts." Eventually, the U.S. Supreme Court "reviewed the *Lee et al. v. Hansberry et al.* case, and it finally ruled in favor of the family's right to occupancy in any neighborhood" (Effiong 30–31).

The play owes much to Langston Hughes. Hansberry knew Hughes's poetry well, and Hughes even visited her family's home during her youth. In fact, *A Raisin in the Sun* alludes to two poems by Hughes. The play's original working title, "The Crystal Stair," takes its theme and imagery from Hughes's poem "Mother to Son." As in "Mother to Son," a mother's influence on her son is a major theme.[12] There are two direct allusions to this poem in the play. On two occasions, Mama is described as climbing a rough staircase: "My— them steps is longer than they used to be. Whew!" (Hansberry 89); and later: "You know them steps can get you after a day's work" (97). Attentive viewers see Mama modeling for her son the determination to keep going even when life provides ample incentives to give up.

The stronger connection is with the poem "Dream Deferred." Hansberry's title comes directly from the first lines in the poem, where Hughes wrote: "What happens to a dream deferred? / Does it dry up / like a raisin in the sun? (1–3). In fact, the play is so committed to emphasizing its connection to Hughes that the entire poem was included on the playbills handed to theatergoers each evening.[13] Critics and reviewers used the language of the poem to describe the play itself, as in this review in the *New York Times*: "Miss Hansberry explodes scornfully when producers are mentioned. . . . When the curtain rises Wednesday night on 'Raisin in the Sun' a dream deferred will mature at last" (Robertson). Often the play is discussed using the dream motif. Hansberry dedicated the play to her mother in "gratitude for the dream" and highlighted these aspects in an interview, noting that "'Raisin' is a play about dreams" (Robertson).

In Brooks Atkinson's review of opening night, readers of the *New York Times* read that "The son is dreaming of success" ("The Theatre"). As if drawn to the final image of Hughes's poem, Atkinson consistently played with Hughes's image of destruction, calling the play a "contribution to an explosive situation" and finding that the play "is likely to destroy the complacency of any one who sees it." Later in the month, Atkinson told readers that "scenes in the script touch off explosions in the performance. But the explosions never give the impression of being arbitrary." Dreams continued to be cited, as Mama is recounted as a woman who has always "dreamed of escaping" ("'Raisin in the Sun'"). The link extended well beyond its premiere. In 1992, Amiri Baraka wrote that the play "is about *dreams*. . . . Walter Lee and Ruth's dialogues lay out his male chauvinism and even self- and group-hate born of the frustration of too many dreams too long deferred" (968). Baraka recounts the play's climax in Hughes's language rather than Hansberry's: "We know the pressures mounting inexorably in this one typical household, and in Walter Lee especially, and of where they must surely lead. It was the 'explosion' Langston Hughes talked about in his great poem 'Harlem'" (968). Even more recent discussions follow suit. According to Soyica Colbert, the 2008 made-for-TV version "proved the lasting appeal of explosive dreaming" (20).

"Shattered Dreams" on the Silver Screen

Eleven days after *Raisin's* Broadway debut, A. H. Weiler of the *New York Times* reported that "practically all the major companies as well as several independent producers already have been bidding for the screen rights." A film would ensure that *A Raisin in the Sun* would leave a permanent imprint on American culture. Moreover, this was expected to be a triumph for African Americans, as producer Philip Rose stated that "it is imperative to us that a movie version should be done with a Negro cast just as the play was. Audiences are proving that they are ready to accept Negros in such a drama as part of American life" (qtd. in Weiler). Rose was accurate in forecasting that the film companies were "not shocked by these stipulations and that their interest was unabated." Leaping from Broadway to Hollywood in such a short time speaks to the cultural phenomenon that was *A Raisin in the Sun*. Not only was all of America taking notice, but the black community counted it as one of the greatest achievements of black culture. Weiler summarizes the entire play in one sentence, using a phrasing that bears an uncanny resemblance to King's first use of the dream metaphor in his speeches: the play deals with "the shattered dreams of a Negro family." It is noteworthy that the play can easily be summarized in such fashion.

Does this use of the phrase "shattered dreams" indicate a connection between this summary and the language of King's sermon? Two years earlier, at Easter, King had first used the words "dreams" and "shattered" within a single phrase. It isn't hard to imagine King's mind being triggered by this line as he prepares for the Holy Week of 1959 by rereading the sermon he had given two years earlier. To be exact, in one sentence King had originally spoken of "highest dreams often shattered," yet now, two years later, this language gets revised to "shattered dreams." Could there even be a relationship between this March 22, 1959, article and King's April 5, 1959, sermon? Could King have been responding to the play?

King read newspapers throughout his life. The two he read regularly during these years were the *Montgomery Advertiser* and the *New York Times*.

It is quite possible that King took special notice of this article in the *New York Times,* since it suggested that a play by blacks, about blacks, and with blacks was set to become a major motion picture. King was attentive to political and cultural events, and the play's success would not have escaped his notice.

If King did gain inspiration from newspaper reports about the success of *A Raisin in the Sun,* he was merely practicing a philosophy he had espoused during his seminary training. King had expressed his theological commitment to what he called "the social gospel" during his first semester at Crozer Theological Seminary (Carson 6: 72). In the fall of 1948, King submitted a five-page outline for his course on preaching in which he expressed principles he would follow throughout his life: "Twentieth century preaching might grow out of a novel or a newspaper article. This was not the case in the first four centuries. The differences between these two are inevitable, for preaching grows out of the times in which the preacher lives" (6: 71). Although he points specifically to the genre of the novel, the logic of King's idea is that contemporary poetry or drama may inspire a preacher's sermon every bit as much as the Bible.

Moreover, King held to his commitment to using newspapers as inspiration. On March 18, 1956, King began his sermon with a quotation from Matthew 10.34–36 but soon turned his attention to recent newsprint coverage of events that surrounded Autherine Lucy's removal from the University of Alabama. King told his parish:

> The next day after Autherine was dismissed the paper came out with this headline: "Things are quiet in Tuscaloosa today. There is peace on the campus of the University of Alabama." Yes, things were quiet in Tuscaloosa, yes, there was peace on the campus, but it was peace at a great price. It was peace that had been purchased at the exorbitant price of an inept trustee board succumbing to the whims and caprices of a vicious mob. (Carson 6: 258)

King not only references the papers as he preaches, but the words he appropriates as his own, those outside his own quotation marks, are ones that he had read approximately six weeks earlier in the *Tuscaloosa News:* "Yes, there's peace on the University campus this morning. But what a price has been paid for it!"[14] The distance between the event and the sermon draws attention to the similar time period between the opening of *A Raisin in the Sun* and his sermon response to it.

Langston Hughes and Popular Culture: Bill Madden

The publication of Hughes's *Selected Poems* and the premiere of *A Raisin in the Sun* (both in March) pushed Hughes's visibility near an all-time high in 1959. During this time, he would be nominated for the Spingarn Award he so deeply coveted, winning it the next year to own the NAACP's highest honor. Hughes's popularity is key to understanding why his poetry would have so deeply appealed to King's sensibilities. Not only was Hansberry invoking Hughes's poetry in the year's most successful play, but another local performer was also making Hughes more accessible than ever. Actor Bill Madden had scheduled a full program to recite a number of Hughes's poems only four weeks after the debut of *A Raisin in the Sun.* As with each request to use his poetry, Hughes was generous in allowing others to use his poems for their own ends. Madden contacted Hughes, clearly enamored of Hughes's "Dream Deferred": "I read your little short poem printed in the program of the Broadway hit 'A Raisin in the Sun.' . . . it is a better poem, as a poem, than the play is a play." Madden's praise veiled a confidence that slowly bled into arrogance as he closed by stating "without any modesty at all, that when it comes to reciting, delivery, and interpretation of your work, I am the best there is (*and I mean the best*)."[15] Madden reminds us that everyone attending the play would have left without any doubt that the play's title was a direct reference to Hughes's poem, as each playbill contained an insert with the complete poem "Dream Deferred."

Hughes did more than give his consent to Madden's recitals. At the bottom of Madden's letter, Hughes notes that he sent a copy of *The Negro Mother* two days after receiving the letter, perhaps thinking that the poems in this collection would make for appropriate subject matter given the rise of the play's success, celebrating, among other things, the role of Mama portrayed by Claudia McNeil.[16] Madden's June 20, 1959, recital, "An Evening of the Poetry of Langston Hughes," was followed by another program the same year, also in New York.[17] Hughes was now so popular that his poems were appearing nearly everywhere.

Hughes's pattern of allowing the use of his poems without expecting royalties had been established in the early 1930s. It continued in 1947 when Hughes was informed that the Progressive Citizens of America had used his poem "Freedom Train" at the largest political rally in the history of Philadelphia. Hughes's poem was not sung by Paul Robeson, as originally planned, but Robeson recited it in front of thirteen thousand people who sat "literally breathless" before erupting in the biggest ovation of the evening." Hughes responded the next day, saying that he was "delighted to know that Paul likes the poem well enough to use it," and he was highly appreciative of being informed of its use as "I had not heard about it before."[18] Although he was informed that Robeson planned to recite it at all the other rallies, Hughes gladly agreed that no permission was required so long as it went to a worthy cause. Two years later Hughes was contacted by the Progressive Citizens of America for permission to use a "modified and condensed version" of his poem "Let America Be America Again." Permission was granted. Hughes received and granted many similar requests. He began his response with "I would be delighted" when petitioned by Zina Provendie to use "I, Too, Sing America" as the main theme of her theatrical and visual presentation of Negro poetry in 1965, and again when Andrew Murray sought permission in 1966 to use lines from "Mother to Son" to title his manuscript. Murray explains that Hughes's poem would be upstaging his own biblical allusion to Jacob's ladder when he writes that he would prefer to use "No Crystal Stair" as his motif.[19]

Although King appropriated Hughes's poems without hesitation, and often without acknowledgment, it is remarkable how many requests Hughes received to use his poetry. Equally impressive, Hughes, ever seeing himself as one voice participating in a much larger collective cause, approved these requests without expecting or requiring royalties. In fact, Hansberry herself asked for and received permission at no charge to use the opening image from "Dream Deferred" for the title of *A Raisin in the Sun*.[20] And as we saw in the introduction, Frederick O'Neal was one of the only people to reimburse Hughes for the use of his poetry. Elated by O'Neal's royalty check of ten dollars, Hughes replied immediately, "You may not believe me when I tell you that this is the *first* time in my natural life that anybody ever sent me *anything* just for reading or reciting a few of my poems."[21]

Hughes's willingness to grant such permission may result from three different factors. First, whether or not Hughes was a Communist Party member, a genuine socialist mentality of sharing marked his life. Second, Hughes had so long tried and failed to achieve true economic success that he simply decided to forgo trying to cash in on royalties. Third, his stance as a representative for his people had instilled a deep sense of community ownership that outweighed any individualistic concept of intellectual property.

Smirnoff Vodka

Hughes's popularity in the African American community rose to new heights with the success of *A Raisin in the Sun*. This is yet another reminder of why

King would have been invoking ideas from Hughes's poetry in this era. Hughes became so popular, in fact, that in October 1959, readers of *Ebony* encountered a calm and cool Langston Hughes promoting Smirnoff vodka. With a wry and knowing smile, Hughes sits at a table and rests his elbow on a white tablecloth as if he is waiting to share a drink with you. He sits patiently thumbing his chin, dapperly dressed in a suit, tie, and pressed white shirt (see fig. 4). Above his thin mustache, Hughes's probing stare seems to ponder what we're waiting for. One glass is poured. Perhaps it's yours, and he has been waiting for you?

The contrast between black and white plays well with the elegance, timelessness, and drama of the moment. In the first line of text, the caption reminds us of the era when advertisements were filled with words. Hughes asks, "Why settle for less than the vodka of vodkas?" Readers are told that Smirnoff is "the vodka most smart people buy and all smart places serve." Italicized to give the partial impression of its poetry, the final idea declares that Smirnoff *"leaves you breathless."*[22]

Hughes's prestige had to be exceptionally high for him to be approached for this endorsement. It is unprecedented that a mere poet effectively contributed to a national advertising campaign of this sort. Smirnoff's campaign featured visible stars from the stage and screen. It began around 1954 with Cedric Hardwicke, who had appeared in more than seventy films. In addition to playing alongside John Wayne in *Tycoon* (1947) and Charlton Heston in *The Ten Commandments* (1956), his credits also included Alfred Hitchcock's *Rope* (1948) and *Around the World in Eighty Days* (1956). In a 1958 ad, Hardwicke asserted that Smirnoff was "the smoothest vodka I never tasted." During the 1950s, Smirnoff ads featured several other stars of television, film, and theater, including Eva Gabor and Tony Randall.[23] Notably, none of these previous stars was black. Nor was Hughes a stage personality. In fact, the ad begins by noting that he is a "famous poet." The advertisement nods toward Hughes's role as a "lyric writer," next acknowledges his role in several dramas, then completes its identification of him as also being a "lecturer and critic." However, the connection to *Raisin* is obvious given Smirnoff's record of highlighting other stars of the stage.

Hughes's popularity was such that he became the first choice of Smirnoff as it sought to capitalize on the success of *A Raisin in the Sun. Raisin*'s success soon led to opportunities for four other stars of the play. By November 1959, Claudia McNeil was promoting Rheingold beer to *Ebony* readers. Behind her on a marquee above a theater, *A Raisin in the Sun* is clearly highlighted as

Figure 4. Hughes in a Smirnoff advertisement in *Ebony,* October 1959.

we read parts of the following lines: "Best in Drama Critics," "A Stupendous Hit," "Bold and Stirring," "Impressive Play, Beautifully Acted," "Language of the Heart," and "Play of the Year." As if the marquee weren't enough, the caption identifies her as an actress in "the Broadway Hit—*A Raisin in the Sun.*" Capitalizing on the play's success, she tells readers, "My Beer's Rheingold— the *Dry* Beer." Next came Earle Hyman, who, like Hughes, pitched Smirnoff as "the vodka of vodkas." Hyman, who would later play Cliff Huckstable's father on the groundbreaking TV sitcom *The Cosby Show*, had recently played Othello. More pertinent to the timing of this ad, he had just begun to play the role of Walter Lee in the London production of *A Raisin in the Sun*. Smirnoff, apparently sensing the play as the locus of where black and white culture were successfully integrating, tapped Ossie Davis and his wife, Ruby Dee, later in 1960. By this time, Davis had replaced Sidney Poitier on-stage due to Poitier's other film commitments. Smirnoff used the success of the play itself rather than its star power. Sidney Poitier never appeared as a Smirnoff spokesman.[24] As if to remind us of just how much attention Hughes received from having a line from his poem serve as the title, Lorraine Hansberry was passed over for Hughes. Despite the fact that she was the author, Hansberry lacked the visual recognition that Hughes had established during his career.

By October 1959, the date when Hughes's ad first appeared, *Ebony* had become a magazine of over 150 pages that included nearly 100 pages of advertisements. More important, it reached more than 650,000 people a month with over half receiving the magazine through direct-mail subscriptions. To contextualize Hughes's status as an advertising spokesman for Smirnoff vodka, it is important to realize that no other alcoholic beverage advertised in *Ebony* before this had featured a spokesperson. In fact, we have to leave the realm of adult beverages to find someone promoting other products. At this time, readers of *Ebony* met the Chicago Cubs baseball player Ernie Banks in his youth endorsing Red Crown canned meats such as Vienna sausage, corned beef hash, chili, and, yes, even pork brains. Dressed in a suit and tie, he declared in large print: "A Big Taste Hit in Any League." The only other celebrity advertising campaigns came from a natural link between the entertainment industry and AMI's popular jukebox. AMI ads linked African American singers with what it boasted was "the world's most beautiful Juke Box" by featuring photographs of well-established stars and brief promotions of that recording artist's latest release. Sammy Davis Jr., Harry Belafonte, Mahalia Jackson, and Nat King Cole were all featured. Langston Hughes was a mere poet who had miraculously garnered enough cultural prestige to promote vodka alongside these stars.

The success of *Raisin in the Sun* resulted in Hughes's final appearance in *Ebony* to promote Smirnoff vodka. By April 1960, his connection with the play had become so well established that he himself simply began referring to "Dream Deferred" as "Raisin in the Sun."[25] A month later, the connection between Hughes and the play was unmistakable as the cover of *Ebony* featured Claudia McNeil holding a small plant, prizing it just as Mama does throughout the play. As the main symbol in the play, this is the figurative raisin that refuses to dry out in the sun. If Mama has her way, it will be planted, tended, and watered in the predominantly white neighborhood of Clybourne Park when the Youngers take residence in their new home. The table of contents can't resist playing with the dream metaphor as the cover article is previewed with a brief but highly suggestive line: "Stardom came to her late in life with shattering suddenness."[26] Hughes's Smirnoff ad is strategically placed exactly ten pages before the lead article. Again, we see Smirnoff capitalizing on the direct associations between Hughes and *A Raisin in the Sun*. Like so many before her, McNeil herself simply can't resist using Hughes's poetry as a source of interpreting her role in the play. Regarding the connections between "Dream Deferred" and "Mother to Son," she says, "I see Lena Younger as Mother Earth, all mothers, trying to realize part of her dreams for herself, and part of her dreams for her children. . . . There's a thin line between the two. Sometimes her dreams come before her children" (Morrison 98).

Despite his appearance before a Senate subcommittee and Joseph McCarthy in 1953 and being haunted by the Communist label ever since, Hughes held an uncommon prestige within the black community. His poetry was amplified on the stage in Hansberry's play, his image was selling vodka in *Ebony*, and King was embedding images from "Dream Deferred" in his sermons and speeches. In magazines, on Broadway, and from the pulpit, Hughes's vast reach seemed to have no limit. But where his words and name could travel, Hughes himself was often barred. The distance between identity and presence is large, and nothing demonstrates this gulf better than the celebration for A. Philip Randolph held at Carnegie Hall on January 24, 1960.

5

"Poem for a Man"

King's Unusual Request

One of Martin Luther King's most surprising encounters with Langston Hughes's poetry occurred in January 1960. With Hughes's popularity as high as it would ever be within the African American community, King invited Hughes to write a poem on behalf of A. Philip Randolph. King, Roy Wilkins, Rev. Harry Emerson Fosdick, Rabbi Joachim Prinz, and Father John La Farge were organizing a celebration of Randolph's seventieth birthday. An overtly socialist thinker, Randolph was long considered the dean of black leaders. He achieved this status because he had championed the first black union when he founded the Brotherhood of Pullman Car Porters, invented the idea of a march on Washington (it was called off in 1942 when President Franklin Roosevelt relented and allowed blacks opportunities to work in defense industries), and, important to this gala, had organized youth marches in 1958 and 1959 to force implementation of the 1954 *Brown v. Board of Education* decision, which outlawed segregation in public schools. King and the other black leaders wanted to simultaneously celebrate Randolph's accomplishments and use that celebration to energize a base dedicated to mass protest and social change.

To prepare for this event, King needed the organizational help, work ethic, and expertise of one of his closest aides, Stanley Levison. King's secretary, Maude Ballou, contacted Levison on October 22, 1959: "Dr. King . . . would like to see you next Thursday, October 29, when he is in New York. He wants to talk over some important matters with you. He will call you sometime late Wednesday night."[1] This meeting led to a letter sent directly to Hughes that included an "unusual request": "Would you feel that you might write and present a poem in honor of Mr. Randolph for the occasion? It would be impossible to describe the significance this creative contribution would give to the event. A poetic tribute by our greatest poet and America's best to one of our purest leaders is a matchless combination."[2] The idea must have appealed to Hughes. Randolph was an unapologetic socialist, and the event was geared to appeal to the masses. Hughes read: "His thousands of friends feel a tribute to him is long overdue. However, the man associated with workers and simple people could not appropriately be honored at the customary banquet where many persons could not attend for lack of ten to fifteen dollars. Similarly, the man associated with mass action can be honored only in a setting of thousands. Hence the tribute will take place at Carnegie Hall, with admission free, on Sunday evening, January 24th, 1960." The setting, featuring both his home city and public access, likely appealed to Hughes every bit as much as the very personal touch of referring to the attendees as "simple people," a nod to Hughes's long-running *Chicago Defender* column, which featured the character Jesse B. Simple as a representative of the common man of Harlem. While the letter was clearly designed to flatter Hughes into writing the poem and attending the celebration, the accolades were not hyperbolic. Hughes was the leading African American poet of the day. Buoyed by the success of *A Raisin in the Sun*, his recent ads for Smirnoff in *Ebony*, and the publication of his *Selected Poems* earlier in the year, Hughes was in high demand.

King's letter went even further in its praise of Hughes's poetry: "To add my personal note—my admiration for your works is not only expressed in my personal conversations, but I can no longer count the number of times and places, all over the nation, in my addresses and sermons in which I have read your poems. I know of no better way to express in beauty the heartbeat and struggle of our people." However, a pronoun in the fourth paragraph of this letter draws attention to the complex process of its composition. The letter states, "This brings us to our unusual request." This "our" seemingly refers to King and the four men whose names appear at the end of the letter after King's signature (the members of the committee organizing the event), but in reality this "our" was much larger than these five men. In fact, the "our" literally refers to the man who composed this letter—Stanley Levison. In addition to the first downstroke in the "M" in "Martin" being broken as if copied, the top loop in the "L" is inconsistent with King's autograph, and the "K" has an opening flourish uncommon for King. Finally, the "J" that begins "Jr." is too understated for King's hand. More obviously, the letter was mailed from New York at a time when King was in Georgia.

The decision to ask Hughes to write a poem was likely made during the meeting Maude Ballou coordinated between King and Levison on October 29, 1959. The most likely scenario based on the evidence is that the general tenor of the letter was established when King spoke with Levison in person, and Levison then composed and mailed it to put their co-created plan into action. While many have noted the contributions that Levison made on behalf of King, seeing the daily operations of just how far, detailed, and exhaustive this support was reminds us of just how critical Levison was to King and the SCLC.

This chapter chronicles the process of securing, writing, and delivering the solicited poem Hughes wrote for the January 24, 1960, salute to Randolph. Although it was read before three thousand people, this poem has never been published. Its two significant references to "dreams" mark yet another early encounter King had with this idea as a result of its being specifically located within Hughes's poetry. Because Levison and King specifically asked Hughes to write a poem that has passed without discussion in the scholarship of either Hughes or King, both this poem and the context surrounding its composition will be explored in detail. In many ways, this poem would never have been written by Hughes, read at the salute, or known and then alluded to by King without the efforts of Stanley Levison. Levison is a critical figure helping us better understand the complex relationship between King's rhetoric and Hughes's poetry.

The Salute to A. Philip Randolph

Levison's efforts on King's behalf were exceptional. Levison worked on King's behalf so that this salute to Randolph not only included a poem by Hughes but also elevated King's status in the eyes of Randolph and the general public. In a three-page letter to King that details Bayard Rustin's current inability to be of help as a result of being in Africa, Levison supplies King with prepared notes for an upcoming NAACP conference and tries to arrange an interview between King and documentary filmmaker Richard Leacock. The fourth item in this December 21, 1959, letter concerns arrangements for the salute: "As I told you in our conversations about the Salute to Randolph, I intend to keep your name in the forefront because this form of association is extremely good public relations. It has evoked interesting and warm responses. One of them was cooperation from Langston Hughes, who wrote a beautiful poem saluting Randolph. I am enclosing his covering letter. I don't have a copy of the poem at hand because it is being duplicated, but I'll send it to you separately."[3] Levison is both proud of this accomplishment and cognizant that this is the one thing that will most impress King. Next, Levison goes into other responses which appear important but not nearly as exciting as Hughes's contribution. He lists a greeting from the president of Ghana, Kwame Nkrumah, that is "as much a salute to you as it is to Randolph," and a letter from Chester Bowles. Bowles, whom Levison characterizes as a potential "dark horse" in the upcoming presidential race, is being encouraged to meet with King in Washington. Finally, Levison notes casually that Eleanor Roosevelt and Senator Hubert Humphrey have committed to attend the salute. Levison's letter spotlights Hughes over each of these important figures. Ending where he began, he says that he has "drafted a 'thank you' note for Langston Hughes," then posts the letter at 1:00 a.m. on December 22, suggesting that he typed this letter at home after the rest of the day's events had been completed.

Levison's thank-you letter for Hughes was retyped verbatim by King's secretary in Montgomery and sent with yet another false signature. It reads: "I cannot say more to express both my appreciation of your poem to Phil Randolph and for your generosity in writing it, than to say it is just what I expected from you. You have added another weapon of the pen to our struggle. We are sincerely sorry you cannot read it, but it will be delivered by Ossie Davis who, as you undoubtedly know, is currently starring in 'A Raisin in the Sun.'"[4]

Levison's choice of words speaks to his own Communist beliefs. It is a stance he shares with Hughes. To declare this poem a "weapon" is to invoke a Marxist metaphor, and it may shed as much light on Levison's motivation for choosing Hughes as it does King's. However, something strange is happening here. Between the original request and the thank-you for the actual poem, this letter assumes that Hughes will not deliver the poem in person, but rather that Ossie Davis will. Why would Davis be reading the poem instead of Hughes?

Hughes had sent King a cover letter and a copy of his poem on December 12, 1959. Addressing "Dr. King," he writes: "I am happy to write a poem to A. Philip Randolph and I am enclosing a copy which you may print in the souvenir program, have read at the testimonial, and use in any other way feasible. My regret is that immediately after the holidays I am going to California and unless some urgent commitment brings me east again, sooner than I expect, it is unlikely that I will be in New York on the night of January 24th.

But perhaps, if you wish, Fred O'Neal or some other skilled performer might be invited to read my poem."[5] How has Hughes learned of the souvenir program? Has he spoken directly with someone involved in the organizational aspects of the event? In his letter, Hughes suggests that Fred O'Neal read the poem. Wouldn't he prefer to read the poem himself? Why can't he arrange his schedule so that he can attend the salute?

Hughes closes his letter with an expression of his admiration for King: "Thank you very much for your kind words about my poetry and certainly I am most pleased that you have used it in your speeches and sermons so effectively. As I have attempted to express to you before, and through my column in the CHICAGO DEFENDER, I have the greatest admiration for you and your work." Just as the statements Hughes received from King via Levison were factual, so are these. Hughes, picking up on the reference to "simple" in the first request, cites the place where his Simple stories were published, the *Chicago Defender*. It appears that Levison, not Hughes or King, arranged to have Ossie Davis read Hughes's poem. Further capitalizing on Hughes's visibility via *A Raisin in the Sun*, a performance by Davis is the perfect way to solidify Hughes's popularity in the eyes of listeners.

It seems likely that Hughes talked with someone close to the salute. The one-day delay in Levison's sending the actual poem results from the fact that it is being "duplicated" so that it can be included in the souvenir program distributed to those who attend. After forwarding the poem to King the day after his earlier letter announcing that he had received it, Levison receives a reply from King on January 5, 1960: "I am happy to know that things are developing so well for the A. Philip Randolph affair. The poem by Langston Hughes is beautiful, and the general public response is wonderful." King's admiration for Hughes is measurable in these first two lines as he acknowledges Hughes's poem but makes no specific mention of the scheduled appearances or contributions of Eleanor Roosevelt, President Nkrumah, Chester Bowles, or Hubert Humphrey. It is Hughes the poet who deserves immediate response, praise, and a thank-you for his contributions. In the middle of changing churches—departing Dexter in Montgomery and relocating to Ebenezer in Atlanta—King shows how much he relies on Levison as he closes with information about the salute itself: "I am now making plans to get a flight which will get me into New York around 6:30, two hours earlier than I had previously planned. . . . I will be contacting you in a few days concerning what I should say in my brief speech. . . . Please keep me informed about Bayard's possible return. We really need his services as soon as possible."[6] The business of securing and arranging this poem from Hughes was one of the many activities Levison engaged in during his time supporting King.

"Poem for a Man"

Hughes began drafting his poem on December 3, 1959. Ten days and five drafts later, he was finished. Hughes titled his contribution "Poem for a Man." Because the poem includes two references to the idea of "dreams" that King himself alludes to in his remarks at this event, the poem deserves a detailed discussion here. Here is the poem in its entirety:

Poem for a man
Who has lived
Seventy years of life
And strife
And emerged grand
In spite of errors here
And errors there.
And pitfalls—
This compromise and that required
That the dreams he sired
Might in part
Be realized.

Poem for a man
Of flesh and blood
And human as you and I
And lost at sea
In waves of other lost humanity,
But holding somehow high
A flag with spar
And star
For you and me.

Poem for a man
Who put his hand
Upon a dream of human dignity
And held it there—

And took his other hand
To try to wipe the mud away,
The mud that splattered everywhere:
"And who are you to think
You lead the Negro People?"

And who are you to ask,
"And who are you?"

Poem for a man
Who plays the checkered game
Of king jump king—
And jumps a President:
That *order 8802*
For me and you
And porters on a railroad car
Who make,
Each time they make a bed,
A hammock on a star
That sings in space
The dawn-song
Of a race.

Poem for a man
All these years
Grand![7]

The poem's title appears at the beginning of each of the six sections. The second strophe reminds listeners that although Randolph appears messianic in stature, he is a man "of flesh and blood, / and human as you and I." In the fifth section, the poem uses the metaphor of playing checkers to suggest that Randolph outplayed Franklin Roosevelt in getting Executive Order 8802 passed in 1941. At the time, most defense plants would not hire African Americans. Randolph, president of the Brotherhood of Sleeping Car Porters, suggested that one hundred thousand people descend on the Capitol to demand the right to work in government factories. Seeking to avoid such a confrontation, FDR signed the executive order, which prohibited discrimination in hiring blacks for defense jobs. In 1963, Randolph helped head the leadership that organized the March on Washington, D.C.

Hughes's poem ends where it started, as the final three lines echo the beginning's sentiments: "Poem for a man / All these years / *Grand!*" Between these bookends, Hughes includes two subtle reminders of Randolph's biography. First, he embeds a phrase that Randolph himself often used, as he lists the phrase "human dignity" in reference to the leader's own concise rhetoric. Second, Hughes's mention of Executive Order 8802 highlights the current implementation of the strategy to march on Washington. Randolph had been playing a key leadership role in the youth marches in the previous two years. According to Levison's letter of request to Hughes, more than fifty thousand people had marched in these rallies.

It is also interesting to note two subtle additions Hughes made to his finished poem. An additional version of Hughes's final draft includes two musical directives. First, Hughes suggests that "Climbing Jacob's Ladder" be sung before his poem is read, with the music hummed "down under" while the words of his poem are read. Is this musical element yet another reason why Hughes might have wanted someone else to read the poem? Second, in his characteristic green ink, Hughes notes at the end of the poem that it should be followed by the song "'Joshua Fit De Battle of Jericho'—and de walls came tumbling down." Placing the poem about Randolph within a chronology that begins with Jacob and ends with Joshua suggests that Hughes is making a comparison between Randolph and Moses.

Hughes's poem activates this inference as he subtly plays with the subject of identity and naming in the third and fourth sections. With questions and answers about "who" being posed and then reversed, these phrases allude to Moses's calling in Exodus 3. Moses wondered if he was qualified, but God reversed these stutterings and revealed himself. Here, the play on "who" also elevates Randolph's standing as one who has stood up to the president of the United States, the oppressive, symbolic pharaoh. Hence Hughes's reference to Randolph's outwitting FDR in a game of checkers appears immediately after this connection between Randolph and Moses.

It is possible that Hughes's musical instructions made their way into the recitation of the poem at Carnegie Hall. It is not difficult to imagine that this typed version was the one passed on to Ossie Davis. Whom else would Hughes have given this copy to? Why would he create another draft with instructions for music if no potential existed for songs to be included for this onetime event? Davis and Hughes had often communicated, and they knew each other well.

Careful coordination characterized this event. While Hughes's poem is not mentioned by the media outlet that covered the event, it is reported that "three distinguished actors—Ruby Dee, John Randolph, and Ossie Davis—read a skit on Randolph's life in which they quoted him as saying: 'The Republican party, representing the corporate interests of the North, and the Democratic, shackled by the Dixiecrats of the South, does not represent the interests of the Negro. The two old parties have failed the Negro'" (Burnham). Perhaps Hughes's poem was read and the musical numbers performed by some combination of these actors.

The interconnectedness of ideas presented from this platform is quite remarkable. Picking up on what these actors portrayed dramatically, Randolph ended the night by declaring marches on the Republican and Democratic Conventions later in the year, because both the presidency and many congressional seats were up for reelection. Randolph's other words added further unity to the events: "We shall not remain quiet, polite, or content until justice is firmly in our hands" (Burnham). The reference to "hands" echoes the key image from Hughes's poem:

> Poem for a man
> Who put his hand
> Upon a dream of human dignity
> And held it there—

Hughes first introduced this dream in the second section of his poem when he wrote of Randolph's ability to see "That the dreams he sired / Might in part / Be realized." A bit roughly, Hughes is suggesting that Randolph was the father of a dream that has only in part been realized. Following the reading of Hughes's poem, Randolph can be heard taking justice "firmly in our hands" from Hughes and amplifying it for his listeners. As such, Hughes's contribution this evening extends well beyond the poem itself.

At the ceremony, King responded to Hughes's poem. Aware of the sentiments of Hughes's musical directives, King references them. We wonder how intensely King had studied the poem or to what degree Levison coordinated this through his own suggestions for King's remarks. On the program, King spoke before Hughes's poem was read. He knew to praise Randolph for refusing to "sell his race for a mess of pottage" (Burnham). The image is an allusion to Jacob stealing his brother's birthright. Jacob was the subject of the song that Hughes envisioned leading into and carrying underneath the cadence of his verses, "Climbing Jacob's Ladder." Interestingly, King reduces Randolph by linking him to Jacob rather than exalting him as Moses. Given his own success with marching, it is possible to imagine King associating himself with Joshua.

More important, King referenced the idea of dreams on this occasion. His handwritten comments for that night begin with a sentence declaring that Randolph "had always had the penetrating insight to dream when the time for a great idea had appeared" (Carson 5: 350). King's comments began the act of doing what they have continued to do until today: King made it appear that Hughes's ideas on dreams came after him. This act of transumption, of making the early seem late and the late feel early, can literally be measured here. Hughes referenced the idea of dreams in two separate stanzas of his poem, each of them being the most memorable image of the poem. The song's reference to the dream in which Jacob sees angels ascending and descending a ladder into heaven reveals that the origin of dreaming here is first invoked by Hughes. However, by taking the stage before Hughes's poem is presented, King introduces the idea of dreaming to the audience that night, thereby reducing Hughes to someone eager to second a motion. King appears to have been the man who brought the idea to the table.

Hughes's poem anticipated Randolph's influence on King. On the first pages of his first typed draft, Hughes created a powerful assertion that did not survive revision. He includes this redacted line at the end of the list of "who" questions that link Randolph with Moses as he plays with ideas of identity. Remembering that this iteration of the poem has already gone from handwriting to type, we read:

"AND WHO ARE YOU TO THINK
YOU LEAD THE NEGRO PEOPLE?"
AND WHO ARE YOU TO ASK
"AND WHO ARE YOU?"
POEM FOR A MAN?

This spacing of the lines, with its lack of an indentation, suggests that, in this draft, Hughes is playing with the idea that Randolph himself is "a poem for a man." While the final draft gestures toward the fact that Hughes has written a poem for a man (hinting at Randolph's first initial, making him the "A man"), this version positions Randolph as a poem waiting to be read by someone else. To extend this idea, Randolph is the poem King read, a text waiting to be read by the next generation. Randolph is the primer King studied, the model to teach him what should be done. In this moment of composing, the poem communicates the idea that King is the man who needed to be inspired by

Randolph. Without Randolph, King would have had no script to follow, no poem to learn from. While it is sometimes difficult to remember a time when King was not the clear and visible head of the civil rights movement, this moment of celebration in early 1960 and this thought in the poem remind us that King was standing in Randolph's long shadow. Moses/Randolph was alive and well. Joshua/King was awaiting his turn. According to Hughes's poem, Randolph was the father of a dream still waiting to be fulfilled. As we now know, Hughes's idea was prophetic.

But we should not reduce this analysis of dreaming to these three men. Levison's role deserves further discussion. Like Andrew Young and Clarence B. Jones, Levison is one of several key advisers who shaped the words King spoke in the years to follow. Here, Levison secured the poem from Hughes, supplied King with a forum that would increase his visibility, and then at least suggested King's talking points for the evening. It is possible that Levison recommended preempting Hughes's poem by introducing the metaphor of dreaming earlier in the program. Another telegram exists in regard to the comments made this evening. In this telegram, sent on January 16, 1960, Levison's suggestions again correspond with the date of King's handwritten notes (Carson 5: 350). This is likely how King received practical guidance from Levison about the comments he should make at the tribute. As such, Levison, King, and Hughes formed an unusual triangle of men all connected in different degrees with the metaphor of dreaming. Without Levison, this point of origin never would have happened. Looking one last time at Levison's first letter to Hughes, we can see that Hughes likely took a prompt (from a letter he believed was written by King himself) that ended up serving as the impetus for the dream image in Hughes's poem. In describing Randolph to Hughes, we read: "He fathered, through mass actions, the first Federal F.E.P.C., which has led to dozens of state F.E.P.C. laws."[8] Having picked up on the "simple" reference earlier in this letter, Hughes may have been prompted by Levison's metaphor of "fathering" to describe Randolph as a man who sired dreams.

Ruby Dee

Hughes did not attend the salute to Randolph. Half expecting to be in California yet not certain that he would be, Hughes skipped the event. (Hughes often had his secretary use "I'll be in California" as a generic excuse to get out of things he did not want to commit to.) Nonetheless, Hughes kept special watch on the event, eager to get word on the reception of his poem. A telegram he sent to Ruby Dee the day after the salute reveals his interest. Hughes sent his telegram to Dee at the Belasco Theater on West Forty-Fourth Street, where *Raisin in the Sun* was still running. His copy of the wire is handwritten in red pencil, the color he often used for lists, telephone correspondence, and other mundane tasks:

> Dear Ruby Dee Thank you very much for what friends in attendance at Randolph Testimonial tell me was your beautiful rendition of my poem last night
> Sorry I had to miss it.
>   Langston[9]

Hughes was in New York the evening of the salute. His calendars and itineraries reveal that he was very busy. He had been in California for the holidays to visit his uncle and a cousin, but he returned to New York on January 7, well before this celebration. He spent January 8 opening Christmas cards and other mail before heading to Brooklyn for a rehearsal. Alfred Duckett was preparing a "ninety minute spiritual spectacular" called *Month O' Sundays* that featured Hughes reading his own poetry to the accompaniment of a seventeen-voice choir known as the Fordhamaires.[10] Other songs and hymns were featured on the program, which was scheduled to be performed at Brooklyn's Antioch Baptist Church on Sunday, January 31. The $1.50 admission fee was being used to pay for a new church organ. Hughes rehearsed on January 11, 16, and 21.[11]

Two other notes on Hughes's calendar are revealing. On January 23, the day before the salute to Randolph, Hughes notes: "Hugh Woodings [*sic*] return to Waldorf Towers." Red pencil notes Wooding's phone number and the fact that a wire has been sent. On January 24, while the salute was taking place at Carnegie Hall, Hughes met with Wooding in his room at the Waldorf Towers.[12]

Wooding, a prominent black lawyer from Trinidad, was the husband of Anne Marie Cousey, whom Hughes had portrayed as "Mary" in his first autobiography, *The Big Sea*. Apparently, Wooding's visit to New York provided an occasion to meet with Hughes. However, since their appointment was scheduled for 4:30, Wooding might have gone to the salute after meeting with Hughes. Why might Hughes have deliberately wanted to miss the salute to A. Philip Randolph?

By the late fall of 1959, Hughes had been working to overhaul his image by linking himself with religion. However, his "deepening involvement in religion seems to have been more of a gambit than a mark of a new personal piety. Perhaps it was also strategic" (Rampersad 2: 306). On November 22, 1959, Hughes published the first of a series of articles in the *Chicago Defender* on religion. In fact, he sent the final five articles in this series to the paper on the same day he sent the two unsolicited poems (discussed in chapter 3) to King in Montgomery. Though not acknowledged by King's or Hughes's secretary, Hughes may even have sent a flier for his poetry recital on January 31 at Antioch Baptist Church.[13] This may explain why Hughes sent King a copy of "Prayer for the Mantle-Piece."

Hughes's reason for being absent from the salute seems clear. After writing on religion in the *Defender*, reading his poems at Antioch Baptist Church, and sending samples of his work to a man of faith, Hughes was immediately reminded that such links to religion could not so easily undo his reputation as a Communist. In fact, "his rising popularity had revived his enemies" (Rampersad 2: 306). Soon after the Randolph salute, the anti-Communist magazine *American Mercury* published the article "Langston Hughes: Malevolent Force," noting that one of Hughes's recent books was receiving intense scrutiny for its alleged anti-American stance by a prominent church group. The article states that "definitive research" on Hughes was needed (2: 306).

Despite the forecast, Hughes decided to risk going out in bad weather. In February, Hughes left for a reading tour, likely optimistic that Hansberry's play and his recent religious campaign would have changed the climate. Even after such popular success, it took little time for him to be reminded just how volatile he still was. Hughes's reading tour was a disaster. In Buffalo a bomb threat "brought a squad of policemen to his reading," where he "read his poems, but nervously" (Rampersad 2: 306). When strong objections were raised, he canceled a reading in Grand Rapids, Michigan. Hughes muttered in a letter, "I haven't got the energy (nor patience) right now to battle their thick headedness" (2: 306). Hughes had grown tired of fighting these battles. The press coverage surrounding an event that included a crowd of three thousand at Carnegie Hall would certainly draw attention, and any printed program including him as a presenter could have brought undesirable attention to the event. Hughes, for his own sake and because of his admiration for Randolph and King, may have wanted to ensure that his presence did not spoil this joyous event. Although New York was Hughes's home and promised a degree of safety from such attacks and bomb threats, it is easy to imagine that Hughes chose to not be present at the salute to Randolph, even if his poem included biblical allusions and was bracketed by spirituals.

"Poem for a Man": Final Revisions

Hughes's "Poem for a Man" has never been published, but Hughes sent a revised copy of it to Ruby Dee and Ossie Davis on September 20, 1964. Hughes, more invested in precision than many give him credit for, made another pass through his poem to revise it before it was sent. He made five deft changes. He broke lines 9–10: "This compromise / and that required." He changed "the" to "That" in the very next line, to form "That dreams he sired." To avoid using the word "mud" twice, he compresses lines 26–27 of the original to read: "To try to wipe away the mud / That spattered everywhere." He also adds parentheses around line 41: "(Each time they make a bed—)."[14] The most significant change occurs before the questions in lines 29–32. Hughes inserts "In questions asked in scorn" to highlight this section's tone. This investment in a poem that Hughes had no intention of publishing reminds us of his commitment to a poem's performance. Moreover, it reminds us that Hughes's approachable poetry should not be devalued for what it may appear to lack in surface complexity. Hughes's style was often journalistic, and his words were meant to be understood. They were compressed until the wood split if given one more twist. It was these qualities that made Hughes so appreciated by Randolph and his audience, and admired by King and Levison.

It is unclear why Hughes made these revisions. One possibility is that he was responding to the fact that Randolph had been awarded the Presidential Medal of Freedom on September 14. While it is tempting to think that Dee and Davis recited or referenced the poem during the ceremony, the timing is odd. Randolph received the award on September 14, and Hughes passed the poem on six days later. Maybe a gathering had been planned upon Randolph's return in which Dee and Davis performed the poem privately for friends.[15]

What is clear is that Hughes's popularity put him in high demand within certain circles in America and abroad. By the end of 1960, Hughes and King would travel together for another celebration. This time the destination was Nigeria.

6

"Youth"

Hughes's Poem and King's Chiasmus

As the first indigenous Nigerian to serve as commander in chief and governor-general of Nigeria, Nnamdi Azikiwe delivered his historic inauguration speech on November 16, 1960. Speaking for about an hour, he boasted that there would soon be seventeen independent nations on the African continent. This freedom movement, he said, was the most spectacular series of events to take place on the continent since the days of the pharaohs. During his address, Azikiwe read a poem that King himself often read in his speeches: Douglas Malloch's "Be the Best Whatever You Are." Soon after, Azikiwe invoked yet another poet, quoting Rudyard Kipling's "If" (Azikiwe 15). Then the speech ended with Azikiwe quoting the poetry of Langston Hughes. After calling on the nation to "look forward to the morrow with hope and charity . . . knowing that the prospects for the future are bright," Azikiwe read Hughes's "Youth" in its entirety:[1]

> We have tomorrow
> bright before us
> like a flame
>
> Yesterday
> a night-gone thing
> a sun-down name
>
> And dawn today
> broad arch above the road we came
> We march. (18)

Of special note, both Martin Luther King and Langston Hughes were in attendance on this historic day. By observing Hughes's international prestige firsthand, King was further motivated to find ways to incorporate Hughes's poetry in his addresses. More important, the immediate effects of this trip allow us to understand how King himself incorporated Hughes's poem "Youth" into an array of speaking occasions.

"Youth"

Twenty days after returning from Nigeria, King wrote to the Montgomery Improvement Association to say that he would be unable to attend its fifth annual Institute on Nonviolence and Social Change: "MAY YOU GO ON WITH THE FAITH THAT UNEARNED SUFFERING IS REDEMPTIVE AND THAT BEYOND THE PRESENT DARKNESS THERE IS AN EMERGING DAYBREAK THAT WILL USHER IN THE WORLDS BRIGHT TOMORROW" (Carson 5: 570). Touching on all three time periods noted in Hughes's "Youth," King's lines mimic Hughes's "sundown name" as a darkness of the present, turn the dawn of "Youth" into an "EMERGING DAYBREAK," and present Hughes's "tomorrow / bright before us" as "THE WORLDS BRIGHT TOMORROW." King also declared that "DAYBREAK" would bring about the "WORLDS BRIGHT TOMORROW." King's repeated uses of "DAYBREAK" came directly from Hughes's dawn imagery in "Youth."

Although King was not introduced to Hughes's poem in Nigeria, his poetic energies had been energized by Azikiwe's quotation of this poem. Although King had used passages from this poem on no less than seventy occasions, prior to his trip to Nigeria he had not invoked the words given above for well over three years. Hearing these lines again reminded King of a phrase from the poem that he had used before but had long forgotten.

One of King's first engagements with "Youth" can be found in a letter he wrote in 1956. Eleven days after his first use of "Mother to Son," on Mother's Day in that year, he alluded to "Youth" in a letter to novelist Lillian Smith. "I have written you a thousand times in my mind," he begins, "but I am just getting to the point of putting it on paper" (Carson 3: 273). In the final sentence of the letter, after saying that those embroiled in the Montgomery Bus Boycott are in a "midnight of injustice," King writes that he believes they will soon "stand in the glow of the world's bright tomorrows" (Carson 3: 274). He has rewritten Hughes's opening idea in "Youth," that "we have tomorrow

/ bright before us." Whereas "bright" had once followed "tomorrow," now it precedes it, just as King had earlier changed "Dream Deferred" to "Shattered Dreams." Whereas Hughes spoke abstractly about yesterday as "a night-gone thing," King now labels it with the more personal reminder of "midnight," and dawn itself is no longer a broad arch but simply a "glow."

Variations on "Youth" appear in almost six dozen places in King's letters, sermons, speeches, prayers, church reports, and public addresses. Because this connection grew more and more complex, flexible, and imaginative, documenting it requires time. The impact of these expressions is central to the development of King's poetic sensibilities.

Because "Youth" becomes so central to King's voice, the poem itself requires further analysis. The poem addresses three periods of time: the bright tomorrows still to come, the night that has passed, and the dawn of today. This structure, turning time into a dark night of suffering and then emerging in the glow of a morning dawn with a "bright" tomorrow still ahead, serves as the basis for how King often encourages his listeners. Its logic is built on the fact that dawn always follows night. King would avoid the awkward constructions "night-gone" and "sun-down" by simplifying them as images of "night" or "midnight." In addition, Hughes's poem ends with the image of marching as the means to usher in this new tomorrow. This focus on the future is captured in the fact that Hughes often referred to this poem as "Tomorrow."[2]

We don't know how or when King first read "Youth." However, it is possible that its first appearance in King's sermon sheds light on how King came in contact with this poem. With regard to speaking publicly, King first alluded to lines from "Youth" in 1956 in the same Mother's Day sermon where he first quoted from "Mother to Son." The fact that there is no evidence of King ever quoting any Hughes poem before May 1956 suggests that King's encounter with Hughes's poetry occurred around this time. It is likely that King had come into contact with Hughes's *The Dream Keeper* around this time as well. Although that collection was first published more than twenty-five years earlier, it was touted as a book for children and has been reprinted more than a dozen times. Notably, "Mother to Son" and "Youth" appear on facing pages in *The Dream Keeper*. It is a fascinating coincidence that King appropriated both of these poems, as they also appear side by side in *The Dream Keeper*. One features the words of a mother determined to encourage her children to keep climbing, and the other declares where that climb will end.[3]

Hughes's "Youth" and Burns's "Man Was Made to Mourn"

A set of quotation marks initiates a revealing journey into King's process of using the words of Hughes's poem "Youth." On May 17, 1956, only four days after delivering the Mother's Day sermon in which he first quoted Hughes's "Mother to Son," King spoke at a dinner for the NAACP Legal Defense and Education Fund. The date itself was set to commemorate the second anniversary of the Supreme Court's decision in *Brown v. Board of Education* to outlaw segregated schools. Appropriating the idea of "maladjustment" from its contemporary use by psychologists, King used the term in a new way to suggest that listeners should become "maladjusted" to segregation and racism as he concluded his speech with the promise of a better future: "It is only through such maladjustment that we will be able to emerge from the bleak and desolate midnight of 'man's inhumanity to man' to the bright and glittering daybreak of freedom and justice."[4] This is the only time in any speech that King put quotation marks around this phrase. They appear in both the published version of this speech and in his handwritten copy. Whom is he quoting? Why is the person *never* mentioned in *any* of King's addresses?

This phrase comes from Robert Burns's 1784 poem "Man Was Made to Mourn."[5] The seventh stanza reads, "Man's inhumanity to man / Makes countless thousands mourn!" (lines 55–56). Whereas King sometimes appropriated the words of Oxenham or Holland, there are plenty of moments when he names or refers to the poet in some way which indicates that the words have come from somewhere else. However, he never mentioned Burns or announced in *any way* that these words came from anyone else. More important, King's quotation marks here are a reminder of the work King has done in both merging and submerging Burns's voice. King understood that these words had come from somewhere else.[6] However, he would appropriate them as his own for the next twelve years.

King's use of the phrase from Burns and his allusion to Hughes's "Youth" first appeared separately. King uses the Burns phrase for the first time ever on February 26, 1956, when he writes in an early outline: "We have seen man's tragic inhumanity to man" (Carson 6: 253). Speaking in the context of the recent lynching of Emmett Till and the mob violence that erupted after Autherine Lucy entered the University of Alabama as the first African American student, King uses the phrase in isolation. That is, the phrase is not linked to Hughes's poem or anything else before Mother's Day of 1956. Significantly, this would be the last time this phrase appeared anywhere on its own.

King invoked his variation on Hughes's "Youth" for the first time on May 13, 1956. In the middle of the same Mother's Day sermon that ended with his recitation of Hughes's "Mother to Son," he told his parishioners to live without bitterness because "Something beautiful will happen in this universe because we were able to look out into darkness and see the pressing daybreak" (Carson 3: 266). On its own, this reference to night and dawn seems innocuous or perhaps even sounds biblical. However, King had never previously used a phrase that depicted this movement from night to day in this way. In fact, previously King had always spoken in the plain biblical language of darkness when he suggested that listeners could "rise out of the dark and dreary valleys of sin and evil, realizing that man's proper home is the high mountain of truth" (6: 179).

When we look again at the way the idea of daybreak coalesces with the lines from Burns's poem, we can trace King's echoes of Hughes's "Youth." In his speech four days after his Mother's Day sermon, King concludes: "It is only through such maladjustment that we will be able to emerge from the bleak and desolate midnight of 'man's inhumanity to man' to the bright and glittering daybreak of freedom and justice" (Carson 3: 286). King has taken ideas from the poems by Burns and Hughes and rewritten them as a single new line.

The fact that each of these poems first appeared separately suggests that they were integrated by King himself rather than simply repeated from a sermon he had read or heard. When King used the poetry of Hughes, he was not mirroring what he had learned from other preachers of the time. That King built a phrase by merging the lines of a white Scottish poet with those of a black poet reveals something about King's poetic mind-set. Here, King can be seen creating something that would stand for years as his signature phrase. This phrase has all the rhetorical fingerprints that indicate it was the sole possession and creation of Martin Luther King. Knowing this brings us closer to King's poetic skills and writing prowess. Moreover, the triplicate structure that the line exhibits would manifest itself again and again in the years to follow.

Chiasmus

King blended Burns's poetry with Hughes's on no fewer than twenty occasions between 1956 and 1961. I will examine this new line as a poetic verse of superior artistry that is best understood as a unique application of the principles of parallelism. This analysis will show how King understood and applied the essential organizing principles of biblical poetry. A brief introduction to four basic types of parallelism is necessary to illuminate the poetic principles at work in King's verse.

The fact that one-third of the Bible is written in poetry is often overlooked. This poetry appears almost exclusively in the wisdom literature, psalms, and prophecy of the Old Testament. It is often based on the placement of subjects within lines rather than the repetition of sounds. The poet's ideas are often captured in the placement of words, and these positions animate meanings beyond the literal meaning. Though not every verse of poetry presented in the Bible follows these principles, dividing these principles into separate labels helps us grasp the effects of individual positions and placements. Nonetheless, we are reminded that any verse can have its own blend of these and other, more complex principles.

There are four types of parallelism.[7] *Synonymous parallelism* communicates the same idea in two ways. For instance, Job 18.5 repeats the same thought twice: "Yea, the light of the wicked shall be put out, / and the spark of his fire shall not shine."[8] "Light" is seen in its parallel, "shine," and "put out" is mirrored in a "fire" that "shall not shine." Repetition offers emphasis, and sometimes the restatement of ideas can offer a subtle variation or intensification of the theme.

An *antithetic parallel* says one thing and then its opposite. Proverbs is filled with such didactic statements that seem to imply that the listener has only two options. For example, readers of Proverbs 14.23 would face a choice between two alternatives: "In all labor there is profit / but the talk of the lips tendeth only to penury." In the Bible, "but" often alerts the reader that an alternative is about to be presented. Here, the imagined reader who is presented as a young man is instructed by his father that he can work and profit or talk and grow poor.

Examples of *climactic parallelism* present extended metaphors that build from start to finish to offer a progressive or unified discussion of one idea.[9] For example, in the space of one verse, Psalm 1.1 offers three progressive verbs that show how a person's level of comfort with ungodliness can grow: "Blessed is the man that walketh not in the counsel of the ungodly, / nor standeth in the way of sinners, / nor sitteth in the seat of the scornful." Each verb moves the subject in a steady progression of growing more and more comfortable with evil behavior as he first simply walks, then pauses enough to stand, and eventually finds himself so enamored that he sits entrapped in the presence of the ungodly.

The fourth and most complex type of parallelism is *chiastic parallelism.* The word "chiasmus" comes from the word "chi," meaning "cross-shaped." A visual makes this organizational pattern easier to comprehend. Coming from the Greek, it is an organizational pattern of writing that resembles the letter X. In chiastic parallel, elements or ideas are expressed sequentially up to a central point, then expressed again in reverse order as the series unwinds. It is one of the most commonly used biblical forms of poetic expression. For example, in his response to Zophar, Job demonstrates his knowledge of God by stating, "He reveals the deep things of darkness / and brings utter darkness into the light" (Job 12.22). This short chiastic structure follows an ABBA structure: the first idea is "reveals" (A), the second idea is "deep darkness" (B), then the idea is repeated backwards with "utter darkness" (B) coming first, and then the idea that is "revealed" is restated as being brought "into the light" (A). Chiastic parallelism has two typical modes of communicating meaning. First, often the X shape reveals movement or progression from the center to the ends of the X to symbolize a shift from one place to another. Second, at other times, the center of the X becomes the most privileged position. In the instance cited above, the darkness is buried and hidden in the center of the X, reminding us of the importance of what is being concealed. However, movement is also captured. As the chiastic structure opens and widens, light reveals what is concealed in the center so all souls can see it.

Infinite varieties and combinations of these and other parallels abound. Furthermore, these categories blur. Of these four distinctive types of parallelism, three apply to King's clincher statement that combines the poetry of Hughes and Burns. King's phrase weaves together elements of climactic parallelism, antithetic parallelism, and chiastic parallelism. It is climactic as it starts with "midnight" then builds toward "daybreak"; the opposite nature of these time referents also supply an antithetic element; the use of Burns's poetry at the center makes it chiastic. As such, King's phrase earns praise for its remarkable artistry because it takes the traditional dynamic of the inner and outer nature of the X and transforms it into a picture of horizontal progression. Rather than picturing this X upright, with emphasis on height and depth, King's phrase turns the shape on its side so that it outlines a movement from the past to the future. Figure 5 shows how both time and this verse move from left to right. King begins with a "bleak and desolate midnight" (A), then places Burns's phrase "man's inhumanity to man" at the center. This phrase is literally a superlative way to center a chiastic structure, as the word

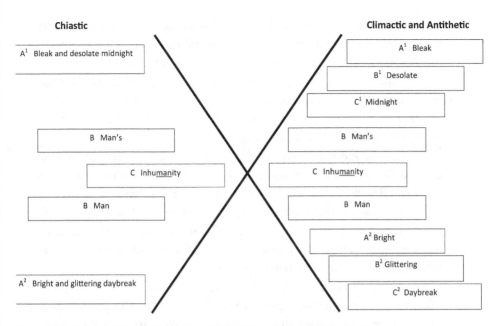

Figure 5. Parallelism in Hughes's "Youth" and Burns's "Man Was Made to Mourn."

"man" serves as both B's in this organizational pattern. Thus, the "man" inside "inhu*man*ity" is literally the center (C) weighted and balanced by two additional "man"s on both sides. The center of the X grows straight out of the "man" inside "inhu*man*ity."

With the second "man" serving as the (B) on the right side of the X, King then moves the listener through this period of difficulty into the "bright and glittering daybreak" (A). As perfect counterweights to "bleak and desolate," King gives us the words "Bright and glittering" to highlight the symmetry at work in his verse. In his first quotation of Burns's line, King used the phrase alone to suggest the violence enacted on the young Emmett Till and the mobs surrounding Ms. Lucy. Now he reassures listeners that the eventual outcome will be a dawn that outshines the darkness of every yesterday.

King seasons his phrase with a dash of the logic that informs an antithetic parallel. He reminds listeners that although today is a "bleak and desolate midnight," tomorrow will reveal a "bright and glittering daybreak." The way these word choices parallel each other highlights not only the balance of this verse but also the antithetic nature of its ideas. Today is "bleak," tomorrow will be "bright." The now is "desolate," but soon it will be "glittering." It is currently "midnight," but it will soon be "daybreak." These opposite states highlight the fact that the present is passing and the future is fast approaching. A word King uses to begin this sentence shows how the antithetic and chiastic modes overlap. King says that we will "emerge" to indicate both the ever-expanding movement outward from violence and into the light but also the progression from dark to light as one state (midnight) is left behind and its opposite (daybreak) will take its place.

Perhaps the most accessible reading of King's phrase comes by looking through the lens of climactic parallelism. The past has been bleak, the now is inhumane, but the future will be bright. This, in one sentence, is the state of things. Here we see that ending a speech or a letter with this complex verse is simultaneously dramatic, artistic, and biblical. We should not be surprised that King constructed such a poetic verse out of others' poetry or that he returned to it on so many different occasions.

We should also not be surprised at King's elusiveness or his artistry. His effectiveness in broadening rhetorical boundaries speaks to his philosophical nature and the issue at the center of the cause. Breaking down old boundaries must begin rhetorically before it can be expected to happen socially. What is remarkable is not the poetic nature of this phrase but the cumulative collision of biblical and secular forces that form it. Here the secular words of two poets and biblical parallelism worked together to inspire those who accomplished actual social integration.

What is all the more remarkable is that we can measure King's desire for this through his signature phrase as it integrates the words of the white Burns with that of the black Hughes. They stand together in verse even before citizens can ride together on Montgomery's buses. In fact, they live together in the pages of history, and they "sat" together on over twenty different occasions as King brought them together with intentionality and purpose. It was the structure of faith, religion, and the parallelism of the Bible itself that enabled them to be united in this way. King integrates the biblical with the secular, white with black, and finally even varying forms of poetry itself as everyone is welcomed, from the Hebrew forms of parallelism to the rhyme of Burns and the free verse of Hughes. Only a poet thinks this way. And only a poet thinks to use such a vast array of poetic principles and poets in this way. In a phrase, this sentence captures King's essence as an orator: borrowing ideas from everyone to blend together something at once wholly old and entirely new. This is always the work of the poet. The poet reorders the words of others in ways no one has ever heard before.

While much important work has been done on King's ability to model integration in the "I Have a Dream" speech he delivered on the National Mall, this chiastic structure offers further insight into the origins of King's strategies. King's most recognizable speech "performs significant rhetorical work by symbolizing the oration's themes of integration" (Vail 64). It does this by merging and integrating voices on many levels to become "iconic" so that the meaning of the text is represented by its form (Vail 64).[10] In this way, the speech communicates in the same way that most art celebrates its subjects.

But three things need to be noted about how King models integration. First, such modeling began long before his iconic speech of 1963. Here, with the African American Hughes and the Scottish Burns, King is successfully integrating sources as early as May 1956. Second, such integration is the most iconic for King's theme when it merges black and white voices. King is not merely interested in merging itself, but merging across racial divisions. The fact that Hughes and Burns represent two very different traditions makes them ideal symbols to integrate. They are not just two ideas King wanted to merge to locate his own voice: he was integrating two different ideals and cultures that had been segregated under the labels of nationality and race. Third, and most importantly, the artistry of such integrative rhetoric is best expressed when none of the voices being integrated is literally named. It is not just that King merges disparate voices in his "I Have a Dream" speech; it is that the new unity that results literally omits the names of all these voices. King's allusive style merges them all into his own voice so that all the parts are symbolically unified. The voices are not simply integrated; each one is merged without ever being named. King intentionally refrains from mentioning a single man or woman by name in the speech at Washington. The speech thus becomes a rhetorical rehearsal for the later performance of social integration. As voices are blurred to a point where they are only identifiable through allusion, they become something both new and harmonious. The ability for such voices to so easily unite stands as the speech's testimonial evidence that actual integration will simultaneously thrive, birth something new, and allow everyone to retain some recognizable sense of individual identity.

The fact that King's chiastic construction stands as one of the first samples of his integrative rhetoric and iconicity extends the arc of King's development back to at least May 1956. What he would do with a single line on this date would eventually develop into a practice he applied to larger passages before expanding this practice until it became the organizing principle for his entire speech in 1963. Moreover, it charts King's fascination with integrative rhetoric as something he mastered through his engagements with poetry. King's poetic sensibilities shaped the overall effectiveness of his rhetoric. It is the rhetorical accomplishment of a chiastic structure that King himself constructed that serves as one of the key motivations for why he quotes it over and over. Knowing the pleasure of accomplishment and the resonant symbolism of the act made this chiastic structure a major element in King's rhetorical arsenal.

King had additional reasons for veiling these two poems. First and foremost, his new phrase often served as the last sentence of his addresses. That was not the time or place to be citing sources and referencing other writers. In fact, King had learned this practice long ago as his earliest sermons end with long collisions of biblical quotations spoken without attribution. Moreover, while part of Burns's poem is taken word for word, King's use of Hughes's poem is more structural than verbal. King knows he can substitute his own words to move from yesterday's midnight to tomorrow's sunrise. What he borrows and thus appropriates is the idea of moving from a dark yesterday to a bright tomorrow. The language is not nearly as significant as the idea. In addition, it is not hard to imagine that King believed that this phrase was now his own. Furthermore, this was public speaking, not academic publishing. The context makes such use not only acceptable but, as we have seen, actually applauded if not required. King had not merely taken a set piece of poetic quotations from Benjamin Mays or Harry Fosdick: he had integrated the voices of two other poets completely on his own.

Burns and Hughes: Marching the High Way

Not long after his first use of this brand-new phrase in May 1956, King put it to use again. With slight variation, it was the summative sentence in his speech on July 23, 1956: "And whenever we decide to do this, we will emerge from the bleak and desolate midnight of man's inhumanity to man in to the bright and glittering daybreak of justice and freedom and brotherhood for all people" (Carson 3: 328). But it is not just the placement of this line that indicates how seminal it was for King. The sheer number of its reappearances also speaks to its importance. And the events of one day in particular illumine why this phrase was so valuable to the civil rights leader.

On August 11, 1956, King began an arduous day by testifying before the Democratic National Convention in Chicago. Joining that of Roy Wilkins, George Meany, Walter Ruether, and A. Philip Randolph, King's testimony aimed at convincing the party to include a strong civil rights agenda as it moved forward. King was called on to begin the session with a prayer, and then he made his statement uninterrupted. In his final line, King declared: "The adoption by this Convention of a strong civil rights plank will aid us in emerging from the bleak and desolate midnight of man's inhumanity to man in to the bright and glittering daybreak of freedom and justice" (Carson 3: 338). Later that night, King received an award in Buffalo, New York. He concluded his acceptance speech by saying that there would be a "time when we shall be able to emerge from the bleak and desolate midnight of man's inhumanity to man in to the bright and glittering daybreak of freedom and justice" (3: 346). King used this signature phrase twice on the same day, first to urge the Democratic Party to adopt a strong stance against racism and later to touch listeners at a banquet.

Hughes's poem ends with the idea of marching, and King's riff on this poem creates some interesting combinations. Throughout his career, King followed his signature phrase with references to walking or marching. On December 3, 1959, he closed his address at the Montgomery Improvement Association's fourth anniversary conference: "I have no doubt that the midnight of injustice will give way to the daybreak of freedom" (Carson 5: 343). His confidence grew into song as he closed with three stanzas of "The Battle Hymn of the Republic." With every stanza ending "his truth is marching on," a phrase also used throughout the chorus, this interesting collision activates even more of Hughes's poem than King may have consciously intended.

On May 17, 1957, King addressed more than twenty-five thousand listeners in New York. Turning his expression into a biblical narrative, he closed by saying that God is "leading us out of a bewildering Egypt, through a bleak and desolate wilderness, toward a bright and glittering promised land" (Washington 200). This connects with imagery from James Weldon Johnson's "Lift Ev'ry Voice and Sing": "lead us into the light / keep us forever in the path" (26–27). King returns to this riff on August 16, 1967, as if paying silent homage to Hughes. Listeners hear a simplified and clearer connection to Hughes's poem: "when our nights become darker than a thousand midnights . . . a power . . . is able to make a way out of no way and transform dark yesterdays into bright tomorrows" (Washington 252). Reactivating the idea of "power" mentioned no less that twenty-three times in a three-paragraph section earlier in this speech, King's cadence loosely rhymes "power" with "tomorrow" here just as he had done in an even more famous speech delivered at the steps of the capitol in Montgomery on March 25, 1965: "But we will go on with the faith, that non-violence and its power, can transform dark yesterdays into bright tomorrows" (Washington 229).

King continued to offer variations on this theme. One of the most interesting examples was when he linked Hughes's "Youth" with John Oxenham's "The Ways." King had used Oxenham's poem since at least 1949, and he also quoted one of Oxenham's hymns on occasion.[11] In his speech "The Crisis in Human Relations," King ended by paraphrasing lines from Oxenham's poem. With the poem's focus on two different roads to take, the "high" being good and the "low" being bad, King dropped the phrase from Burns and ended his speech: "If we will but choose the high way we will emerge from the bleak and desolate midnight of corroding injustice into the bright and glittering daybreak of freedom and justice."[12] Here, Burns's "man's inhumanity to man" becomes simply "corroding injustice." In the context of the "high way," King's "corroding" seems to activate the idea of the rust that can build on a car during travel.

In 1956, King spoke variations on ideas from Hughes and Burns from every stage. The chiastic line was also called on to communicate the hopes and aspirations of the citizens engaged in the Montgomery Bus Boycott at one of the most important moments in King's life. Having led the citizens of Montgomery through the successful boycott, King chose these same words as the final sentence of his statement to announce that it had reached a successful end: "With this dedication will we be able to emerge from the bleak and desolate midnight of man's inhumanity to man into the bright and glittering daybreak of freedom and justice" (Carson 3: 487). King's declaration links poetic vision with political equality.

Those who heard King speak often departed with the submerged phrases of Robert Burns and the optimism of Langston Hughes ringing in their ears. Hopeful and futuristic, these expressions always pointed to a future not quite realized. During 1957, audiences heard this dream of the future in the last line of addresses delivered on February 6 and 8 and on September 2. King even built this theme into the title of a sermon, "A View of the Dawn," which was published in *Interracial Review* in May 1957. King must have been pleased to have left his readers with a line that collapsed ideas from both Burns and Hughes. The line continued to serve as King's summation of the future when he used it to conclude his remarks in 1959 on January 14, May 11, August 20 and 21, and September 17.[13] The full line, with Burns and Hughes together, didn't leave King's repertoire until November 16, 1961 (Washington 53). This means that for a period of more than six years, King used this line to end his speeches, sometimes twice in the same day, and often on consecutive days. From 1956 to 1961, this sentence was one of King's go-to lines when it came time to end an important letter, statement, or address. He was no longer imitating Hughes: the ideas from "Dream Deferred" and "Youth" were now concepts King owned.

The Montgomery Bus Boycott and Fred Shuttlesworth

King believed deeply in the power of poetry. His belief can be measured in the large number of appearances of this line in 1956. The Montgomery Bus Boycott is an illuminating context for how and why it became so embedded in his mind. Remembering that King had encouraged the African American community to march on its feet for freedom and justice, it seems unsurprising that King ended his address with this imagery when he declared the end of the bus boycott at the Holt Street and First Baptist Churches. On December 20, 1956, King took up the topic of tired feet. More than once he declared that over the course of the last twelve months they have all "kept going" (Carson 3: 486).

But his final sentence that evening did not echo Hughes's "Mother to Son." Instead, King declared: "With this dedication we will be able to emerge from the bleak and desolate midnight of man's inhumanity to man to the bright and glittering daybreak of freedom and justice" (Carson 3: 487). The next day, King, E. D. Nixon, Ralph Abernathy, and Glen Smiley rode an integrated bus through the streets of Montgomery. Hughes's poetry not only laid the foundation for enduring the boycott but also pointed to the destination they believed was emerging. Determination is built on hope and inspiration. King supplied it through poetry. Unnamed and uncounted citizens not only accepted it but held fast to this hope as they became walkers with the dawn.

I revisit this occasion here to frame another significant invocation of this inspirational line. No document better captures the force of King's poetry than a letter he sent to Fred Shuttlesworth, the pastor of Birmingham's Bethel Baptist Church, six days later, on December 26, 1956. In this handwritten letter, King used poetry to sustain a critical effort in the civil rights movement.

Following the court order to desegregate buses in Montgomery, black citizens in Birmingham were met with violence when they attempted to claim that right for themselves and ride local buses. Worse, Shuttleworth's church was bombed on Christmas night. During a mass meeting, members of the Birmingham community filled another church that night and decided to call off their challenge to the city's segregated busing. When King was alerted, he sent a telegram from Montgomery imploring them to rethink their decision. King's letter applauded the twenty-one riders who had been arrested. Writing as if he were Hughes's speaker in "Mother to Son," King called for them to "keep moving toward the goal of justice. Keep riding the buses on a non-segregated basis. Keep living by the principle of non-violence" (Carson 3: 496).

At this important moment, King called on his deepest reserves to inspire Shuttlesworth and his followers. He turned to two images from "Youth": "Those of use [sic] who stand amid the bleak and desolate midnight of man's inhumanity to man must gain consolation from the fact that there is emerging a bright and glittering daybreak of freedom and justice" (Carson 3: 496). In this crucial hour, it was not Paul, John, Matthew, Luke, or Mark whom King called on to rally spirits. It was the poetry of Langston Hughes and Robert Burns. King promised them they would one day "stand in the glow of the world's bright tomorrows" (3: 496). The letter reads as if one dose of poetry was not enough, so King prescribed two.

It is one thing to invoke the poetry of Hughes to inspire those who are listening to a speech; it is quite another to change people's actions. Upon reading the telegram, Shuttlesworth and his fellow protesters immediately reversed their decision. Hughes's poem is not merely part of the poetic flourish that ends King's letters; it is not just a powerful way to end an address or the means to gain credibility among the imaginative; and it is not just a way for him to embrace his cultural roots. No, King's words transformed the people of Birmingham. The four hundred citizens who met to discuss the best way forward were swayed that night by King's poetic missive. And if they heard echoes of Hughes's poem, they knew that all who had come before them were imploring them to continue to march. As Shuttlesworth read this message from King, King's authority and Hughes's hope coalesced in a triumphant return to protest. The group voted to continue to ride, encouraged that their actions would make a difference and believing a bright future lay ahead. The darkness around them was deep, but Hughes and King kept them focused on the dawn.

Personal Metaphors

King invoked echoes of Hughes's poetry to connect with the shared cultural traditions of his audience. The intensity and depth of these invocations leads us to consider if King himself had internalized Hughes's poetry on such a deep level that it became the means by which he expressed his own experiences. In recalling one of the darkest hours of his own life, King appears to reveal what Hughes's poetry meant to him emotionally. Are these metaphors the ones that helped define and steady his own nerves?

In an undated, handwritten draft from his book *Why We Can't Wait*, King recalls how he felt when he was arrested in Birmingham in the spring of 1963. In the draft, which included some material that did not appear in the final version, King confessed: "Altogether, I had spent three days in solitary. This kind of confinement is a thing which a person cannot forget. In the mornings the sun would rise, sending shafts of light through the black hole which was my home. You will never know the ominous meaning of darkness until you have lain in such a hole, know that sunlight was streaming through and *still* unable to see anything but darkness. . . . [T]he realization was that truly, I had never been in actual solitary confinement."[14] He concludes: "In the midst of deepest midnight, daybreak had come. I don't know whether the sun was shining in that moment. Nevertheless, once again, I could see the light."[15] Although the statement ends with King refocusing attention on the spiritual implications of "light," the language of poetry seems to live here as well as King once again activates the metaphor of dawn. Is King merely trying to connect his feelings with his reader, or was he genuinely trying to ease his own anxieties as he ministered to himself?

The metaphors of midnight and dawn appear throughout King's addresses and writings after May 1956. Reflecting two years later on the Montgomery Bus Boycott, King uses this imagery to convey a sense of calm in the midst of trials. Recalling how the group of leaders reacted the night after Rosa Parks was arrested, King writes: "The clock on the wall read almost midnight, but the clock in our souls revealed that it was daybreak" (Washington 427). Midnight itself is the centerpiece of King's August 16, 1967, sermon, "A Knock at Midnight," in which King asserts that "Midnight is the time when all moral values lose their distinctiveness." Not unexpectedly, King's hope against such disillusionment comes in the phrase "However dark it is now, morning will come." When King asserts soon after this that "he is not worried about anything now," his earlier use of "midnight" in this sermon seems to be on his mind.[16] King's choice to turn Hughes's awkward phrases for darkness into his own "midnight" in his chiastic line suggests that he was doing even more than making Hughes's ideas more accessible: King may have also been personalizing at least one experience that occurred near midnight.

In many instances, King emphasizes and reemphasizes the timing of one experience in his life so that "midnight" itself becomes imbued with deep personal meaning. The experience sometimes referred to as "the vision in the kitchen" took place on January 26, 1956. In fact, it may be no coincidence that "midnight" is invoked in King's chiastic phrase for the first time only four months after this event. In *Stride toward Freedom*, King describes the calm that came over him on that night. Weary from helping initiate and sustain the Montgomery Bus Boycott, and facing continuous threats to both himself and his family, King reports that after one particularly disturbing phone call that threatened his life, he wandered into his kitchen and sat beside a cup of coffee. King identifies the time of this crisis as "midnight": "I decided to take my problem to God. With my head in my hands, I bowed over the kitchen table and prayed aloud. The words I spoke to God that midnight are still vivid in my memory: . . . 'I am afraid . . . I am at the end of my powers. I have nothing left. I am at the point where I can't face it alone.' At that moment I experienced the presence of the Divine as I had never experienced Him before. . . . Almost at once my fears began to go. My uncertainty disappeared. I was ready to face anything" (*Stride* 125). Is King saying that it was literally around midnight, or is he speaking metaphorically and declaring that this was a "midnight moment" in his life?

King also seems to invoke metaphors born from his appropriation of "Mother to Son," "Youth," and "Dream Deferred" during other experiences. Learning that his home has been bombed, King calms the audience before him at the church. Fearing they may become violent, he admonishes them with "Let us keep moving" because they should trust that "what we are doing is right" (*Stride* 126). Having used the theme from "Mother to Son" to calm his parishioners, King arrives at his home where he offers an idea that almost reads as a fresh rephrasing of "Youth" to settle down the angry men and women gathered there. With his wife and daughter safe, King calms this crowd by ending this "midnight moment" with the hope of dawn: "If I am stopped, this movement will not stop, because God is with this movement. Go home with this glowing faith and radiant assurance" (128). Writing with hindsight, is King inserting ideas he had preached long after this event into his recollection of the event itself, or had he truly found such imagery here spontaneously and then later added it to his addresses? Regardless of the process, these metaphors were not merely elements King used to develop his rhetorical persona: at times they seem to have became so deeply ingrained within him that they flowed into life itself.

King appears to personalize imagery from Hughes's "Dream Deferred" in much the same way. Another undated draft begins: "Some of my personal sufferings over the last years have also served to shape my thinking." After declaring that he has been "battered," King crosses out the words "I must admit that at times the load," replacing them with "I have felt that I could no longer bear such a heavy burden." Is King self-censoring an allusion to Hughes's "heavy load"? He ends this section by building toward a conclusion, "when fears have lurked forth and dreams have been shattered," but he crosses this out.[17] However these words look on paper, we need only listen to King deliver "Unfulfilled Dreams" on March 3, 1968, to gather how personal these metaphors could sound. On this occasion he declared earnestly and solemnly that "our dreams are not fulfilled" before setting his focus for the sermon at hand: "Life is a continual story of shattered dreams" (Carson, Holloran, and Shepard). Here, less than a month before King's assassination, we can hear how the idea of "shattered dreams" had grown immensely personal.

Versatility: Letters and Prayers

The number of important people who were encouraged by imagery that originated in Hughes's poetry is staggering. Rosa Parks herself sat in wonder as King concluded his address on September 2, 1957, at the Highlander Folk School's twenty-fifth-anniversary meeting. Immediately after a paragraph that ends with the driving intensity of "We must not slow up. Let us keep moving," King declared: "We will be able to emerge from the bleak and desolate midnight of man's inhumanity to man into the bright and glittering daybreak of freedom and justice" (Carson 4: 276). King also uses these words of encouragement in correspondence with Roland Smith and Daisy Bates over the Little Rock Nine in September 1957: "Keep struggling with this faith and the tragic midnight of anarchy and mob rule which encompasses your city at this time will be transformed into the glowing daybreak of freedom and justice" (4: 279).

King was moved to invoke this imagery again and again. In an August 30, 1957, letter reassuring Vice President Richard Nixon that recent civil rights legislation was a step in the right direction, King closes: "With persons like you occupying such important positions in our nation I am sure that we will soon emerge from the bleak and desolate midnight of man's inhumanity to man to the bright and glittering daybreak of freedom and justice for all men" (Carson 4: 264). The next day, he conveys the same idea to Billy Graham: "We are gradually emerging from the bleak and desolate midnight of injustice into the bright and glittering daybreak of freedom and justice." He then ends his letter by reiterating: "they that stand with him stand in the glow of the world's bright tomorrows" (4: 265). Here, the only difference is that King drops Burns's phrase "man's inhumanity to man."

Occasionally, King invokes this phrase early in a speech rather than saving it for the end. King addressed the legislature of Hawaii on September 17, 1959, only a month after Hawaii became the fiftieth state. He began: "As I think of the struggle that we are engaged in in the South land, we look to you for inspiration and as a noble example, where you have already accomplished in the area of racial harmony and racial justice what we are struggling to accomplish in other sections of the country, and you can never know what it means to those of us caught for the moment in the tragic and often dark midnight of man's inhumanity to man, to come to a place where we see the glowing daybreak of freedom and dignity and racial justice" (Carson 5: 278).

King sometimes embedded this phrase in the final prayer to close his sermons. When he delivered his mock letter to American Christians at the Dexter Avenue Baptist Church in Montgomery on November 4, 1956, he blurred the genres of sermon and epistle. "Paul's Letter to American Christians" closed with a prayer that imitated the way Paul ends his letters to those in Ephesus and Corinth. King's final lines read: "And now unto him who is able to keep us from falling, and lift us from the fatigue of despair to the buoyancy of hope, from the midnight of desperation to the daybreak of joy, to him be the power and authority, forever and ever. Amen."[18]

King's performances of this script remind us how interchangeable these moving rhetorical parts are in his arsenal. When King delivered another version of this same "letter" a year and a half later, on June 3, 1958, his benediction varied again: "And now unto Him who is able to solve the race problem if we will cooperate with Him. And now unto Him who is able to transform this cosmic energy into constructive force. Now unto Him who is able to transform this tragic midnight of injustice into a glowing daybreak of freedom and justice. To Him be the power and authority, majesty and dominion, now, henceforth, and forever more" (Carson 6: 346). These comparisons of sermons with the same title, subject matter, and organization remind us of King's penchant to vary language for the sake of keeping his ideas fresh. Though always seeking to improve delivery through changes in expression, King retains the underlying structure.

Poetry was much more than part of King's rhetorical persona. It resided in his heart, flowed from his pen, and rose from his lips in every context. His ability to merge his own ideas with those of Burns and Hughes reveals his artistic capabilities. Extending well beyond the resonance with "Youth," another poem by Langston Hughes was silently hovering at the end of King's most famous addresses. As we will see in the following chapters, this poem's central idea was the dream of a new world.

7

"I Dream a World"

Rewriting Hughes's Signature Poem

On June 6, 1961, Martin Luther King delivered the commencement address at Lincoln University, in Pennsylvania. He began by introducing the idea of the American dream: "As you go out today to enter the clamorous highways of life, I should like to discuss with you some aspects of the American Dream" (Washington 208).[1] Given that Lincoln University is Hughes's alma mater, it is no coincidence that King ended this speech with the chiastic line he had built by integrating Burns's "Man Was Made to Mourn" with Hughes's "Youth": "We will be able to emerge from the bleak and desolate midnight of man's inhumanity to man in to the bright and glittering daybreak of freedom and justice" (216). More important, King's first major point in his speech indicates a linguistic link between Hughes's poem "I Dream a World" and King's dream.[2] For the first time in his life, King uses the phrase "dream of a world": "The American dream will not become a reality devoid of the larger dream of a world of brotherhood, and peace, and good will. The world in which we live is a world of geographical oneness and we are challenged now to make it spiritually one" (209).

King's capacity to think thematically about the relationship between a small American dream and a larger world dream of brotherhood bears a striking resemblance in theme, structure, and diction to the dream Hughes portrays in "I Dream a World." Hughes had called for a world of unity, marked by peace and freedom, and King singles out "peace" in the sentence above. As King continues, he comments on the challenge to unify the world: "If we are to survive today and realize the dream of our mission and the dream of the world, we must bridge the gulf" (Washington 211). The irony is piercing.

In this sentence, King joins the dream of the civil rights movement ("our mission") and the "dream of the world." King is seeking to inspire Lincoln University graduates with the same rhetoric that their own alumnus made famous by stating that these dreams stand united. The context, diction, and ease with which this reference takes place suggests that King was already aware of this interdependence.

Why did King link Hughes's poem with his own vision? The relationship between these two dreams dates back to King's first enunciation of the beloved community. To understand the significance of this link, we must explore the history of the poem itself. "I Dream a World" is tied to the libretto Hughes wrote for the opera *Troubled Island*. Because "I Dream a World" is central to the dreams of both Hughes and King, we will explore each of these contexts fully. This chapter documents King's engagements with Hughes's poem "I Dream a World" to show how King internalized and then re-created Hughes's dream. As we will see, King echoed Hughes's vision of a better world long before he returned to redeem Hughes's metaphor of the dream.

Troubled Island

In 1949, Hughes's libretto was set to music by the African American composer William Grant Still and mounted as an opera under the title *Troubled Island*. In the opera, "I Dream a World" is sung by the character Martel, whom Hughes describes as "an elderly slave, later Chief Counselor."[3] The history of this poem within this context is important for better understanding the poem's theme. In 1936, Hughes completed one of several drafts of his play *Troubled Island,* which eventually served as the basis for the opera. The words that became "I Dream a World" first emerged from Hughes's 1936 drafts. In the opera, Emperor Jean-Jacques Dessalines outlines his goals as the new leader of Haiti. He wants nothing to do with France or with the European world, but simply "a land where black men / Govern—Free" (*Collected Works* 6: 30). Martel, in contrast, wants integration, and he responds with the lines of "I Dream a World," suggesting that he has "an even bigger dream than that":

I dream a world where man
No other man will scorn,
Where love will bless the earth
And peace its paths adorn.

I dream a world where all
Will know sweet freedom's way
Where greed no longer saps the soul
Nor avarice blights our day.
A world I dream where black or white,
Whatever race you be,
Will *share* the bounties of the earth
And every man is free,
Where wretchedness will hang its head,
And joy, like a pearl,[4]
Attends the needs of all mankind.
Of such I dream—
Our world!

Hughes stitches the poem together by repetitions of "I dream a world" be-
tween the poem's main ideas. This use of visionary anaphora is the poem's
distinguishing feature. The first appearance of this phrase eliminates hatred
between all men, as this new world is now one of "love" and "peace." The sec-
ond asserts that this new world is one in which everyone is free. No man is
owned by another man, and men are treated as human beings, not property.
This is also a world in which "greed" has been abolished. Third, in its most
celebrated lines, the poem disrupts the cadence of the anaphora and inverts
the title to declare "A world I dream." Paralleling the cadence of "I have a
dream" more than any other section of the poem, this section repeats its own
themes as it asserts that whether you are "black or white," everything will be
shared and everyone will be free. Following the tenets of communism, the
poem envisions an integrated world where money and capital are distributed
equally. "Joy" itself results when the needs of the poor are met.

"I Dream a World" in Print and Politics

Hughes's "I Dream a World" first appeared in the July 19, 1941, *Amsterdam
News*. Published in New York, this paper catered to African Americans. For
ten cents, readers were greeted on this Saturday by a headline declaring that
Secretary of War Henry L. Stimson was denying that the United States had
plans to occupy Liberia. Marve and Joe Louis's divorce was also front-page
news. Hughes's poem appeared in a section titled "Poet's Corner," which fea-
tured three poems. The first prophesied ruin to men who "tread on others'

I dream a world where man

No other man will scorn,

Where love will bless the earth

And peace its paths adorn.

Langston Hughes

Figure 6. "I Dream a World" Christmas card, front and inside. Artwork by Rockwell Kent. (Beinecke Rare Book and Manuscript Library at Yale University.)

toes" and show "haughtiness and hate." The second chronicled African Americans' rise out of slavery and ended by asserting that God "created a world of equity and love." This served as a natural transition to Hughes's contribution, which envisioned a world where men of every race would "share the bounties of the earth" (11). Evidence for the world Hughes dreamed could be found in the brief article that appeared directly below Hughes's poem. As if to model how these bounties could be shared, the press's "Helping Hand Department" reminded patrons to send in their requests for clothing. Another article requested volunteers to serve on a committee to help free soldiers who were court-martialed during World War I, and another complained that the official agreement to employ Harlem workers to drive local buses had yet to result in a single new change in drivers. The appearance of Hughes's poem in the *Amsterdam News* reminds us of the poem's political overtones.

Though it is less familiar today than many of Hughes's other poems, "I Dream a World" was Hughes's signature poem.[5] As figure 6 shows, its lines were incorporated on Christmas cards that featured artwork by Rockwell Kent. The poem was even included in the program for Hughes's funeral. The centrality of "I Dream a World" to Hughes's poetry can best be summed up in the fact that it held a commanding place as the closing poem of his public readings (Rampersad 2: 25). A variation on this poem would later hold this same prestigious position in several of King's most memorable speeches.

Hughes Testifies before Joseph McCarthy

On March 21, 1953, Hughes was summoned to appear before Joseph McCarthy and the Senate Permanent Subcommittee on Investigations of the Committee on Government Operations. He immediately began to prepare a written statement that would help shape the most important defense of his life. Although this statement was never formally delivered to the committee, what Hughes wrote reveals how he tried to negotiate a complex balance of anger and anxiety. Having to reduce his entire life to five pages, Hughes faced the daunting task of denying that he was a Communist (which also directly implied he was an atheist) and defending his life's work, all the while resisting being bullied and intimidated to surrender his right to free speech. In his testimony, Hughes stated twice that he was never a Communist. On March 26, his testimony was broadcast on radio and television.[6]

Hughes ended the written statement he prepared with "I Dream a World." Having set the poem within the context of his opera (thereby carefully re-historicizing it as something about Haiti and not the United States), Hughes states that the poem "expresses my own personal feeling in regard to social and political relations." Because it closes the section of his statement where Hughes planned to assert his right to free speech, and follows directly his argument that the United States has changed and can continue to change, the poem can be read as confrontational. While McCarthyism is dividing the world into capitalists and Communists, Hughes subtly links the image of Jean-Jacques Dessalines from *Troubled Island* with McCarthy. Where the emperor hates France, McCarthy hates Russia. In contrast, Hughes, like Martel, offers a dream of integration. This context highlights the "material well-being" that Hughes alludes to in the paragraph before the poem. "I Dream a World" does not just proclaim love and peace; it declares an end to capitalist principles and the abandonment of "greed" and "avarice." Hughes highlights this in his personal copy of the poem, where he underlines the word "share."[7] Hughes's notes on his copy of the poem suggest that he was intent on using the historical events in Haiti to comment on current social issues. In the lower righthand corner of the poem we read that this is "an Opera with overtones for today." In comparing the differences between several drafts of this poem, we can see that this private copy bears the greatest resemblance to the one Hughes planned to deliver in person. Only on this copy and the one he planned to read before the committee is the word "share" underlined, suggesting that the "today" Hughes is thinking of is 1953. The confrontational nature of this choice is highlighted by the fact that Hughes himself did not deliver the prepared draft that concluded with this poem. Perhaps he feared that the veiled attack would be understood. The comments he delivered publicly after the private hearing he had on March 24 may also suggest that the committee negotiated a truce by which it would go easy on Hughes in public if he agreed to be compliant. If so, being compliant meant not ending his prepared statement by reading "I Dream a World."

"I Dream a World" is deceptively subversive. Hughes had taken the American dream and expanded it to the world by wondering aloud why the promises of American democracy had yet to be achieved internationally. Three years later, Martin Luther King would invoke these same subversive qualities.

King's 1956 Speeches: "Facing the Challenge of a New Age"

To better understand the complex ways in which King first engaged with "I Dream a World," we have to examine a series of speeches King delivered in

1956 under the interchangeable titles "The Birth of a New Age" and "Facing the Challenges of a New Age." By examining each speech individually, we can see unique developments in King's rhetorical approach to using this poem. King spoke in New York City on December 15, 1956, before an integrated audience gathered at the Commodore Hotel. The event was intended to highlight the needs of rural schools. As King took up his subject of desegregation in these schools, he cited the 1954 landmark case *Brown v. Board of Education*. King began by referencing the Supreme Court's decision in *Brown*: "To all men of goodwill, this decision came as a joyous daybreak to end the long night of human captivity. It came as a great beacon of hope to millions of colored people throughout the world who had a dim vision of the promised land of freedom and justice" (Carson 3: 472).

The body of King's speech outlines the evils of segregation. Alluding to Hughes's "Dream Deferred," where Hughes asks if deferred dreams "fester like a sore," King states that segregation is a "festering sore" that "scars the soul of both the segregator and the segregated" (Carson 3: 474). King invokes Josiah Holland's "Wanted" to make the point that great leadership will be necessary to eliminate segregation in the nation's schools. However, King never acknowledges Holland or his poem, despite using its ideas. Strengthened by a resolve to suffer for good and a drive to be the inspirational leader he was speaking of, King declares that through the transformative approach of nonviolence "We will be able to emerge from the bleak and desolate midnight of injustice to the bright and glittering daybreak of freedom and goodwill" (3: 478).

King may have picked "goodwill" here and in his introduction rather than the word he more often used, "justice," because it was just ten days before Christmas. He then swings into a passage that sounds just as poetic: "If we do this we will be able by the help of God to create a new world. A world in which men will be able to live together as brothers. A world in which men 'will beat their swords into plowshares and their spears into pruning hooks.' A world in which men no longer take necessities from the masses to give luxuries to the classes. A world in which men will respect the dignity and worth of all human personality" (Carson 3: 478–79). King makes no mention of a dream; instead, he focuses on the new creation itself.

King then inserts a quotation that serves to unite theology with poetry. After speaking words he has borrowed from Archibald Cary about Lookout Mountain and the molehills of Mississippi, King delivers his final line: "And when that happens, the morning stars will sing together and the sons of God will shout for joy!" (Carson 3: 479). This quotation from Job 38.7 is noteworthy because of its use of the word "joy." In fact, the complete sequence of ideas mirrors Hughes's "I Dream a World." Like Hughes, King uses the refrain "A world" to begin each of four thoughts. The elimination of the dream metaphor initially masks the connection to Hughes's poem, but the parallels quickly become clear once we remember that Hughes spoke not just of a "dream" but of its product, a new "world." Where Hughes's poem ends with the image of "joy like a pearl attending the needs of all mankind," King ends his sequence with a biblical verse that not only uses the word "joy" but also embeds joy to signal the creation of the "world." This joy is at once secular and sacred.

King's use of similar passages earlier in 1956 clarifies how Hughes is being engaged. On December 3, in Montgomery, King ended his speech very similarly. Again, he ushered in his climax by signaling readers to a new world rather than a dream: "There is nothing in all the world greater than freedom" (Carson 3: 462). Soon after he went into the same four refrains beginning with "a world in which men" (3: 462). Hughes's poem uses the word "man" four times; so does King. Whereas King says "in which" after his refrain, Hughes says "where." Look how these lines read with the full addition of Hughes's refrain and the simple change from the "in which" construction to the "where." When we set King's words as verse, it is easy to see how his ideas look and sound the same and communicate the same themes as Hughes's poem:

> I dream a world where men
> will live together as brothers.
> I dream a world where men
> will beat their swords into ploughshares
> and their spears into pruning hooks.
> A world I dream where men
> respect the dignity and worth
> of all human personality.
> Where men will no longer take
> necessities from the masses
> to give luxuries to the classes
> of such I dream our world!

The structural similarities are evident. We hear the internal rhyme of "dignity" and "personality," and the theme of brotherhood is present in the same syntactical position as in Hughes's poem. Moreover, King catches the high frequency of the whispering "s" in the Hughes's poem. King gives his listeners "swords," "ploughshares," "spears," and "hooks." He writes of "necessities," "masses," "luxuries," and "classes," just as Hughes more softly used "wretchedness," "its," "attends," and "needs." Each invokes the future tense just once. Hughes writes "wretchedness will hang its head," and King says "men will no longer take necessities."

The thematic similarities are also apparent. King's second idea in this sequence is an allusion to Isaiah 2.4, which speaks about a world at peace; the end of Hughes's first idea calls for a world where "peace its paths adorn" (line 4). King next suggests that this world includes a sharing of resources and the abolition of greed; Hughes's second idea declares that "greed no longer saps the soul" (line 7). Next, King paraphrases lines by A. Philip Randolph regarding the need to treat African Americans as persons rather than as property; Hughes's third statement declares hope for a world where "every man is free." Finally, King adds a quotation from Job so that its final word is "joy." "Joy like a pearl" is Hughes's final image in "I Dream a World." We can almost imagine King working to include this final connection: in an August 11, 1956, speech he added the word "joy" as he paraphrased Revelation 11.15. The word "joy" appears *nowhere* in the original verse from Revelation. Here, he seeks out a quotation that has the word "joy" embedded in it from Job, switching the tense from past to future as if to suggest that "joy" itself was the image King was after as he sought to add new life to Hughes's old imagery. It was the success of moments like this that allowed King to continue this practice of rewriting. Though it was nearly an untraceable inflection in his voice, King was already dreaming of a new world in 1956.

But why would King riff entirely new lines based on the structure of "I Dream a World" when he had so often quoted or paraphrased lines from so many other poets in this speech? If questions themselves were the stylistic key to King's linking "Dream Deferred" to his own "Shattered Dreams," we must answer this important question: How is King using anaphora in the speech where he first rewrites "I Dream a World"?

King's use of this ending in his speeches dates to August 11, 1956, when he delivered "The Birth of a New Age" in Buffalo. The organizational pattern of this speech reveals that King's final section is not merely an example of anaphora. Several signs point the listener toward the importance of the speech's ending. By carefully examining the intricacies of this structure, we can uncover King's motivation for rewriting Hughes's "I Dream a World."

Figure 7 illustrates the chiastic structure of King's speech.[8] King estab-

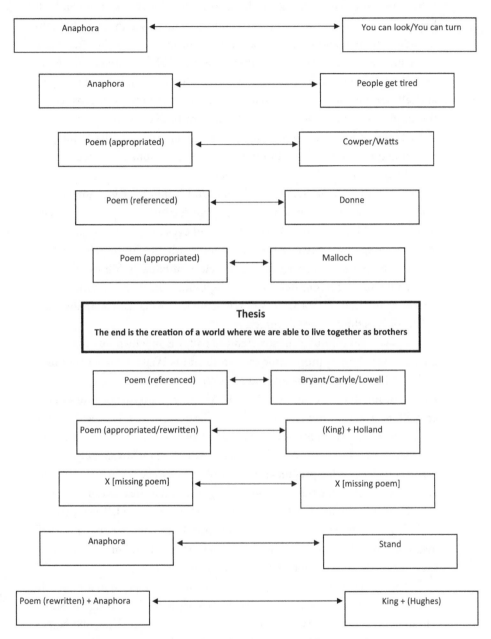

Figure 7. Parallelism in King's "The Birth of a New Age" speech, Buffalo, New York, August 11, 1956.

lishes this pattern early to inform his purposeful alterations at the end. He begins by previewing two of the most important images in the speech. In the introduction he mentions that civilization is currently caught in a "deep and tragic midnight" (Carson 3: 340). Then he writes: "There comes a time when people get tired of being pushed out of the glittering sunlight of life's July and left standing in the pitying state of an Alpine November" (3: 340). While the emphasis seems to be the switch from warmth to cold, the speech is asking listeners to focus unconsciously on the imagery of light. The "midnight" mentioned earlier and the "glittering sunlight" mentioned here will be key ideas he returns to at the end of the speech.

Between these references to "midnight" and "sunlight," King embeds two extended invocations of anaphora. In four consecutive sentences he says either "We could look to" or "We could turn our eyes to" (Carson 3: 340). This variation prepares the reader for a critical disturbance in the speech's final paired example of matching anaphoras. He immediately follows this first use of anaphora with four new lines of anaphora: "There comes a time when people grow tired" (3: 340). It is noteworthy that King uses anaphora, not epistrophe, as the cadence of choice.

King has also carefully constructed the patterns in which he invokes poetry. He begins by appropriating the words of his Watts/Cowper set piece, and then he references "one man" as he paraphrases lines from Donne. Later, King appropriates the poetry of Malloch. After these three invocations of poetry, King eases toward the center of this chiastic structure. He speaks of the "end" no fewer than six times, and he alerts the listener to the importance of his current statements when he uses the word "center" twice in this same paragraph. Then, King presents the focus of his message when he says: "The end is the creation of a beloved community. The end is the creation of a society where men will live together as brothers" (Carson 3: 344). The repetition of "The end is the creation" signals that the pattern established up to here will begin to unwind. King is also alerting us to look to the end of his speech for the creation of a place where men will live together as brothers.

Because King included three poets before this central point in the speech, we can now expect three separate invocations of poetry. Following his earlier pattern of alternating between appropriation and reference, King first names all the authors in his set piece from Carlyle, Lowell, and Bryant, as these unified lines represent a single integrated reference to poetry in his mind.[9] We now expect two more invocations of poetry, and this is where things get interesting. King appropriates Josiah Holland's poem "Wanted." He then skips a poem that should be overtly referenced in his pattern, offers only the first of what should be two sets of anaphors, and then delivers his rewritten verses of "I Dream a World" featuring anaphora. What rhetorical reason did King have for constructing a pattern only to clip it at the end?

The answer rests in King's theme. The rhetorical movement of this speech literally models his speech's focus on the idea that an old world is passing away and a new one is being born. Because this clipped ending is the most significant section of the pattern, everything in this section (beginning with Holland's poem) deserves added discussion.

Rewriting the Poetry of Hughes and Holland

Intentionally refraining from alerting his audience that he was using anyone else's ideas, King speaks poetry in the form of prose as he first rewrites and then paraphrases ideas from Holland's "Wanted." Though he names Holland in other speeches, King engaged ideas from "Wanted" in this speech without informing his listeners that the words were not his own.

Because King does not signal that the ideas to follow were from anyone else, those in the audience would not have known where King's thoughts ended and Holland's began. King's own prose is suspended after he declares: "We have got to have leaders of this sort who will stand by courageously and yet not run off with emotion" (Carson 3: 345). After this, he offers a hybrid poem whose first six lines he rewrote, followed by eight lines that he reordered and rewrote from Holland's poem. The result loosely resembles Holland's original sonnet:

> We need leaders not in love with money
> but in love with justice.
> Not in love with publicity
> but in love with humanity.
> Leaders who can subject their particular egos
> to the pressing urgencies of the great cause of freedom.
>
> God give us leaders.
> A time like this demands great leaders.
> Leaders whom the fog of life cannot chill,
> men whom the lust of office cannot buy.
> Leaders who have honor.
> Leaders who will not lie.

Leaders who will stand before a pagan god
and damn his treacherous flattery. (Carson 3: 346)

The first six lines feature a chiastic structure and an ABCCBA rhyme scheme. Then, after paraphrasing part of the first line of Holland's poem, King jumps to Holland's ninth line and mentions the fog, which he then combines with the poem's third and fourth lines by joining "lust" with "buy." He then skips line five and arrives at a near-perfect line six before avoiding the awkward "demagogue" by simplifying it to merely "god." He also drops the image of "winking" in Holland's sonnet, which is not dependent upon any other word here for rhyme.

King's riffing on and appropriation of Holland's poem are part of this speech's overall rhetorical strategy. King's typed speech was right before him. Recognizing King's insertion of "fog" from line nine of Holland's poem is critical to understanding King's rhetorical strategy. Holland's poem is a sonnet. Its first eight lines offer a plea, and the final six describe the current state of a world waiting for this plea to be answered. The ninth line of a sonnet is called the volta, because it is where the poem takes a critical turn. By invoking the word "fog" from this volta in line nine and moving it out of place, King draws attention to the fact that this whole poem itself is serving as a turning point in the speech. This is why he leads into this hybrid poem by stating, "This is a tense period through which we are passing, this period of transition" (Carson 3: 345). All the other poems he references are quoted accurately; beginning here, half of this poem is written by King, the rest by Holland. King constructs his poem this way to symbolize the fading of an old world that is soon to be replaced by the new. This strategy can also be seen in the fact that in other contexts—that is, speeches in which he was not talking about a new world replacing an old one—King alerted listeners that these ideas from Holland were not his own and did not move line nine in such dramatic fashion.[10]

By placing a poem here that is partially his own and partially Holland's, King maintains the alternating pattern of allusion and quotation he has used throughout the entire speech. Moreover, the farther he gets into the speech, the more the original thoughts, words, and ideas pass away as something new comes forth. This progression reinforces King's theme. But ending the pattern of alternation with Holland's poem and his own rewritten lines would have left the speech on the edge of a new world not yet born. The speech would read like a sonnet without a sestet. King has one more poem for his listeners.

The speech's structure dictates that a third and final poem should appear in order to counterbalance the three offered earlier. Moreover, this poem's author should be identified. However, King has already begun to break the pattern he has established in this speech by blurring his voice with Holland's.

In the sequence, King skips the next expected poem. Instead, the first of what should be two invocations of anaphora appears as the beginning of the conclusion when King uses the word "stand" exactly four times in the second-to-last paragraph. Expecting another reference of four consecutive anaphors, King instead creates a new emblem for his idea of the beloved community.

This final section of the speech is based on King's declaration in the center of this chiastic structure that "the end is the creation of a beloved community" (Carter 3: 344). Having already pointed us to the "end," primed us for another poem, and left us expecting another instance of four consecutive anaphors, King now rewrites Hughes's "I Dream a World." King's final lines read:

We will be able to move into this new world, a world in which men will live together as brothers; a world in which men will no longer take necessities from the masses to give luxuries to the classes; a world in which men will throw down their sword and live by the higher principle of love. The time when we shall be able to emerge from the bleak and desolate midnight of man's inhumanity to man into the bright and glittering daybreak of freedom and justice. That there will be the time we will be able to stand before the universe and say with joy—the kingdom of this world has become the kingdom of our Lord and our Christ! and he shall reign forever and ever! Hallelujah! (3: 346)

King gives us three instances of anaphora when he repeats the phrase "a world in which." Introducing his vision of a new world, he repeats a line from the speech's focal point: "we will be able." The use of three anaphors when we expect four suggests that the disruption in the sequence is of paramount importance. But these four lines are also poetry. To replace the missing anaphor, King takes his rewritten lines of Hughes's "Youth" and merges them with the unacknowledged quotation from Burns: "The time when we shall be able to emerge from the bleak and desolate midnight of man's inhumanity to man into the bright and glittering daylight of freedom and justice." And, just in case we have not noted the patterns King has worked so hard to build, King offers a grammatical slip to purposefully draw added attention to this line: it is a sentence fragment. The entire speech coalesces in this space. King's central thesis, his patterned use of poetry, and his use of anaphora meet in a passage that features two examples of poems he has rewritten based on works by Hughes. King has modeled a new world to fulfill the speech's pattern: in exactly four lines, he has integrated poetry and anaphora.

Moreover, the introduction's notions of a "deep and tragic midnight" and "glittering sunlight" have been redeemed in this rewritten line that features "midnight" and "daylight." The fragmented grammatical structure supports the idea that this world is close but incomplete. The speech's themes are captured in the lines where King literally shows the old poetry passing away and his own poetry emerging. The rhetorical needs of this speech also lead King to take the structure from "I Dream a World" and rewrite its verses. His rhetorical movement is complete as old poems emerge as something completely new to model the idea of the old world passing away to usher in the new. This poetic act was forecast in the word "creation," which King uses twice in the center of the speech's chiastic structure. King fulfills his promise to show us an end where the beloved community is created by integrating poetry within his final example of anaphora.

Viewing this speech as a whole, we see that what once was a dream Langston Hughes spoke through the character of Martel in *Troubled Island* was rewritten and spoken by Martin Luther King for the first time on August 11, 1956. In a turn of uncommon coincidence, the name "Martel" translates as "Martin," the man now speaking a similar dream to the world, not from a stage or in Haiti but before those desperate to see a similar dream realized in America.

The connection seen here in the August 11, 1956, speech in Buffalo between "I Dream a World" and "Youth" is also important for another reason. In the speech above, King's line from "Youth" is connected to this poem's idea of a new world. The title of one of King's lost sermons also appears to link "Youth" with another idea from "I Dream a World": "Dreams of Brighter Tomorrows."[11] Although the text of this undated sermon has been lost, its title and subject matter suggest that King engaged Hughes's poetry by merging ideas from these two poems within it.

The structure of "I Dream a World" made the poem easy for King to rewrite. He simply linked his lines through the preacher's cadence of anaphora. In fact, the presence of anaphora in this poem may have been one of the things that King found most attractive about it. Sometimes, the poem's focus on a new world allowed King to activate overtones of the Second Coming; on other occasions, he used it to express dreams, both secular and sacred. While a first glance would lead us to suspect that King's three uses of the phrase "a world in which" are simply his own anaphoric creations, the pattern of the August 11 speech reveals that King was rewriting Hughes's "I Dream a World" and integrating it with his old line from "Youth."

What impressions did "I Dream a World" make on King's imagination? By internalizing Hughes's ideas through the act of rewriting, King engaged with those ideas on a level that is far more intense than quoting or even reciting. Such acts of rewriting are an investment with long-term rewards; paraphrasing is always a loan you pay back to the source. By rewriting Hughes's ideas with this degree of personal investment, King made Hughes's ideas his own.

Not only had this integration perfectly modeled King's theme on this occasion, but its placement at the end of this patterned sequence suggests that these are the most important lines in the speech. Wyatt Tee Walker once asked King what his "top priority was in planning a sermon—'Your three points?'" King replied, "Oh no. First I find my landing strip. It's terrible to be circling around up there without a place to land" (qtd. in Lischer, *Preacher King* 139). King's answer suggests that he decided on his ending before planning any other section of his addresses. By stating this final idea in the form of something poetic, he further highlights the importance of this passage. This critical aspect of an address is what some preachers refer to as "making gravy." C. T. Vivian, an associate of King's, explains, "there are two ways to make gravy. One of the ways . . . is that you cook meat—prepare your sermon—you take it out and you've got the grease there and you mix some extraneous stuff—flour that wasn't in the original grease, and then you stir that up pretty and you've got gravy . . . the other way to make gravy is to put on the pressure cooker . . . and you press all your elements down and you keep turning up the heat . . . you put your meat in . . . so that when you take the top off the gravy has come to the top naturally up out of the meat. That was Martin" (qtd. in Lischer, *Preacher King* 139).

Over time, the number of voices King incorporated in his dream would grow. Given the early date of this connection, the dream was as secular as it was sacred, and it was poetic long before it was prophetic. As King continued to press this specific dream, his own rewritten poem based on "I Dream a World" would always be the gravy; anything else was merely seasoning.

The Beloved Community

Given King's ability to rewrite a poem built on anaphora, we may wonder if Hughes's "I Dream a World" was the source of inspiration for the speech itself, as its themes and patterns stand so deeply unified. After all, this is King's poetic representation of his principle of the beloved community. King's decision to rewrite Hughes's poem and use it to develop his idea of the beloved community has major implications. As scholars have long recognized, the beloved community was "the capstone of King's thought," as all his "intellectual concerns were directly related to the priority he assigned to 'the Beloved Community'" (Smith and Zepp 119). Given the thematic focus on economic injustice in Hughes's poem, we can now ask what role Hughes's poetic dream served in shaping King's philosophy, knowing that King "frequently chastised the United States for its economic system that withheld the necessities of life from the masses while allowing luxuries to be monopolized by the few." If King "believed fervently that one of the major goals of the United States should be to bridge the gap between abject poverty and inordinate wealth" then, in King's mind, "The Beloved Community would be the manifestation of God's intention that everyone should have the physical and spiritual necessities of life" (Smith and Zepp 123). But was it a manifestation of God, or was it born from Hughes's metaphor? Perhaps it was both. After all, "Metaphor, instead of being selected after and apart from the discovery of ideas, occurs anterior to, and actually generates, the discovery of ideas" (Osborn 130). Like Hughes, King "could not envision the Beloved Community apart from the alleviation of economic inequity and the achievement of economic justice" (Smith and Zepp 125). His first enunciation of the beloved community occurs in a context where the secular meets the sacred as Christianity merges with communism.

This question is of paramount importance to understanding one of King's highest principles. Ira Zepp has argued that "King's devotion to the realization of the beloved community was his primary goal. It was the organizing principle of his life and around which all his thought and activity centered. His writings and his involvement in the civil rights struggle were illustrations of and the footnotes to this fundamental preoccupation" (207). Neither the theme of economic justice nor the term "beloved community" was an original creation of King's. The philosopher Josiah Royce used the term "beloved community" in his 1908 book *The Philosophy of Loyalty,* and it is likely that King encountered a positive assessment of it as he studied Walter Rauschenbusch's *Theology of the Social Gospel* during his doctoral training at Boston University (Zepp 209). Rauschenbusch spoke of "the similarity between the Second Coming and Marx's vision of a classless society" (Branch, *Parting the Waters* 74). Blending biblical quotations with the cadence from Hughes's poem perfectly balances these ideals.

If Royce's term epitomized the spiritual elements of King's vision, Hughes's poetry merged perfectly as its secular counter. As we will see in chapter 8, "The figure of the dream is used by King as an instrument to communicate the content of the beloved community" (Zepp 220).[12] King's ability to make a rewritten version of Hughes's poem "I Dream a World" stand as the representation of the beloved community adds further resonance to the connections between Hughes's poem and King's dream. Clearly, then, Arnold Schuchter is right to assert that King's idea of the beloved community "express[ed] more than a religious point of view" (569). As Lewis Baldwin writes, King's concept of the beloved community "represented a peculiar blend of insights from black culture, the Bible, liberal Christian theology and ethics, the American democratic heritage, Niebuhrian Christian Realism, and Eastern and Western philosophical traditions" (*Beloved Community* 3). Hughes's poetry is one element of "black culture" that Baldwin is suggesting. As David Bobbitt writes: "The black religious tradition of the hope for freedom and reconciliation, the social gospel of Rauschenbusch, and the theory of personalism, all converge in King's concept of the Beloved Community" (14). Now we also know that this concept has direct ties to poetry. The presence of "I Dream a World" at this stage in King's development of the idea of the beloved community is of critical significance. It reveals the key role Hughes's poetry played as King developed and communicated his concept of the beloved community. As we will see in the following chapter, by the fall of 1962 King was beginning to articulate his dream of the beloved community in an unforgettable way.

8

"I Have a Dream"

King Speaks in Rocky Mount

It is not surprising that King created his most memorable set piece featuring the phrase "I have a dream" on November 27, 1962.[1] King spent the "first ten days of October" of that year in Atlanta, working on his book of sermons titled *Strength to Love* (Garrow, *Bearing* 221). That fall King had spent a good deal of energy thinking about and refining his best sermons. His revisions to his sermon "Unfulfilled Hopes" reveal his preoccupation with the metaphor of dreaming during this period.

For the tenth chapter of *Strength to Love*, King revised his April 5, 1959, sermon "Unfulfilled Hopes" and gave it the new title "Shattered Dreams." In this handwritten draft of "Shattered Dreams," King traces the word "dreamed" three or four times before moving on to his next word. Hence the word "dreamed" itself shows up bold and dark in an unmistakable blue ink against the background of his yellow legal paper.[2] King's tracing captures his personal investment in the metaphor of dreaming as this word appears in the sentence "We as a people have long *dreamed* of freedom." Moreover, there is also a measurable pause in an earlier section of this draft when King stops after writing: "This is a central question, for we must determine how to live in a world where our highest hopes are often _____." In regard to rhyme and rhythm, the word that would best fit here is "deferred." King decides, instead, to strike "often" and write "not fulfilled." A few pages later, his repeatedly traced "dreaming" is once again the trope he cannot move past. In late 1962, dreaming was very much on King's mind.

✦ ✦ ✦

E. Stanley Jones

In addition to his engagements with Hughes's "Dream Deferred," King had engaged with the dream metaphor well before this time. King was well acquainted with the 1944 book by E. Stanley Jones titled *The Christ of the American Road*. King had high regard for the white preacher's works. As early as 1957, he had used ideas from Jones's 1925 book *The Christ of the Indian Road* to deepen his understanding of Gandhi and his culture. However, by 1959, King was drawn to a particular passage in Jones's 1944 book. Ten pages into his third chapter, Jones writes:

> What and where is America? America is a dream—unfulfilled. A dream of equality of opportunity, of privilege and property widely distributed; a dream of a place where class is abolished and where a man is a man, a place where race and birth and color are transcended by the fact of a common brotherhood, a place where humanity as humanity can begin a fresh experiment in human brotherhood that will be a new beginning for the race as a whole, a place where all our gifts and resources are held not for ourselves alone but as instruments of service for the rest of humanity—that is the dream. (60)[3]

When King delivered a speech before a gathering of the AFL-CIO in Miami at their annual convention on December 11, 1961, he closed with these words:

> This will be the day when we shall bring into full realization the American dream—a dream yet unfulfilled. A dream of equality of opportunity, of privilege and property widely distributed; a dream of a land where men will not take necessities from the many to give luxuries to the few, a dream of a land where men will not argue that the color of a man's skin determines the content of his character; a dream of a nation where all our gifts and resources are held not for ourselves alone but as instruments of service for the rest of humanity; the dream of a country where every man will respect the dignity and worth of human personality—that is the dream.
>
> When that day comes, the fears of insecurity, the doubts clouding our future, will be transformed into radiant confidence, into glowing excitement.[4]

A sentence-by-sentence breakdown of this sequence proves illuminating. The first two main ideas come directly from Jones, while the third and fourth are King's. The fifth is from Jones's text, and the sixth is from King. The final line is from Jones. Hence, Jones is represented in the lines that begin and close the passage plus two other sentences, while King's three ideas appear in between. Structurally, the white Jones and the black King work side by side, rhetorically allowing King to model integration. Rhetorically, King is expanding upon what he had already accomplished with his one-sentence verse that merged Burns and Hughes.

As we trace to its origins King's use of Jones's text to model integration, we learn that King first used this passage on May 11, 1959, in a speech delivered in Washington, D.C. That was exactly five weeks after he delivered a sermon about shattered dreams in the wake of the onstage success of *A Raisin in the Sun*. This raises an interesting question. Had the audience's response to the idea of dreams been so positive that King sought out a mainstream source so that he could address this topic free of recognizable allusions to Hughes when he spoke to integrated audiences? Whatever King's motive, the result is a new passage that reads like a prose poem as it blurs the lines between King's poetry and Jones's paragraph:

> Then and only then will we be able to bring into full realization the dream of our American democracy—a dream yet unfulfilled. A dream of equality of opportunity, of privilege and property widely distributed. A dream of a land where men will not take necessities from the few to give luxuries to the many. A dream of a land when men do not argue that the color of a man's skin determines the content of his character, where they recognize that the basic thing about a man is not his specificity but his fundamentum. A dream of a place where all our gifts and resources are held, not for ourselves alone but as instruments of service for the rest of humanity. The dream of a country where every man will respect the dignity and worth of all human personality, and men will dare to live together as brothers—that is the dream. Whenever it is fulfilled we will emerge from the bleak and desolate midnight of man's inhumanity to man into the bright and glowing daybreak of freedom and justice for all of God's children. (Carson 5: 202)

Once again, King ends his speech with a line that can be read as a complex poetic form of parallelism that integrates lines from Hughes and Burns. King's other poetic mode of choice here is internal rhyme. King finds an internal rhyme in Jones's quotation between "equality" and "opportunity." The extension of this rhyme in Jones's original "privilege" and "property" is likely the reason King kept these lines and replaced others from the original passage. Embedded within these lines, King rhymes "necessities" with "luxuries," seeming to revel in the rhythmic flourishes in "specificity" and "fundamentum." Off rhyme exists between the opening "h" sounds in "held" and "humanity." Strong end rhyme also appears symbolic in the closely connected "together" and "brothers" as the words themselves are extremely close to each other, enacting the theme expressed. End rhyme appears in the final words, "dignity" and "personality."

To merge his voice with Jones's in this prose poem, King included his own rewritten lines of "I Dream a World." This results in a passage that is not exactly prose yet not completely poetry either. The lines King included above as his own all appeared in the poem he created when he rewrote lines from Hughes's poem. King's ability to transfer his own earlier verses about a new world into this passage featuring dreams highlights the aspect of dreaming that was absent from the surface of the poem King first spoke in August 1956. On August 11, King's speech contained a latent connection to the metaphor of dreams.

Given King's decision to marry his first rewritten lines of Hughes's poem from 1956 with this new passage from Jones, this new passage contains one key remainder from Hughes's poem. Despite the clear presence of Jones and King, this passage simultaneously submerges the cadence of Hughes's poem. A textual comparison of the words of Jones, King, and Hughes reveals that the anaphor "dream of a land" can be read as King's latest revision to Hughes's "I Dream a World." Not repeating the word "dream," Jones's original passage only repeats the word "place"; however, the passage King delivers repeats "the dream of a land," "the dream of a place," and "the dream of a country." Located at the beginning of King's lines, these examples of anaphora mirror Hughes's poem. This inflection goes almost unheard because of the louder amplifications of Jones and King.

This verbal remainder can be found on other occasions as well. Even when King compressed all these ideas as he introduced or concluded speeches on the American dream, this cadence continued to linger in the phrase "the dream of a land":

I should like to discuss with you some aspects of the American Dream. For in a real sense, America is essentially a dream, a dream as yet unfulfilled. It is the dream of a land where men of all races, of all nationalities and of all creeds can live together as brothers. The substance of the dream is expressed in these sublime words, words lifted to cosmic proportions: "We hold these truths to be self-evident, that all men are created equal, that they are endowed by their Creator with certain unalienable rights, that among these are life, liberty, and the pursuit of happiness." This is the dream. (Washington 208)

Here the voices of Hughes, King, and Jefferson receive a moment of amplification as they unite within a space bracketed by the words of Jones.

In all these instances, King's audible anaphoric repetitions of "the dream of a land," "the dream of a place," and "the dream of a country" redeem the rhythms of Hughes's poem. These more expansive constructions demonstrate how King continued to add other voices into his dream as he moved closer to 1962. As he does, the presence of anaphora itself becomes the lingering surface remainder from Hughes's "I Dream a World"; however, given its prominence as both the earliest and eventually the most memorable feature of his dreaming, this connection is a critical component allowing us to hear the full resonance of King's metaphor.

Here, anaphora itself is the oral trait King continues to exalt as an echo of African American heritage mastered in folk pulpits and preserved in Hughes's "I Dream a World." In fact, when King read Hughes's poem, his first connection may have been to imagine the poem's speaker as an old-time folk preacher. As such, this specific and repeated incorporation of the cadence of "I Dream a World" results in what we might term *metanaphora*. Metanaphora occurs when a metaphor is repeated through anaphora. Here, the metaphor is a dream repeated in varying iterations of "the dream of a land." By 1962 the dream metaphor will become repeated in the anaphor "I have a dream." Although metaphors are inherently untraceable, and repetition can turn any word or phrase into an anaphor, it is noteworthy that, except for the two cases listed above, there are no other examples in King's addresses of an original anaphor activating a metaphor.[5] The result is that a trace remainder of Hughes's poem is captured in each of these refrains. As we listen, we hear Hughes's poetry being redeemed by King. On a larger scale, Hughes's poetry is at the center of King's rhetorical project to model integration, from its earliest origins to its most complex expressions.

All this reminds us that King's frequent invocation of the idea of dreaming supplied him with ample motivation and opportunities to revisit this subject as he maintained a hectic speaking schedule. The repetition of the dream alone would provide grounds to take a new slant on this topic. His penchant for revision, his desire to say something old in a new way, and the context that came from knowing each moment—all of these pushed King to develop his poetic persona at a time and in an atmosphere that privileged poetry from every stage. King needed a memorable way to communicate the civil rights movement's goal of integration. What he created was both inspirational and unforgettable.

Rocky Mount, North Carolina

When it came time to deliver a speech from the podium, Martin Luther King always knew exactly where he was. We have already seen this in his address at Lincoln University. This was never more apparent than when he took the platform to speak in the high school gym in Rocky Mount on November 27, 1962. King created a focus for his speech that evening by telling more than eighteen hundred listeners:

> This evening I would like to use as a subject from which to speak "Facing the Challenge of a New Age." And I guess in making a civil rights speech, it is improper to take a text from the Bible, but tonight I want to take a text. Many, many centuries ago a man by the name of John was in prison out on a lonely, obscure island called Patmos. . . . He thought about many things, he thought about the old Jerusalem. But in the midst of all this, he lifted his vision to heaven. He saw a new heaven and a new earth, the new Jerusalem, descending out of heaven from God. And if you will turn over in the Book of Revelation, you will find these words: "Behold, I make all things new, the former things are passed away."[6] And in a real sense, those of us who live in the twentieth century are able to say with John of old, "I see a new heaven and a new earth. I see the new Jerusalem descending out of heaven from God." An old order is passing away, and a new order is coming into being.[7]

Revising and updating his series of speeches from 1956, which ended with his rewriting of lines from Hughes's "I Dream a World," King made rhetorical history this night by once again taking elements from Hughes's old poem and making it new. Having previously activated the image of a new world on several occasions, tonight King shared his dream with the audience.

The school where King delivered his speech was named for Booker T. Washington, who had stopped in the city in 1910. Located along a major rail route, Rocky Mount claimed Washington's legacy in part by naming the segregated black school after the famous leader. King understood Washington's contribution to America. Growing up in Atlanta, King had attended that city's segregated Booker T. Washington High School for two years (Garrow, *Bearing* 34–36). King had quoted Washington four months earlier when he said: "Let no man pull you so low as to make you hate him" (Lewis 162).

King also seems to have been familiar with Washington's most famous public address. Speaking at the Atlanta Exposition on September 18, 1895, Washington had captivated an audience with his oratorical skills. His speech was reprinted across the country, taught in black schools, and even included in his autobiography, *Up from Slavery*. Washington ended his speech: "far above and beyond material benefits will be that higher good, that, let us pray God, will come, in a blotting out of sectional differences and racial animosities and suspicions, in a determination to administer absolute justice, in a willing obedience among all classes to the mandates of law. This, coupled with our material prosperity, will bring into our beloved South a new heaven and a new earth" (161–62). When King begins his speech in Rocky Mount by saying that John saw "a new heaven and a new earth," he is picking up where Washington's most famous address left off. By the time he finished delivering his fifty-five-minute speech that evening, King had shaped the visions of John, Washington, and Hughes into something unforgettably new.

The sermon genre has come to occupy a privileged position in the African American literary imagination. As Dolan Hubbard has shown, the tradition of exceptional preaching in the black community demands that the "preacher revives a system of values that are dormant in the black community" (16). This often includes inviting the community to join in as the preacher creates a "new world by transcending the narrow confines of the one in which they were forced to live" (Levine 32–33). As Hubbard notes, preaching itself is best when it becomes an "oral poetry" (4). King's speech at Rocky Mount fulfilled the speaker's charge to "embod[y] the Aristotelian notion of poet as creator and receiver. . . . [T]he preacher stands in the prophetic tradition of John of Patmos" (17). However, King is also reviving secular values.

The revised version of "Facing the Challenge of a New Age" that King delivered in Rocky Mount blends three distinct energies: inspirational elements of a sermon, an energized response from the crowd reminiscent of a mass meeting, and the political activism of a civil rights speech. The coalescence of these emotions is yet another example of King's ability to model integration. Not only does the speech end with a version of the "I have a dream" sequence, but that sequence is immediately preceded by the "How long? Not long" set piece that he made famous when he used it in his address at the end of the march from Selma to Montgomery in March 1965. The speech concludes with King repeating "let freedom ring."

After King first gave this speech on August 11, 1956, its taut organizational structure slowly loosened until it became more and more free. The structure of this speech exchanges the intricacies of the chiastic structure for a pattern built on numbers. Despite having abandoned the overall chiastic structure, King still pays considerable attention to the number of repetitions in his invocations of anaphora. This November 1962 speech bears the same cadence from six years earlier. Structurally, the speech has three main points followed by another four. King separates these themes and introduces this structure with well-placed uses of anaphora. He uses the phrase "people get tired" three times to preview his first three points; later, he uses "How can one avoid being depressed" four times to mirror the four main points that follow. It is important to remember that Hughes's "I Dream a World" uses four anaphors as well. Having dropped the overall chiastic structure, King is no longer worried about alternating between citing and appropriating the poetry he invokes. The lines from Cowper and Watts are clearly noted as poetry, Donne is named directly, and the words of Malloch sound as if they belong to King.

Intentional Mistakes

King ends his speech by doubling his cadence of anaphora and delivering eight refrains of the metanaphor "I have a dream." This set piece replaces the passages that appeared throughout other editions of this speech that spoke about a new world. Most notably, King offers three intentional mistakes to highlight the fact that he is dreaming of a new world. Not only has he rewritten John's revelation, Booker T.'s assertion, his own previous speeches, and Hughes's poetry, but he now pricks his listeners' ears with intentional mistakes intended to show how a new world will replace the old one.

First, King creates a new county at the very end of this speech when he says: "I have a dream that one day down in Sasser County, Georgia, where they burned two churches down a few days ago because Negroes wanted to register and vote, one day right down there little black boys and little black girls will be able to join hands with little white girls and little white boys and walk the streets as brothers and sisters." Hailing from Georgia, King knows that there are counties in his state with monikers such as "Bad Baker" County and "Terrible Terrell" County. However, Georgia does not have a Sasser County. King had visited the city of Sasser just eleven days earlier, where he spoke at a ceremony to commemorate the burning of two churches.[8] He had also just raised ten thousand dollars from Nelson Rockefeller to restore these buildings (Branch, *Parting* 639). King invents a fictitious Sasser County because his dream of a future world contains a place that looks so unlike present-day Georgia that the counties deserve better names. Sasser is now in "Terrible Terrell" County; when the new world arrives, it will be replaced by a better and brighter Sasser in which children of all colors are free to play with each other.

Second, although he accurately named the city in which he is speaking only two sentences earlier, in the middle of his dream King asserts that "One day right in Rocky Mountain, North Carolina, the sons of slaves and the sons of former slave owners will meet at the table of brotherhood." As with its southerly sister, the town of Sasser, the new order will so change the habits of this county that the segregated Rocky Mount will become the integrated Rocky Mountain. The shift indicates a new level of freedom enjoyed by all its citizens.

Third, King saves his most dramatic intentional mistake for a quotation from Isaiah 40.4–5. It is a passage he knows so well by heart that his error highlights the triumph of his rhetorical strategy. At the place in the speech where he has moved into his fifth refrain of "I have a dream," King says: "I have a dream tonight. One day every valley shall be exalted and every mountain shall be made low. Crooked places will be made straight, the rough places will be made strange, the glory of the LORD shall be revealed and all flesh shall see it together." King audibly pauses before speaking the word "strange"; the word he should say here is "plain." With his three changes in this section, King has literally turned the *plain* places of Sasser, Georgia, and Rocky Mount, North Carolina, into Sasser County and Rocky Mountain. As if he were John (not Amos or Isaiah), these new, *strange* places are places that King wants everyone in the audience to imagine. King knows that nothing is more memorable than when it is mispronounced. He casts part of this vision as biblical, but the cadence in this metanaphor comes directly from Hughes's poetry.

"How Long? Not Long"

To more fully understand King's "I have a dream" passage, we have to examine the section that immediately precedes it in this speech. King's poetic persona begins to reveal itself near the end of this speech. As if reactivating ideas embedded in the two anaphors he used earlier when he spoke of people being "tired" and then "depressed" at the sight of suffering, King combines these feelings when he signals this move to his conclusion: "I know some of you, and suddenly all over, we get weary." This shift from "I" to "we" leads King to imagine that his listeners are asking, "How long will it take to solve this problem?" And then, previewing the type of poetic element soon to come, King takes ideas he will soon quote and imaginatively rewrites them: "How long will prejudice blind the visions of men, darken their understanding, drive bright-eyed wisdom from her sacred throne? Somebody's asking tonight, when will wounded justice be lifted from this dust of shame to reign supreme among the children of men? When will the radiant star of hope be plunged against the nocturnal bosom of this lonely night, plucked from weary souls the manacles of fear and the chains of death? How long, somebody's asking, will justice be crucified and truth be buried?" In asking "How long?" exactly four times in this section, King reestablishes the cadence of organizing his ideas in sets of four that links this speech with its 1956 predecessor.

This establishes a cadence King builds off of and then alters for effect in the two main sections that follow. The question "How long?" activates memories of biblical poetry, as it appears in no fewer than five psalms.[9] Though "How long?" appears elsewhere in the Bible in some rather innocuous questions, the repetitions invoked here by King most closely resemble the first two verses of Psalm 13:

> How long wilt thou forget me, O Lord? for ever?
> How long wilt thou hide thy face from me?
> How long shall I take counsel in my soul,
> having sorrow in my heart daily?
> How long shall mine enemy be exalted over me?[10]

In his speech, King further links these repetitions of "How long?" by poetically restating ideas centering on the idea of a "throne" that he will continue to extend in his own way before revealing their origin. This culminates in King's declaration that one day "Christ will rise up and split history into AD and BC so that even the life of Caesar must be dated by his name."

The rhyme between "history" and "BC" gives way to the repeated trochaic feet in "Caesar" and "dated." The irony of these rhymes comes in the fact that the two-syllable "Caesar" is replaced by the one-syllable "name" embedded within the final anapest. The effect of this rhythm is that the one-syllable

"Christ" replaces the two-syllable "Caesar," thereby mirroring the idea expressed by King.

Unlike the hidden inspiration of Hughes, King reveals the origin of these riffs and identifies the poets he has just been mimicking. After answering his own question of "How long?" with a triumphant "Not long," keeping the cadence of four anaphors, King says:

> There is something in this universe that justifies Carlyle in saying, "No lie can live forever." There is something in this universe which justifies William Cullen Bryant in saying, "Truth crushed to earth will rise again." There is something in this universe which justifies James Russell Lowell in saying,
>
> Truth forever on the scaffold,
> Wrong forever on the throne,
> Yet that scaffold sways the future,
> Behind the dim unknown
> Standeth God within the shadows,
> Keeping watch above his own.
>
> There is something in the universe which justified the Bible in saying "You shall reap what you sow."

By collapsing the distance between the Bible, the words of poets and writers, and his own voice, King previews his dream of a new world.

Chiastic Form

The differences between this speech and the passage King built from the ideas of E. Stanley Jones can be measured in the repeated structural element of chiasmus. This structure unified the entire August 11, 1956, speech, and it is now compressed into the speech's signature refrain, "I have a dream." In comparing this version of "Facing the Challenge of a New Age" with its original version, we notice that one structural element has been activated in a new way. As we saw in the last chapter, King's August 1956 speech was organized around a strict chiastic structure. However, this November 1962 version does not use this structure to unify the speech; rather, King organizes the "I have a dream" section into a loose chiastic form. Given the speech's history of being organized around patterns of four, the exact number of anaphors Hughes used in "I Dream a World," King begins with the opening statement: "And so, my friends of Rocky Mount, I have a dream tonight.[11] It is a dream rooted deeply in the American dream."[12]

From this point in the sequence, King creates a loose ABCD DCBA structure through the remaining refrains of "I have a dream." He sees a world in which "little black boys and little black girls will be able to join hands with little white boys and little white girls and walk the streets as brothers and sisters." This theme of integration is a sure sign of the freedom that appears in his final statement of the sequence: "I have a dream tonight that someday we will be free." In the context of King's vision of what the civil rights movement hoped to accomplish, integration was synonymous with freedom. For the B sections of this organizational structure, King begins with an allusion to Acts 17.26: "The sons of slaves and the sons of slave-owners will meet at the table of brotherhood, knowing that out of one blood God made all men to dwell upon the face of the earth." This statement is paired with another that gives added emphasis to unity, as King's corresponding line reads: "I have a dream tonight. One day my little daughter and my two sons will grow up in a world not conscious of the color of their skin but only conscious of the fact that they are members of the human race." King seems to be linking his own voice with the writings of another doctor, Luke, who wrote the book of Acts.

The middle sections of King's sequence depicting his dream are the tightest in regard to his organizational structure. Moreover, like the last matching pair, King deliberately connects the ideas of individual speakers. Just as his voice is a match for Luke, he connects ideas spoken by Jefferson and Christ. One of the effects of this pair is to show a connection between the core values of America and Christianity. King's third pair of matching sentences affirms that "one day men all over this nation will recognize that all men were created equal and endowed by their creator with certain inalienable rights." This is paired with Christ's directive that "one day men will do unto others as they would have them do unto them." Linking Jefferson and Christ creates the effect that both the fundamental creed of America and the call from the leader of brotherhood could be equally fulfilled in the new world that King is dreaming of. Finally, the center of this structure prominently pairs the words of Amos and Isaiah. These declarations of justice coming to the Earth highlight a future still to come, a new world where "justice will roll down like waters and righteousness like almighty stream." He then turns the chiastic sequence toward its matching verses with the intentional mistake in his quotation from Isaiah 40.

The structural choice to reemphasize the quotation from Isaiah has several advantages. The quotation itself is the turning point in this loose chiastic structure. Having started to unravel the first four ideas, this line receives added attention because of King's mistake. Moreover, it unifies the speech by highlighting the very place that King has foreseen. With its mountain imagery, King's line creates a noticeable resonance with the intentional shift from Rocky Mount to Rocky Mountain.[13]

If we read this chiastic structure from the center out, King's dream suggests that the new world to come is one in which the ideals of both Jefferson and Christ will become a reality so that members of the human race, all created equal, will know and experience freedom measured specifically in the form of integration. This chiastic structure enables King to communicate the thought that a transformation of this world will lead to a unity that results in freedom. This dream of freedom is one that King lingered over as he wrote and revised his sermons by hand, particularly over this phrase: "We as a people have long *dreamed* of freedom." To what degree did King's revisions to his sermon "Shattered Dreams" trigger this invocation of dreaming?

Here, the chiastic structure that binds the "I have a dream" passage is more than an organizational strategy. By linking the refrains of "I have a dream," King seems to be aiming for something that closely resembles poetry. This version reads like a first-draft attempt at writing a poem built on metanaphora and parallelism.

It is important to note that the metaphor of dreaming is not found in any of the passages that King quotes here. Neither Amos, Isaiah, Christ, Luke, nor John claims the metaphor. While Amos, Isaiah, and John could be said to have had "visions," King's choice of diction and, just as important, cadence leads to another place. His use of this dream as an example of metanaphora at the end of *this* speech points directly to Hughes's "I Dream a World." King's use of the dream metaphor may even have been triggered by revisions he made to his sermon "Shattered Dreams." The fact that this refrain surfaces for the first time in the speech from which King's closest use of Hughes's poetry about dreams occurs reveals that the origins of King's dream are deeply intertwined with Hughes's poetry.

In August 1956, King used the essential argument of his speech to imagine a new world. In 1962, he is literally dreaming of a new world. Beginning in 1959, King spoke of "shattered dreams"; now, despite the recent failure of the Albany campaign, he declares that his dream is alive and well. He had activated every facet of Hughes's metaphor. The text box on page 173 reveals how King presented this dream by once again altering the order of words in Hughes's poetry. King's dream is merely an updated version of his concept of the beloved community. As such, it is no wonder that Drew Hansen found that "Much of the substance of the 'I have a dream' set piece appeared in a series of speeches in which King looked forward to . . . a new world" (118). This is true because these were all revisions to the same speech: "Facing the Challenge of a New Age."

Reordering Hughes's Words

Poem	Hughes	King
"Youth"	tomorrow bright	bright tomorrow
"Dream Deferred"	dream deferred	deferred dreams
"Brotherly Love"	love you still	still love you
"I Dream a World"	I dream a world	I have a dream

As can be seen above, Hughes's opening words in "Youth" ("we have tomorrow / bright before us") have been rearranged. King takes Hughes's words that started on the left and slides them in circles until they end up on the right. Where "bright" once followed "tomorrow," now it precedes it, just as King switches "dream deferred" to "deferred dreams." King does the same thing with the word "still" when he delivers lines from Hughes's poem "Brotherly Love." Similarly, three of the four words in his repeated phrase "I have a dream" are also found in Hughes's anaphor "I dream a world."

Like his "How long? Not long" set piece, King's dream knits together equal elements of the secular and the sacred. Had King not rewritten Hughes's imagery of the dream, this sequence would have been too dependent upon sacred elements, using only Jefferson's statement as a counterbalance. The refrain itself strikes the balance King imagines by supplying a needed element of the secular. Hughes's poetry is the key representation of African American culture.

Moreover, everything King states in the final eight minutes of his speech is either a direct quotation or a measured allusion. *Nothing* in these last three set pieces is wholly original. Anything truly original would have undermined the speech's theme and stripped the rhetorical force from King's expressiveness. The idea of the speech is that the old is being transformed into the new.

The dream itself is best understood as an idea King encountered in Hughes's poetry before transforming it into a poetic structure of his own by making it as inclusive as possible. This dream touches the realms of poetry, prophecy, and politics so that each listener might hear an echo of something he or she knew best. The unifying structure of King's dream models the integration both he and his listeners seek. In regards to content, the common language of religion becomes a unifying language around which all levels of listeners could relate. But where the dream needed stitching, King used poetry as his unifying refrain.

"Let Freedom Ring"

Tracing the origins of this speech to 1956 reveals that the use of four anaphors is not only responsible for the number of times King repeats several organizational phrases, thus allowing him to symbolically double the number of examples in his dream section, but is also responsible for understanding the specific number of lines King devotes in his "let freedom ring" set piece to end his speech. The implications of this cadence have not been adequately considered. King delivered this rewritten set piece for the first time on December 4, 1956. He ended this version of "Facing the Challenge of a New Age" with a passage built on a sequence of four. The original passage came from Archibald Carey's 1952 address before the Republican National Convention. Carey's version contains the words, ideas, and theme King used; however, the repetition and cadence came from King's own hand.

After reciting the lyrics of "America" (also known as "My Country, 'Tis of Thee"), Carey said: "That's exactly what we mean—from every mountainside, let freedom ring. Not only from the Green Mountains and the White Mountains of Vermont and New Hampshire; not only from the Catskills of New York; but from the Ozarks in Arkansas, from the Stone Mountain in Georgia; from the Great Smokies of Tennessee, and from the Blue Ridge Mountains of Virginia" (Carson 3: 463n23). Given its list of states, the passage suggests that the freedom in the North should be extended to the South. Whereas Carey lists three states in the North and five in the South, King strikes a perfect balance of four in each region in all his addresses from 1956 to 1961.[14] King's early penchant for rhythmic and numerical balance leads him to divide his list into two equal sets of four when he speaks on these occasions. From Carey's list he keeps one state from the North (New Hampshire) and two from the South (Georgia and Tennessee), but in adding new states he uses creative adjectives to describe the mountains themselves. In his speech at Rocky Mount he refers to the "heightening Alleghenys of Pennsylvania" and "the curvaceous slopes of California." As Garry Wills notes, this mountain imagery "picks up on other mountain language in the speech—the heights from which Amos's waters of justice roll down . . . the mountains turned into a royal progress route in Isaiah" (224). These links are intensified in a speech where King turns Rocky Mount into Rocky Mountain.

As we can see at the very end of this 1962 speech, King departs from his balanced approach to listing these states. Instead of listing four northern and four southern states, King gives five northern states and four southern ones. Coming on the heels of a speech that uses strict numerical sequencing, it is curious that King has altered the balance. The appearance of this imbalance immediately after King gave his audience a taste of his dream may suggest that this "let freedom ring" section captures more of a picture of the current reality, namely, that freedom is allowed to exist more in the North than it does in the South.

In Rocky Mount, King ended his speech by calling for equal freedom for everyone. By the end of this unique speech, he had rewritten, alluded, or referenced ideas from Archibald Carey, Booker T. Washington, William Cullen Bryant, James Russell Lowell, Thomas Carlyle, the Old Testament prophets Amos and Isaiah, Psalms, Revelation, Thomas Jefferson, and Langston Hughes. Most importantly, he had begun the first step of shaping his dream into the form of poetry. Presenting his dream as a poem not only reactivates the roots of the imagery King made his own; it also speaks to King's personal investment, dynamic skills, and rhetorical values. In the next chapter we will examine how King's poetic skills continued to mature, reaching their zenith when he shared this dream in 1963 in Detroit.

9

"The Psalm of Brotherhood"

King at Detroit's March for Jobs

The March for Jobs, held in Detroit on June 23, 1963, was one of the largest gatherings of protesters in U.S. history. Martin Luther King was invited to be its featured speaker. King's offices in Atlanta buzzed with requests for information, requests for advance copies of the speech, statements, and interviews as over thirty calls came into the office on June 10 alone. King's father was so excited about the attention sure to come from the upcoming event that he even directed his son to alert the newly elected Pope Paul VI in hopes the pontiff might take notice of the march. Later that day, King received a call from Medgar Evers regarding a potential visit by King to Mississippi.[1] King made flight plans for the trip to Detroit, then canceled them so he could travel to Washington, D.C., for a meeting with the president.[2]

Over the years, King had established a close relationship with the people of Detroit. With the support of influential men such as William Ruether, who headed the United Automobile Workers Union in Michigan, King quickly started receiving financial support from this area for the civil rights cause. By the spring of 1963, Ruether had raised "$160,000 from unions to get protestors out of jail in Birmingham. No one but big labor could offer such support. . . . [T]he union had a powerful Washington office that helped to defeat filibuster threats in the U.S. Senate in order to pass civil rights laws" (Honey 74–75).

On June 23, after a procession that included "125,000–150,000 people" filling a "twenty-one block area after marching down Woodward Ave." (Honey 74), a crowd of ten thousand packed Detroit's Cobo Hall to hear performances by Dinah Washington, the Four Tops, and other musical groups.

King's face was displayed on the program cover. Appearing seventh on a program that featured twenty-eight speakers and musical performances, Dorothy Ayers read the poem "Freedom March." James Weldon Johnson's "Lift Ev'ry Voice" was performed, as was "The Star-Spangled Banner." One choir sang "Do You Want Your Freedom" set to the music of "Climbing Jacob's Ladder" and another sang "We Shall Overcome." Finally, after being introduced by Congressman Charles Diggs, King took the stage.

In his speech that evening, King presented a revised version of the dream he had first spoken of eight months earlier, in Rocky Mount, North Carolina. This chapter will examine the poetry behind the dream that King communicated to his listeners as he combined the structural elements of parallelism with auditory principles of prosody.

King's Address

We cannot underestimate the significance of this speech in the development of King's poetic sensibilities. King ended his address with his own poem. Each line of this "Psalm of Brotherhood" featured the refrain "I have a dream," and it was the first time King spoke these words on a national stage.

In preparing for Detroit, King rewrote the sequence he had delivered in Rocky Mount, further refining his dream of a world where integration was a reality. In this higher-profile context, his decision to submerge Hughes's poetry within his speech was an act of purposeful defiance. In 1963, King was not about to forfeit the prize of civil rights by acting recklessly. The day before, Attorney General Robert Kennedy, Assistant Attorney General Burke Marshall, and President Kennedy had each successively told King to expel from his camp the suspected Communists Jack O'Dell and Stanley Levison. Despite having been warned about the dangers of such associations, King embedded a controversial poet's ideas within his speech.[3] Submerging Hughes within his speech in Detroit wasn't dangerous—he had always succeeded in hiding the poet's ideas under the cover of new language. On this particular day, however, King's was an act of defiant subversion in which he spoke truth to power through the reinvented metaphor of a subversive poet. The irony radiated in the fact that power was made to listen to something it thought it had effectively silenced.

King expresses his dream at the culmination of his address in what are effectively ten lines of free-verse poetry. About halfway through the speech, he subtly prepares listeners for the poem to come by using the phrase "now is the time" five times. His use of anaphora in this middle section reveals his creativity in two ways. First, his initial invocation of "now is the time" features his own rewriting of words that President Kennedy had delivered live on national television on June 11. That day, Kennedy had federalized the Alabama National Guard and assigned them to accompany two African American students as they entered the University of Alabama. That night, before referencing the events in Birmingham, Kennedy had declared, "Now the time has come for this nation to fulfill its promise."[4] King uses this idea in his own way in Detroit when he says: "Now is the time to make real the promise of democracy."[5] (Two months later, King would say, "Now is the time to open the doors of opportunity to all of God's children" [Washington 218], an allusion to the blocked entrance at the University of Alabama.) By restating "Now is the time" in anaphora, King not only draws attention to Kennedy's speech but also suggests that both he and the president are stating the same idea.[6]

Second, King is not invoking metaphor in the next line of his speech when he says, "Now is the time to transform this pending national elegy into a creative psalm of brotherhood." Although the speech as a whole is not as multifaceted as his speech from August 11, 1956, where he ended by rewriting Hughes's "I Dream a World," King is nonetheless previewing the end of his speech in the same way. He is telling us that his speech will end with a "psalm of brotherhood." As expected, King signals the connections between this passage and the end of his speech through the use of anaphora. Here, King introduces five consecutive phrases with the words "Now is the time." This use of five anaphors, the only sustained instance in the speech before the conclusion's ten metanaphors of "I have a dream," is significant, since it previews the later doubling to ten verses. With a symbolic intensification, Kennedy's promise gives way to King's poem. As he had in August 1956, King is again using a line near the middle of his speech to preview the poetry waiting at the end.

That both of these speeches create a poem of "brotherhood" further connects their purpose, theme, and anaphoric cadence to Hughes's "I Dream a World." King's "Psalm of Brotherhood" is his perfected revision to the dream he delivered in Rocky Mount. In 1956 he *spoke* of a new world; today he would *dream* of one.

King's decision to end his speech with a poem featuring the refrain "I have a dream" can be further contextualized in two ways. First, the subversive undertones of King's choice would resonate with a community that was well

attuned to Marxist ideology. "By the 1960s, blacks in Detroit had had signifi-
cant exposure to Marxism" (Dawson 200), and "black auto workers [had]
come to identify Marxism with people willing to fight for the black causes"
(Geschwender 80). According to Michael Dawson, at this time "several
types of Marxism were available; there was the CPUSA, and the great black
Trotskyite intellectual C. L. R. James spent much of World War II in Detroit.
James and Grace Lee Boggs were both active among black auto workers as
well. Marxists had a long history of struggle both in and out of the auto in-
dustry, in and out of the union, and in and out of the CPUSA" (200). Such an
atmosphere could have guided King's decision to use a passage that included
overtones of Hughes's poetry.

Second, King had ended a speech in Cobo Hall two years earlier by re-
peating a refrain that centered on dreams. On April 27, 1961, he had told fifty-
seven hundred union members and their guests that "economic justice and
the brotherhood of man" were within reach. "This dream can be realized," he
said, but "before this dream is realized, maybe some will have to get scarred
up a bit; before the dream is realized, maybe some will have to go to jail;
before the dream is realized, maybe some will have to face physical death"
(Honey 30). With exactly four refrains that feature dreams to be fulfilled
rather than deferred, King matches the four metanaphors in his earliest ver-
sions of "Facing the Challenge of a New Age."

It is important to view King's 1963 address as a revision of his speech in
Rocky Mount. Both dreams are built on the foundation of the new world
he presented in 1956. The diction, theme, and structure reveal that King has
compressed the pattern he spread out over the course of his 1956 speech and
reduced it into a single poem. King has taken the ten chiastic elements that
unified his 1956 speech and concentrated them into a single ten-line poem.

We will treat King's "Psalm of Brotherhood" as poetry. While it is com-
mon to address these dream passages as if King were a prophet, it is often
overlooked that prophets often use the genre of poetry to communicate to
their people. Biblical prophecy is often recorded, spoken, and transmitted in
the genre of poetry. King's "Psalm of Brotherhood" is both prophetic and po-
etic.

King's Psalm

On its own, King's "Psalm of Brotherhood" is as chiastic as his entire August
11, 1956 address, "Facing the Challenge of a New Age." As we examine the

entire sequence, we note that it is often set off as ten separate lines, or verses, when reprinted. This format helps to highlight the organizational principles of each verse. King introduces this psalm by saying: "I go back believing that the new day is coming. And so this afternoon, I have a dream. It is a dream deeply rooted in the American dream." Then he begins the psalm:

I have a dream that one day right down in Georgia and Mississippi and Alabama, the sons of former slaves and the sons of former slave owners will be able to live together as brothers.

I have a dream this afternoon that one day little white children and little Negro children will be able to join hands as brothers and sisters.

I have a dream this afternoon that one day men will no longer burn down houses and the church of God simply because people want to be free.

I have a dream this afternoon that there will be a day that we will no longer face the atrocities that Emmett Till had to face or Medgar Evers had to face, that all men can live with dignity.

I have a dream this afternoon that my four children, that my four little children will not come up in the same young days that I came up within, but that they will be judged on the basis of the content of their character, not the color of their skin.

I have a dream this afternoon that one day right here in Detroit, Negroes will be able to buy a house or rent a house anywhere that their money will carry them and they will be able to get a job.

Yes, I have a dream this afternoon that one day in this land the words of Amos will become real and "justice will roll down like waters, and righteousness like a mighty stream."

I have a dream this evening that one day we will recognize the words of Jefferson that "all men are created equal, that they are endowed by their Creator with certain unalienable Rights, that among these are Life, Liberty and the pursuit of Happiness." I have a dream this afternoon.

Figure 8. Martin Luther King, Cobo Hall, Detroit, June 23, 1963. (Photo courtesy of the Detroit News Archives.)

> I have a dream that one day "every valley shall be exalted, and every hill shall be made low; the crooked places shall be made straight, and the rough places plain; and the glory of the Lord shall be revealed, and all flesh shall see it together."

> I have a dream this afternoon that the brotherhood of man will become a reality in this day.[7]

Through his psalm, King presents his vision for a new world. This passage expands upon the structures he had used to organize his 1956 speech and the chiastic line that resulted when he combined Burns's "Man Was Made to Mourn" with Hughes's "Youth": "We will be able to emerge from the bleak and desolate midnight of man's inhumanity to man into the bright and glittering daybreak of freedom and justice" (Carson 3: 346).

Although the refrain and metaphor of King's psalm is his "dream," the theme of the poem is that "we will all be able to live together as brothers."

King announces this in the first verse, where he says that he has a dream that one day "the sons of former slaves and the sons of former slave owners will be able to live together as brothers." From this point on, the sequencing of King's ideas is of critical importance to understanding this prophetic poem. Just as he had done with "Youth," King organizes his ideas in a structure that merges the chiastic, climactic, and antithetic. Moreover, he does it in exactly the same triplicates, such that three negative ideas are countered by three positive revisions.

Figure 9 illustrates how King has organized his ideas. His first idea (living as brothers) is thematically paired with his tenth idea (brotherhood). His second idea (black and white children holding hands) is mirrored by the ninth idea (the new would will be seen by everyone together). Then, ideas three, four, and five pair with ideas six, seven, and eight, respectively (the first three focus on negative things that King no longer wants to happen, while the last three mirror these themes to speak of how things will change in the future). To better understand how these ideas mirror one another in this complex organizational pattern, I will amplify each pair of ideas in the following sections.

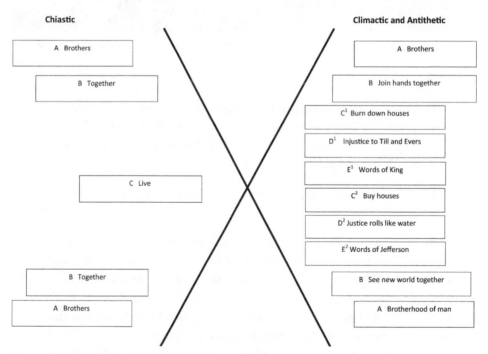

Chiastic

A Brothers

B Together

C Live

B Together

A Brothers

Climactic and Antithetic

A Brothers

B Join hands together

C^1 Burn down houses

D^1 Injustice to Till and Evers

E^1 Words of King

C^2 Buy houses

D^2 Justice rolls like water

E^2 Words of Jefferson

B See new world together

A Brotherhood of man

Figure 9. Parallelism in King's "I Have a Dream" speech, Detroit, June 23, 1963.

Brotherhood

The first verse introduces the central theme of King's psalm. In King's prophetic vision, black slaves and white masters can "live together as brothers." This is the first "A" in the diagram. This idea dates back to the three speeches King first delivered in 1956. It is the same idea that begins his first rewriting of Hughes's "I Dream a World." It is also the definition of the beloved community: "The end is the creation of a beloved community. The end is the creation of a society where men will live together as brothers" (Carson 3: 344). During the address in Detroit, King couples this idea with the final thought of this section as verse ten repeats the vision's theme. The matching "A" on the diagram comes in the final line of the speech in this chiastic pattern as King says that his dream is that "the brotherhood of man will become a reality."

Together

It is no accident that a passage designed to communicate people living together would reemphasize the idea of unity. In the first "B" in the diagram, King gives us a picture of white and black children who are standing together as they "join hands as brothers and sisters." While it is easy to focus on the prophetic nature of King's ninth verse, as it borrows ideas from Isaiah 40.3–4, the theme of this passage is the emergence of a new world in which equality prevails. This equality is described in geographical terms as the high being made low and the crooked becoming straight. What is critical to understanding King's larger rhetorical goals is the fact that Isaiah's prophecy ends with the declaration that "all flesh shall see it together." Not only is this new world coming, but it is a world everyone will see *together*.

Live

Just as he had done so often by pairing the images of "bleak and desolate midnight" with "bright and glittering daybreak," King's third, fourth, and fifth verses all correspond directly to verses six, seven, and eight to form connections that are at once climactic and antithetical. Verses six, seven, and eight demonstrate the opposite of verses three, four, and five, and each one speaks to the theme of "how to live." Each pair of triplicates deserves a side-by-side comparison.

When King mentions in verse three that his dream includes a world where "men will no longer burn down houses," he is indicating that America's black citizens currently face domestic terrorism.[8] It is impossible to have the life promised by the Constitution when life itself is under constant threat. The antithetic in verse six offers the positive counter to this imagery: a place where "Negroes will be able to buy a house or rent a house anywhere." King exchanges burned houses for ones that black families can buy. The move from "burn" in the old world to "buy" in the new world shows the climactic and antithetic nature of these parallels and captures the climactic progress forward where things that once happened will soon be replaced by their direct opposites.

In verse four, King speaks of the unjust acts of lynching and murder when he references Emmett Till and Medgar Evers. These two citizens were literally killed and not allowed to live. Verse four's parallel, verse seven, speaks of a future world where "justice will roll down like waters." Given the fact that Till's lynched body was found in the Tallahatchie River, Amos's statement could not be more antithetic. Hence, King's structure highlights the change from injustice to justice. Notably, King substitutes "justice" for the original biblical term, "judgment." "Justice" more clearly completes his chiastic structure, indicating the deliberate nature of King's construction.

The similarities between verses five and eight would have been the easiest ones for listeners in Cobo Hall to recognize. Although it is often forgotten today, one purpose of King's speech was to inspire greater participation in the March on Washington, planned for August. King's support of the new civil rights bill then before Congress is the context that unites these two verses. Earlier in the speech King focused on Lincoln's Emancipation Proclamation, and in the paragraph before his "I have a dream" sequence he said, "we also need your support in order to get the civil rights bill that the President is offering passed. . . . [T]his bill isn't going to get through if we don't put some work in it and some determined pressure."

Verses five and eight focus on legal rights and their ability to enhance quality of life. Verse eight quotes Jefferson's statement regarding the "unalienable Rights" of "Life, Liberty, and the pursuit of Happiness" and then notes that these rights have not been "recognized." The problem, of course, is that these rights have not been protected. We can see this emphasis in King's fifth verse most clearly by comparing it with the way he usually presented this idea in previous speeches. In his first use of the phrase "content of his character," King used the word "argue" in place of "judge." On May 11, 1959, King told listeners that he hoped America would be a land where "men do not argue that the color of a man's skin determines the content of his character" (Carson 5: 202). This phrase appears again two years later as King describes "a dream of a land where men will not argue that the color of a man's skin determines the content of his character."[9] Because we often think we know King's dream so well, this use of the word "argue" almost sounds foreign. King's choice to revise his older "argue" with the newer "judge" is no accident. King is signaling his listeners to the critical idea of enforcement of the law in Detroit's speech when he substitutes "judged" for "argue." As a result of this change, the phrase as we now know it has become much more powerful and memorable as King altered it to complete the demands of a parallel structure focused on the subject of justice.

The poem's most important organizational cue comes in verse five, which moves us away from the negative depictions of current living and toward the positive dreams of life in the future. King begins verse five by suggesting that the past is something he wants to move away from: "I have a dream this afternoon that my four children will not come up in the same young days I came up within." As in verses three and four, he asserts that the past has led to tough living. Moreover, this allows him an opportunity to invoke the same negative language that he used in those two verses. With his phrase "will not come up in," the consistent patterning of these phrases cannot be overlooked. In verses three, four, and five, some negative phrase is used: "will no longer" in verses three and four, and "will not come in" in verse five. In contrast, verses six, seven, and eight speak in the positive and future sense of what "will be able," "will become real," and "will recognize."

The turn that highlights the antithetic and climactic nature of this poem occurs in verse five. The first half includes a "will not" construction, but the second half of the verse shifts toward what is to come: "they will be judged on the content of their character, not the color of their skin." Next, verses six, seven, and eight will move the organizational pattern forward in a climactic manner as "will" replaces the "not."

Verse five may be the most personal verse in this poem. It begins with an idea that could be an allusion to an oft-repeated prayer of King's father, and it ends with one of King's own most famous lines. In 1961, two years before King gave this speech, his father testified that "My prayer was always—Lord, grant that my children will not have to come the way I did" (Baldwin, *Balm* 105). In verse five, King appears to be transitioning from the prayers of his father to the day that he himself envisions for every one of God's children.

By pairing verses five and eight, King is elevating himself as the rightful and righteous black counter to the historical white figure of Jefferson. King speaks on what the future should hold, and his rhetoric highlights the fact that the current racism, according to which one is judged by "the color of one's skin," will be replaced when we recognize that "all men are created equal." It is a piece of biting irony that King employs the old words from the Declaration of Independence to mark his ideal future. It is as if he is saying that what has been decreed in the past is still waiting to be realized. Given their similar structure and the interrelationship of King's more common chiastic structure, verses three, four, and five are where midnight ends, and verses six, seven, and eight mark where the dawn begins. This larger-than-life moment pushes King to enlarge the chiastic structure he first perfected with Burns and Hughes.

But none of this represents the most important element of this structure. Taken as three individual sections, verses three, four, and five show how we are currently *not* living together as brothers. The next three verses proclaim King's vision of a future where recognition of everyone's rights *can* allow people to live together as brothers. As the left side of figure 9 shows, the chiastic structure literally moves from brothers together living without rights to legal rights that enable us to live together as brothers. It is not just the pattern that is important; what matters most is what the pattern communicates through its order. $A + B + C^1 + D^1 + E^1$ equals "brothers together living without rights," while $C^2 + D^2 + E^2 + B + A$ equals a world where "recognizing rights lets men live together as brothers." With this "Psalm of Brotherhood," King enunciated his dream with the force of biblical prophecy as he spoke with visionary conviction and the skills of a poet.

The Poetry Within

Each verse of King's psalm invokes additional poetic strategies as well. Elements traditionally used in free-verse poetry are also embedded in this chiasmus as the worlds of black and white commingle, breaking down all distinctions between Gentile and Jew. Verse one includes extensive alliteration on the letter "s": "I have a dream that one day right down in Georgia and Mississippi and Alabama, the sons of former slaves and the sons of former slave owners will be able to live together as brothers." Has King lifted the key sounds from "Mississippi," where Till and Evers had been murdered, to riff off that state's dominant letter? This repeated "s" sound can be read as the imaginative trigger that leads King into his own highly alliterative first verse, which makes use of no less than twelve of these sibilants. By highlighting the state of Mississippi, King simultaneously previews his reference to Till and Evers in verse four.

Verse two seems to be a riff on the anthem "We Shall Overcome" when King imagines that "one day little white children and little Negro children will be able to join hands as brothers and sisters." Whereas this civil rights anthem proclaimed that "we will walk hand in hand someday," King declares that "one day" these children will join hands. King's reference to "one day" in seven of the ten verses can also be regarded as a riff on the "someday" that appears throughout "We Shall Overcome." Is King also previewing the chiastic structure of this larger sequence with the order in which he places these ideas? As with his combination of Hughes's "Youth" and Burns's "Man Was Made to Mourn," two separate entities ("little white children" and "little Negro children") join hands to emerge as "brothers and sisters." On its own, this verse can be read as a climactic parallel where the two separate and antithetic entities end unified as family members.

King uses parallelism to communicate togetherness, as literally all the parts of verse two must work together to achieve a coherent model of prosody. Each is described with three words, mimicking the transformation of King's "bleak and desolate midnight" into a "bright and glittering daybreak." Moreover, King is communicating a progression in this poem's refrain that blurs elements of "We Shall Overcome" with "Youth." In all ten verses, King also uses opening phrases such as "afternoon," "day," and "evening." The "new day" he invokes to bracket this poem simultaneously fulfills scripture, satisfies the hopes of "We Shall Overcome," and embraces the inevitability of earthly time exhibited in "Youth." Such a strategy could not be better placed, as it immediately precedes the three contrasting pairs that follow.

In verse three the listeners heard: "I have a dream that one day men will no longer burn down houses or the church of God simply because men want to be free." While "simply" and "free" form a subtle off rhyme, they are spaced so close together that King's rhythms point to "burn" and "church" as forming another repetition of "ur" sounds. These subtle examples remind us that the repetition of the refrain "I have a dream" creates an anaphoric pattern that is buoyed by the repetition of the phrase "one day." Given that "We Shall Overcome" was literally sung earlier on the program, King's repetition of "one day" strikes ears as a riff on the song's repeated use of "someday." Hence, every one of King's lines is building off strategies that are well established in song and poetry.

Next, verse four displays a much more effective use of off rhyme. In a complex and nuanced poetic strategy, King uses sounds to create statements that subtly communicate the distance between the past, the present, and the future: "I have a dream this afternoon that there will be a day that we will no longer face the atrocities that Emmett Till had to face or Medgar Evers had to face, that all men can live with dignity." With the syntactic placement of his off rhyme between "atrocities" and "dignity," King suggests that such atrocities are undignified. The "s" in "atrocities" puts these rhymes slightly out of true and makes them just as possible to repair socially as they would be to alter poetically. The blunt force that comes from repeating the word "face" reminds us of the means by which one of these victims was murdered, conjuring up the casket photographs of Till that showed his bloated and mutilated face. Here, the sounds echo the sense. Moreover, the loss of Medgar Evers was being felt deeply that day. After King spoke, the largest choir of the evening sang a tribute to Evers, and a special offering was taken up to create a scholarship fund for Evers's children. The spirit of the event also pushed King to try to overtly link Evers's recent murder with a lynching as a means to point out the need to respond with nonviolence now, just as Rosa Parks and the Montgomery Bus Boycott had eight years earlier.

Verse five reveals the embedded rhymes within King's dream. The repeated sounds here are as calculated as they are effective: "I have a dream this afternoon that my four little children will not come up in the same young days that I came up within, but they will be judged on the basis of the content of their character, not the color of their skin." King introduces the idea of "in" with "come up in," then compares it with the time that he "came up within." His dream for the future is bound up in a comparison that imagines a completely different sociological ideal. The new system of values will be based on the content of one's character, not more of the same old system founded on judgments based on "skin." "In," "within," and "skin" are auditory variations on the same form of old-world thinking. While offering a sonic progression of the norms that people have lived in, are living in, and will live in, King is finely tuning each syllable so we can hear that the "within" which matters most is the one beneath the skin. The character *within* is what King aims to substitute for this era's norms. With his internal off rhymes, he has successfully contrasted the internal with the external.

Verse six also invokes the dissonance of off rhyme. Here he uses the word "house" twice as an item that citizens will either rent or buy, and then he gives added emphasis to the location of these homes as he repeats the "r" sounds in "anywhere" and "carry." Just as verse three used this same cadence between "burn" and "church," and then "simply" and "free," King's word associations are overt enough to convey artifice yet subtle enough to go unnoticed by those not expecting poetry.

King's quotation from Amos in verse seven appears to highlight alliteration with its repeated "s" sounds, but the verse really seeks to make yet another connection through off rhyme, just as the previous four verses have. While "justice," "waters," "righteousness," and "stream" all feature strong "s" sounds, the King James Version that the speaker was so familiar with would have emphasized these sounds even more, as it includes "as" twice in place of King's "like." By substituting "like" for "as," is King trying to make sure listeners don't accidentally pair this verse with verse one, which used these "s" sounds even more often? Where we heard a double repetition of near off rhymes in the paired third and sixth verses, here King offers a single off rhyme that mirrors the single one in verse four when he uses "real" and "stream." The presence of "re" in both of these words is emphasized by their placement within the cadence of this verse.

King's final use of off rhyme in this sequence, in verse eight, offers powerful semantic implications. On its own, Jefferson's declaration uses the final "s" sound to link "rights" with "happiness." This connection suggests that one's "happiness" is inextricably linked to one's ability to enjoy all the privileges and "rights" of citizenship. This phrase, which King did not recast, contains its own off rhyme. However, King likely highlighted this connection by dropping the opening section of the quotation. Previously, King had usually introduced these lines with "We hold these truths to be self-evident" when he used them embedded within his introductory passage based on Jones. By eliminating this phrase, the connection between "rights" and "happiness" is further highlighted and divided by just the right amount of distance to help them connect within this cadence.

Because neither of King's last two verses uses off rhyme, his choice to employ this poetic strategy in the middle six verses (three through eight) may have been intentional. He had the powers of alliteration and perfect rhyme at his disposal, and as we have seen, he invokes his refrain in the form of anaphora in each of these verses. What does the medium of off rhyme suggest about the meaning King might be trying to convey? If a poet were trying to link two sets of verses that each contained identically corresponding ideas, he would invoke pure rhymes. Why does King use off rhyme?

Using off rhyme exclusively within these three paired verses links them stylistically in the same way that they have already been connected thematically. In other words, King is using the same poetic strategy of off rhyme to further match verses three, four, and five with their corresponding opposites, verses six, seven, and eight (see fig. 10). The result is that each of these pairs is matched both thematically and stylistically. More important, King could not have selected a better poetic device for these three pairs (CDE), as he is in the larger process of connecting ideas that are both similar *and* different. Off rhyme captures the tension of the real-life situation in which things are dissonant. Off rhyme highlights how King introduced three verses that speak of how things are "now," only to replace them with three corresponding verses about how things should be in the "future." Hence, just as each off rhyme is slightly out of true, King's prosody communicates that each is still waiting to be perfected. Off rhyme is not perfect, but fixing it is possible. King has communicated the same idea in two different ways. First he used parallelism to show us the antithetic and climactic nature of his dream; here he uses the poetic principles of the English language to show how the present is not quite what the future needs to be. There is a dissonance. Passing the civil rights bill will bring the finality of a major chord.

That King intentionally used off rhyme becomes clear when we examine his poetic strategy in verse nine. This verse marks the moment in this poem where King is communicating the idea of "togetherness" with its matching pair, verse two. In verse nine King does not use assonance, alliteration, rhyme, or off rhyme as his poetic strategy; instead, he invokes the same type of internal prosody he used in the corresponding second verse as he now gives us the words of Isaiah 40.4. Set off as poetry, the words of a man crying in the wilderness read as follows in the original King James Version:

Every valley shall be exalted,
and every mountain and hill shall be made low:
and the crooked shall be made straight,
and the rough places plain.

Isaiah's words are examples of climactic and antithetic parallelism. They turn valleys into hills, turn mountains into valleys, straighten the crooked, and make every rough place smooth. Not only is the entire sequence of ten verses ordered by this parallel logic, but so is this verse's and its matching pair, verse two.

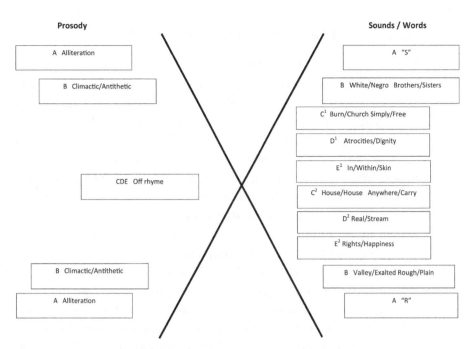

Figure 10. Prosody in King's "I Have a Dream" speech, Detroit, June 23, 1963.

While verse ten has visual approximations of rhyme, the true sound values of these words do not form an off rhyme. While the double "o" in "afternoon" and "brotherhood" and the "y" that ends "reality" and "day" appear as visual rhymes, neither sound is ultimately consistent enough to label either as true off rhymes. What does repeat is the alliterative "r." As such, this verse can more definitively be read as invoking alliteration, just as its pair, verse one, clearly does. Moreover, it appears in highly charged words that unify the major themes of this passage. "Dream," "afternoon," "brotherhood," and "reality" collectively summarize all the poem's major ideas. The fact that each word contains an "r" sound is not as significant as the fact that the words themselves characterize the ideals of the entire poem: King's *dream* this *afternoon* is that *brotherhood* will be a *reality*. Hence, in addition to the extraordinary organizational structure of this chiastic poem, each of King's internal verses can be read as using prosodic principles that correspond as well. Verses one and ten invoke alliteration; verses two and nine form individually climactic and antithetic parallels; verses three through eight all invoke off rhyme. King cast his dream in the pattern of chiastic parallelism, and we can see how he used this structure to create an unimpeachable argument that feels as inevitable as any psalm in the Bible.

The Dreams of the Prophet Daniel and Langston Hughes

Immediately after he finished his performance of this poem, King invoked consecutive allusions to coalesce the voice of the Old Testament prophet Daniel with that of Langston Hughes. The next three lines of the address read: "And with this faith I will go out and carve a tunnel of hope through the mountain of despair. With this faith, I will go out with you and transform dark yesterdays into bright tomorrows. With this faith, we will be able to achieve this new day." In the first line, King offers a complex allusion to Daniel, who interpreted King Nebuchadnezzar's dream by "describing a stone that smashes a figure made of precious metals, ore and clay" (K. Miller, *Deliverance* 144). In the book of Daniel, the rock is hewn by God to bring about a final and perfected world; here, King allusively activates this passage and Daniel's dream by creatively altering its symbolic imagery.

The second line is a straightforward allusion to Hughes's "Youth." Transforming "dark yesterdays into bright tomorrows" establishes King in the role of the new dream keeper. King is holding fast to all the dreams brought to him by the world's great dreamers. Just as King ended his 1956 rewrite of Hughes's "I Dream a World" with an allusion to "Youth," he makes this same connection here again. He has dropped the connection to Burns's poem today, because he is not submerging Hughes with Burns: this sequence, built of binaries, is integrating the prophetic visions of Daniel with the poetic dreams of Hughes. The sacred Daniel and the secular Hughes merge here as an explanatory footnote to King's dream. This text suggests that King's sources of inspiration for his dream also include the prophet Daniel and the poet Hughes.

In his third line, King says that this transformation will result in a "new day." This "new day" simultaneously activates imagery from the book of Daniel's fifth kingdom, the "one day" hoped for in "We Shall Overcome," and the new day of the world's bright tomorrows promised in Hughes's "Youth." Hence, King's dense composition seems bent on activating as many associations as possible for a diverse set of listeners. Some recognize the scripture they know, others hear the song they have been singing, and still others see a poem they have read—or some combination of these three.

In these lines, King is slowly transitioning between the pronouns "I" and "we." In the line from Daniel, King claims that he himself will complete this act when he uses the first-person pronoun "I." In a speech that must be heard, not read, King's exaggerated lengthening and overamplified enunciation can be heard in the way he delivers the "I" in both of the above lines. This suggests that King intended this "I" to be very important. It is so important because its goal is to move from a single and individual dream to a collective belief. Hence, in the second line he says, "I will go out with you" to suggest that the upcoming march will be collective. Together and collective, King overenunciates the word "we" when he next declares that "*we* will be able to achieve this new day." Just as Daniel's and Hughes's dreams began as something individual, their greatest effects came when each became collective. Daniel's dream affected the behaviors of King Nebuchadnezzar and then Babylon; Hughes's dream affected Martin Luther King and then America. Each dream is successful when it moves beyond a personal vision to become a collective belief. In this context, connecting Daniel with Hughes reminds us that King sought to integrate not only Jews and Gentiles, blacks and whites, Protestants and Catholics, but also the secular with the sacred, the progressive left with the conservative right.[10]

Intentional pronoun shifts such as this one are as common in the psalms as the portrayal of a collective "I" is in Hughes's poetry. Hughes's early reputation as one of the leading figures of the Harlem Renaissance resulted from the archetypal speaker he presented in his poem "The Negro Speaks of Rivers." In this poem, Hughes's speaker uses the pronoun "I" to transcend time from Egypt's Nile to Eden's Euphrates River. In this and other poems, Hughes's speaker creates an identity by merging it across the boundaries of time and place. In the largest sense, a similar merging is taking place in King's "Psalm of Brotherhood" as the prophets Isaiah and Amos find expression with the voices of Jefferson and King's father. Here at the end, King is merging his identity sequentially with Daniel and Hughes. Next, audience members themselves are invited into this collective group. Poets are known by the arrogance of their allusions. King is imploring his listeners to claim this same audacity. He intensified everyone's sense of ownership when he declared that this dream would become collective. King has been claiming the dreams that were dreamed before in order that these dreams can be rightfully claimed by others. Stated more personally, King wants his dream to become yours. To miss this point is to misunderstand King's complex use of the pronoun "I." King's Detroit dream suggests we have been misreading the rhetorical purpose of the "I" in "I have a dream." This purpose is revealed here when King transforms his "I" into a "we."

Although King applied the organizational structure of his entire August 11, 1956, speech to this revised poem, whatever might have been left of "I Dream a World" is now three steps removed from its original: the revision of a revision of a revision. This is why, despite King's initial attraction to the vision and anaphora of Hughes's poem, the impact of King's deep engagement with "I Dream a World" is nearly unrecognizable. Yet King likely believed that he had merely given Hughes's poem new validity by activating an imaginative association with its key refrain.

In delivering this "Psalm of Brotherhood," King had legitimized the anaphoric cadence so common in African Americans' conceptions of call and response. He had challenged the prosaic world of politics with the artistry of poetry. He had restored poetry to its primal context by making it a staged performance. He had triumphantly demonstrated poetry's ability to inspire legislative and social change by asserting the poet's rightful place in the Republic. In the following chapter, we see how King extemporaneously recalled many of the lines from his "Psalm of Brotherhood" when he delivered his most famous speech just two months later at the March on Washington.

10

The March on Washington

Veiling Hughes's Poetry

When Andrew Young, one of King's closest advisers, stopped by King's room the night before the March on Washington, "he noticed that King had crossed out words three and four times, looking not only for the right meaning, but also the right rhythm. Young thought that King was composing the Washington speech as if he were writing poetry" (Hansen 69).

It appears that King had not intended to say anything about his dream or what had become his "Psalm of Brotherhood" on August 28, 1963. During his address, the singer Mahalia Jackson called out to King from her seat just behind him: "Tell them about the dream, Martin!" (Hansen 57). After King delivered three more sentences from his text, she called to him a second time. King then set aside his prepared text to deliver lines from memory as best he could of what had become his "Psalm of Brotherhood," each beginning with "I have a dream" (58). Soon, people in the crowd began shouting, "Dream some more!" and "Keep on dreaming!" (Harrison and Harrison 176). Using a phrase that now sounds like an odd mixture of "Mother to Son" and "I Dream a World," the crowd eventually exploded: "Dream on! Keep dreaming! Keep dreaming!" (Hansen 60). The words King ended up delivering that day are now so well known that by 2008, "recognition of King's words among American teenagers had reached 97 percent" (Sundquist 2).

It is important that we reconsider how Langston Hughes's poetry informed King's most public moment. Because King's speech has already received so much critical attention, this chapter will offer a brief reanalysis. As we have seen, the apex of King's original poetry came when he delivered his "Psalm of Brotherhood" before ten thousand listeners in Detroit. What has not been noted is that the long trajectory of King's growth as a poet resulted in several previously unrecognized traces of his engagements with Hughes's poetry that appeared in this historic speech. Locating those traces is important not only for documenting how Hughes's poetry became a key inflection in King's voice but also for understanding a defiant aspect latent in this speech. What has confounded so many readers who have sought to locate Hughes's ideas in King's words is that neither this speech nor King's general rhetorical practices allow for simple one-to-one comparisons between individual Hughes poems and King's words. It is only by tracing the long trajectory of King's speaking habits that we can illuminate the rhetorical implications of King's allusions.

King's "I Have a Dream" speech, delivered during the March on Washington, contains traces of his lifelong engagements with Hughes's poems "I Dream a World," "Youth," and "Mother to Son." The following sections will address those connections.

"I Dream a World"

First, given all the evidence presented up to now in regard to the development of King's metanaphor "I have a dream" and its relationship to Hughes's "I Dream a World," King's famous refrain echoes the cadence, theme, and structure of this poem. The spontaneity of King's delivery at this event results in closer parallels to Hughes's original poem than we might expect. To see this, we first have to rethink how we interpret King's famous dream passage.

King's Detroit speech is often viewed as a mere prelude or a longer, more complete version of the dream he delivered on the National Mall two months later. Tracing the process by moving forward, rather than backward, reveals that the complexity and artistry of King's "Psalm of Brotherhood" makes the Washington version of King's dream a truncated version of King's poem. This is important, because King himself would never write a better poem than the one he delivered in Detroit. However, hearing the more famous version of King's dream reminds us that performance trumps form. The historic nature of the March on Washington, its unparalleled visibility, its unceasing video repetition, and King's extemporaneous delivery allow it to rightly outshine the meticulously crafted poem he wrote for the audience in Detroit. But without the long process of rewriting and delivering ideas from Hughes's poem, King's well-known riffs could never have been spoken with such eloquence and force.

Read from past to present, the sequence of phrases that began with "I have a dream" that King delivered on August 28, 1963, was not the perfect poem but rather the memory of a poem. In Washington, King was quoting from his own poem. Part of the gleam in his eye as he looked over the crowd resulted from the satisfaction of having Mahalia Jackson request that he recite his own poetry. Understanding that King actually repeated lines of his own poetry confirms many descriptions of King's delivery of these phrases: "King virtually assumes a stance of poetic or mystic reverie" (Leff and Sachs 83).

King presented only six refrains of his "Psalm of Brotherhood" at the March on Washington, and it is important that we do not "stand in awe of a speech just because it occupies a prominent place on the canvas of history. Rather, we should endeavor to understand it and evaluate it on its own terms, as a real response to a particular situation" (Wenzel 179). In number, King's six refrains fall short of the ten chiastic lines he presented in Detroit or the eight he spoke in Rocky Mount, North Carolina, in 1962. No deep parallel structure binds the six refrains that King delivered in Washington.[1] King relied on metanaphora alone to link his ideas, and this cadence was an echo of the one featured in Hughes's "I Dream a World." Rather than disappointing the audience, these half-riffed expressions created the sense that King was speaking from the heart.

The effects of this spontaneity are significant. Read against the context of the sequence he so carefully prepared and delivered in Detroit, the lines beginning with "I have a dream" that King shared in Washington do not comprise a poetic masterpiece. Without its complex chiastic structure, King's address leaves the poet sounding like a prophet. Sounding like a translation, the sequence lost its poetry and left us only with the prophecy. King riffed mismatched lines from a psalm that had been presented in Detroit in the form of a prophetic poem. Although the deep poetic structure was dropped, the surviving prophetic elements have guided our discussions of King's dream to this day.

The fact that King's metanaphor "I have a dream" binds this section of his speech together brings this version of the dream back closer to Hughes's "I Dream a World," which was also held together without any ornate parallel structure. This is important: King's effortless return to the colloquial pattern of Hughes's poem means that this version of the dream resembles Hughes's poem more closely than the complex chiastic structure King composed for Detroit. Because it was bound by anaphora but not by chiasmus, King's most famous sequence more closely resembled Hughes's "I Dream a World" than any he had delivered since 1956.

Structurally, this dream was far more secular than sacred. Judging by history's response, it was the free-verse, jazz-like improvisation that communicated King's theme the best, not the multifaceted, geometric patterns of parallelism. Quite simply, this dream is more authentic. King, more natural in this state, performed with greater approachability, confidence, and authenticity. This authenticity led to a performance that outshone the craftsmanship epitomized by his "Psalm of Brotherhood." Speaking in Washington, D.C., King rediscovered that impassioned metanaphora alone (such as the poem of August 11, 1956) communicated even better than the intricacies of chiasmus. As a result, all future performances of King's dream remained loosely bound by anaphora and epistrophe, and the complexities of an extended chiastic structure were abandoned. King understood that to move an audience he needed only the cadence and repetition resembling Hughes's poem, not the formal structures of parallelism.

"Youth"

Although King used the phrase "my people" in this speech, this phrase seems to have nothing in common with one of Hughes's most popular poems, "My People."[2] However, King used imagery he had developed from Hughes's poem "Youth" in two places in this speech. As we have seen, this was typical for King, who had used these lines since 1956. Here, King's third sentence of his address makes use of the imagery of "daybreak" as he states that the Emancipation Proclamation came "as a joyous daybreak to end the long night of captivity" (Washington 217). King returns to this imagery later in this speech with the phrase "bright day" when he asserts that "The whirlwinds of revolt will continue to shake the foundations of our nation until the bright day of justice emerges" (218). It should come as no surprise that King would invoke this language. The occasion, a literal march on Washington, is the perfect moment to include imagery rewritten from Hughes's poem. Though reworded by King, the imagery of "Youth" has clear traces in this speech.

"Mother to Son"

King also invokes the language of Hughes's "Mother to Son" in his speech. In the context of a march, and even using the idea of walking in the same sentence, King asserts with Hughes's speaker that "We cannot walk alone. And as we walk, we must make the pledge that we shall march ahead. We cannot turn back" (Washington 218). Whereas King had often spoken within the context of the Montgomery Bus Boycott by appropriating this idea into "we cannot stop now," here he returns to the literal language of line fourteen in Hughes's poem when he says "turn back." These brief glimpses of the invisible Hughes remind us of the lingering effects of the red scare and King's own subversive qualities. King may have been asked to remove O'Dell and Levison from his inner circle, but he was leaving Hughes submerged in his rhetoric.

King's Integrative Rhetoric

Having located three definitive remainders of King's engagements with Hughes's poetry in this speech, we will now explore some aspects of this address that are far less clear. It is important to note that such speculations are necessitated by King's decision to refrain from naming anyone in this speech. His use of integrative rhetoric required that he refrain from acknowledging or referencing anyone by name. King even maintains this rhetorical strategy throughout the section he performs from memory. As Mark Vail has argued, the audience's ability to recognize King's allusions "allows the rhetor to integrate the audience into the speech," as "the audience becomes an active participant in the speech making process" (59). Every audience that encounters this speech unconsciously completes King's metaphors. Because of each listener's personal association with the various metaphors King incorporates in this speech, these metaphors "gain rhetorical force" because they are "hardly unique" (Vail 59). This, in part, enabled King to "straddle the boundary between a black and white audience" as he fused his sources to reach a variety of listeners present in this national audience (Sharman 102).

King's speech becomes emblematic of the theme of integration. In asking Americans to integrate, King's speech purposefully integrates the voices of numerous unnamed speakers. King refrains from naming a single person in his speech. Lincoln is suggested but never named as King begins by speaking of a "great American, in whose symbolic shadow we stand" (Washington 217). The tension that results from our ability to recognize King's allusions to Lincoln pleasantly pulls us closer to his themes, while our inability to recall the name of George Wallace when King mentions only the governor of Alabama pushes us away from knowing the speech's cultural history. The rhetorical integration of these sources enacts America's creed; here *E pluribus unum* is tangibly experienced as out of many voices, one emerges. This speech was an auditory rehearsal for a social performance still to come. Listeners were intellectually integrating every voice King invoked, whether or not they knew its origin. King was demonstrating that social integration was also possible.

If King's integrative rhetoric owes anything to Hughes's poetry, its trajectory can be measured as King began modeling such integration on the rhetorical level when he first combined Burns's and Hughes's poems to form a single line of poetry. It expanded further when he alternated his own lines with ones from E. Stanley Jones. It continued when he created his "Psalm of Brotherhood." It reached new heights here, as every quotation is allusively integrated into all three sections of King's speech.

King's speech took the idea of integration beyond anything King had ever attempted. Every voice in King's speech became an instrument that sounded more unified with every measure. This occurred as King wrote an entire speech that modeled integration. Ever conscious of the speech's guiding rhetorical principle, he even delivered the lines he recited off script from memory without naming Jefferson, Wallace, or Isaiah.

The Speech's Deep Structure

Reading King's speech imaginatively, by noting where more than images emerge, results in some fascinating possibilities. Artists are often unable to name the sources of their thoughts. It is possible that some of King's rhetorical appeals in this speech demonstrate that Hughes's poetry had settled deep into his unconscious. If we consider this possibility, the speech takes on several new and intriguing aspects. Having already established that this speech owes some of its imagery to three of Hughes's poems, it becomes interesting to examine whether something from these poems is revealed in the speech's deep structure.

Broadly speaking, King's speech has three main sections.[3] It begins with the metaphor of a check that the marchers have come to cash, continues in the middle section by calling on the marchers to return to the South, and then ends with the dream. The dream sequence has already been addressed at length. It is interesting to consider to what degree King's one new idea, the idea that "we have come to cash this check," one that has initially come back marked "insufficient funds," might be linked to Hughes's deferred dream. The word "deferred" itself has connections to money, as we often speak of "deferred payments." Is King unconsciously invoking Hughes's poem, or, clearer still, the literal image of a check used in Hansberry's *A Raisin in the Sun,* when he declares that "America has defaulted on this promissory note insofar as her citizens of color are concerned" (Washington 217)? After all, the plot of Hansberry's play centers around what each character would do to fulfill his or her deferred dreams when the check for ten thousand dollars finally arrives.

On a literal level, King suggests that "When the architects of our republic wrote the magnificent words of the Constitution and the Declaration of Independence, they were signing a promissory note" (Washington 217). King has turned the American dream into a check on which America has deferred payment.[4] Collapsing the images, the realization of the America dream has been deferred. Considering this logic, we are reminded that King specifically addressed housing needs in his speech in Detroit, and the fact that he might begin here with the idea of a deferred dream is not just a clever way to play with the word "defaulted" and find "deferred" as its synonym. In fact, this reading provides a surprising insight into one possible frame for this speech.

In his speeches, King was fond of presenting an idea in the introduction and then expanding it in his conclusion, thus bookending the speech's ideas. As such, this reading considers the likelihood that, as he had done in so many of his speeches, King is letting his introduction anticipate the themes that his final dream sequence answers and fulfills. In other words, King begins holding a deferred dream in his hands and then ends by delineating what that dream represents. The symbolism of the check cannot be read without its connections to what it really stands for—the Constitution's declaration that "We hold these truths to be self-evident; that all men are created equal."

When King rolls into his "I have a dream" section, his check metaphor is clarified to mean a payment that has been too long deferred. This reading gives King's ending its purpose as a sustained and direct effort to speak about dreams. Is this why he begins the final section with the odd word "still" when he declares, "I still have a dream"? Is it prompted in any way by his mention of the "slums and ghettoes of our Northern cities" that immediately precedes this statement and resembles descriptions of Harlem itself? Is King implying that despite its deferral, he is *still* holding onto his dream?

This possible connection to "Dream Deferred" has several precedents. Jesse Jackson stated that this is "a speech describing nightmare conditions" (qtd. in "Nonthreatening Dreamer"). Keith Miller suggests that "King devotes the first half of his address not to celebrating the dream but to cataloging a nightmare" (*Deliverance* 23). Although King sometimes invoked the nightmare imagery, on other occasions he wrote that the founders had never intended that liberty should be "doled out on a deferred-payment plan" (*Why We Can't Wait* 128). Even those who comment on his August 28, 1963, speech refer to the promissory note as something that has undergone a "seemingly endless deferral" (Sundquist 89). Furthermore, King himself consistently linked money, food, and deferment on other occasions in complex ways. He used the term "deferred" to document the costs of reimbursing those who have been "cheated for centuries" when he wrote: "inferior education, poor housing, unemployment, inadequate health care . . . will require billions to correct. Justice so long deferred has accumulated interest and its cost for this society will be substantial in financial as well as human terms" (Washington 314).

King would also use the word "deferred" in his May 28, 1964, address at the NAACP Convocation on Equal Justice. On this occasion, King began his speech by drawing attention to the ideas of Hughes's poem and Hansberry's play by using "deferred" in place of "deterred": "We must not be deferred by those who argue that laws and judicial decrees cannot change the heart."[5] Then, as if combining the financial implications of the word with Hughes's food imagery, King amplifies this use of "deferred" when he states: "A piece of freedom is not enough for us as human beings nor for the nation of which we are a part. We have been given pieces, but unlike bread, a slice of which does diminish hunger, a piece of liberty no longer suffices. Freedom is like your life. You cannot be given life in installments." Hughes's food imagery used throughout "Dream Deferred" commingles with freedom, liberty, and life that has been paid out in installments. Standing alone, King's comments in this speech sound unclear and muddy; however, the move from "deterred" to "deferred" earlier in this speech hints at the potential that King is taking measured liberties by combining food and installment checks with Hughes's "Dream Deferred" in a complex way.

This use raises questions about the degree to which King intended to deliver the final prepared section of his speech that day in Washington. In other words, the speech King delivered reads like a thoughtful, well-compressed address on lost dreams and the need to continue to pursue those dreams. It may be no coincidence that at one stage of the planning process, four days before the march, King had two ideas he liked most. Based on feedback from his advisers, King had just this "bad check" section and his "I have a dream" sequence (Hansen 66). Had he presented only those two sections, this speech could read as one that begins with a deferred dream and ends with the dream of a new world. No clearer mirroring of the themes from Hughes's own poems could be imagined.

Is it possible that King privately imagined that he could deliver the "I have a dream" section off script? Had he learned something from seeing the response Robert Frost received when he did this two years earlier on a national stage in the very same political setting? To use Frost's own language, did King's dream sequence happen "accidentally on purpose"? Did he consider that delivering this section extemporaneously would make him seem even more poetic and prophetic? Having spoken extemporaneously all his life, King would have known he could do this nearly as well as Frost. This might help to explain Harry Boyte Jr.'s statement that he heard King rehearsing the "I have a dream" section the night before the speech.[6] Is there any chance that King was merely *performing* spontaneity? These are difficult questions to answer, but the overall structural unity of the speech King delivered justifies such questions.

In the middle section of the speech, King alludes to lines from "Youth" with the force and certainty of what we know to be another Hughes poem, "Mother to Son," when he declares, "We cannot turn back." But rather than highlighting the march toward Washington, King exhorts his listeners to "go back" to the South, where the most difficult work still remains to be done. This is where the rough stairs must be climbed. With the metaphor of the check, marching, and his dream, it is not difficult to find in all three of King's main ideas a resemblance to the poems King most often invoked when he engaged Hughes's ideas. The speech's three-part structure might be said to revolve around themes from "Dream Deferred," "Mother to Son," and "I Dream a World." It is interesting to note that, without connecting his findings to Hughes's works in any way, David Bobbitt's analysis of the speech observes that the speech's three metaphoric clusters address imagery with distinct parallels to Hughes's poetry (73–83). The most telling clue to the connection to Hughes's poems comes when King himself reflected on this historic day during "A Christmas Sermon on Peace" in 1967. On that occasion, he compressed imagery from these same three Hughes poems in precisely this order.

King appears to revisit all his major invocations of Hughes's poetry in his 1963 speech on the National Mall. As such, the members of America's dominant culture who listened to the speech were unconsciously accepting the logic of a poet they detested. This could only result because Hughes's ideas were discreetly separated from his subversive identity.

Deceptively Subversive

Because of the way King engaged Hughes's works throughout his life, plotting the exact intensity of such influence cannot be accomplished by merely comparing Hughes's finished poems with the speech King delivered on the National Mall. Perhaps King did not have Hughes's poetry consciously on his mind as he arrived at the core structure of his speech, but Hughes's poetry was a defining presence in all that had brought King to this point. As such, its impact can be considered more tangible than the visible traces of its reworded lines in this speech. More important, King had learned to harness the motivational aspects of poetry. Hence, poetry was at the center of the rhetoric that drove a key element of the civil rights movement. The fact that no one could forget King's dream testifies to poetry's place in politics and its lasting mark on our cultural consciousness.

The fact that Hughes was effectively submerged speaks to the development of King's poetic sensibilities. However, in the historical context of King's speech, it also speaks to the cultural climate of the era. To understand this speech's rhetorical appeals, we must understand King's ability to simultaneously activate and conceal Hughes's ideas through these allusions. Stated succinctly, King's "I Have a Dream" speech is not only inclusive but also deceptively subversive. By blurring, reinventing, alluding, and rewriting ideas from Hughes's poetry, King embraced the roots of African American art and culture. But more than that, standing in the shadow of the Lincoln Memorial as he spoke to a national audience, he championed integration by engaging a mode of rhetorical defiance. Because of Hughes's reputation as a subversive, his poetry had to be concealed on this historic occasion. By coyly alluding to Hughes's poems "Mother to Son" and "Youth" and by rewriting "I Dream a World," King subversively spoke truth to power through the diction, themes, and cadence of a man whom power thought it had silenced.

Conclusion

Extending the Dream

Martin Luther King and Langston Hughes were linked in other unexpected ways. Less than three weeks after King delivered his address at the National Mall, the composer Irwin Heilner sought permission from King to set to music the "deeply moving and poetic climax" of the "I have a dream" section of King's speech.[1] In his correspondence, Heilner included newspaper clippings regarding songs he had recently composed using lyrics from Hughes's poems "Southern Mammy Sings" and "Democracy."[2] Heilner received permission, and by early 1964 he had set these two Hughes poems and King's "poetic" piece to music. Other requests followed. In April 1967, Robert Bialeck asked if King could recommend black performers to appear in a newspaper advertisement or formal program protesting the Vietnam War. His "Artists of Conscience" list included only Harry Belafonte, Sidney Poitier, Sammy Davis Jr., Duke Ellington, Louis Armstrong, and Langston Hughes.[3] A few months later, a graduate student in Italy, Lia Bosonetto, intent on writing his thesis on Hughes, wrote King to request information about "the man" himself, as he assumed the two were personal friends.[4]

One of the most unusual connections involved a collection of Hughes's poems published as a tribute to King. In 1968, Spanish translations of fifty-three of Hughes's poems were published in honor of King's death. The collection, *Yo También Soy América: Poemas de Langston Hughes,* appeared in Mexico only six weeks after King's assassination. The editor began the collection with two of Hughes's poems that featured the metaphor of dreaming, "Dreams" and "The Dream Keeper." The collection also gave new resonance to the last lines of Hughes's poem "Militant," featured later in the collection:

For honest dreams
Your spit is in my face
And so my fist is clenched
Today—
To strike your face. (lines 11–15)

With the rise of black militancy in the late 1960s, King's recent assassination, and these two men's attentiveness to the idea of dreaming, publishing these lines in this context reanimated the voice of a younger Hughes. These lines captured the growing anger of both the nation and a sympathetic world against those who sought to extinguish the dreams of both King and the oppressed.

This conclusion addresses four additional intersections between the worlds of Hughes and King. Because this book has thus far focused primarily on King's responses to Hughes's poetry, three of these links center on Hughes's responses to King. First, during the week following King's speech in Detroit in June 1963, Hughes revised one of his most successful plays, *Jericho-Jim Crow*, and we will examine the play in this context. Second, Hughes's poem "Dream of Freedom" will be considered as Hughes's response to King's use of the metaphor of the dream. Third, in a speech he delivered in Ghana in 1962, Hughes encouraged his listeners with the same focus on dreams that King himself used. Finally, King's most visible invocation of Hughes's poetry came when the preacher quoted the poem "Let America Be America Again" in his denunciation of U.S. involvement in Vietnam in one of his most powerful speeches, "Beyond Vietnam: A Time to Break Silence."

Hughes's *Jericho-Jim Crow*

While King was preparing the speech he would deliver in Detroit on June 23, 1963, Hughes was hard at work writing a play. On June 20, Hughes finished the script for what he called his "song-play" about the civil rights movement, *Jericho-Jim Crow*, which would become "the most extravagantly praised of Hughes's works in theater" (*Collected Works* 6: 254). The play was the culmination of Hughes's various experiences with dramatic works ranging from his long-running *Mulatto* in 1935 (373 performances) to the near-hit *Street Scene*, several gospel plays based on biblical themes, and of course the opera *Troubled Island*.

Hughes dedicated *Jericho-Jim Crow* to "the young people of all racial and religious backgrounds who are meeting, working, canvassing, petitioning marching, picketing, sitting-in, singing and praying today to help make a better America for all, and especially for citizens of color" (*Collected Works* 6: 254). The play addresses racism as it has evolved through the generations, shifting its appearance under the cover of various strategies of oppression.

Hughes's complimentary copies of *Jericho-Jim Crow* make it clear that King was a key source of inspiration for the play. King's name appeared at the top of Hughes's list of eighteen people slated to receive autographed copies. The next three were King's companions in the cause: Wyatt T. Walker, Ralph Abernathy, and Fred Shuttlesworth. Three days before King's first nationwide expression of his refrain "I have a dream," Hughes mailed an autographed copy of the bound script to King. In his signature green ink, Hughes wrote: "Especially for Martin Luther King (whose name—and imprint—is here) with admiration, Sincerely—Langston Hughes, New York, June 20, 1963."[5] Hughes's choice of the word "imprint" is revealing. Hughes seems to be signaling King that the actions and approach characterized in the play reflect King's own strategies for change—strategies that include marching and singing under the flag of nonviolence. The young boy who appears onstage at the start of the play announces that he has a "hundred thousand" names. When this boy identifies himself by running together the names of ten prominent men in African American history, King's name appears prominently in the middle of the boy's list, which includes Frederick Douglass and Nat Turner.

King's "imprint" is especially visible in the play's title. When Hughes sent King his script, the working title was "Jericho-Jim-Crow-Jericho," which visually captures the idea that Jim Crow will come tumbling down as a result of being surrounded on both sides by this new Joshua. In the biblical story, God instructs Joshua and his band to blow a trumpet once a day and then march around the city of Jericho. On the seventh day, the walls came tumbling down. The idea that simply marching would result in the overthrow of racism parallels the logic at work in the book of Joshua.

The play opens with two trumpet blasts, reminding the audience of the biblical story. Hughes's main female figure is also young, and she, too, carries a range of names, from Autherine Lucy to the antilynching crusader Ida B. Wells-Barnett. In one of the first musical numbers, the singers call out three consecutive lines of "I'm on my way and I won't turn back" (*Collected Works* 6: 258), mirroring the determination that the mother in Hughes's "Mother to Son" longs to hear from her son:

Aint gonna let nobody turn me around
turn me around, turn me around
Aint gonna let nobody turn me around
keep on walkin' keep on talkin'
keep on marchin' to the freedom land. (*Collected Works* 6: 258)

Hughes's references to King come when the play turns its attention to contemporary events. After portraying the sit-in movement with references to "Segregated cokes and Segregated malt" (*Collected Works* 6: 273), Hughes conjures up images of Autherine Lucy's struggle to attend classes at the University of Alabama. Hughes engages in a typical call and response by having several characters repeat variations on the phrase "I woke up this morning with my mind on freedom" (6: 273–74). Then Hughes references King as the boy speaks: "somehow I got elected leader of this demonstration." The reference to King's rise as leader of the Montgomery Bus Boycott leads to the declaration: "We are going to march! March! . . . we'll keep marching until it works" (6: 274).

Immediately after King spoke in Detroit, Hughes requested the return of his original scripts for "Jericho-Jim-Crow-Jericho" and started a new list to keep track of where to send the new versions of his text. He underlined in red pencil the names of those who had returned the first scripts. Five people returned the first script, including Harry Belafonte and John Hammond at Columbia Records. Hughes noted that James Peck had "discarded" his first copy. Then Hughes noted that he had already sent updated versions of the script to King, Abernathy, and Daisy Bates on June 27, 1963.[6]

On King's copy, Hughes's new inscription reads: "Especially for Martin Luther King, whose name is in this play, Sincerely, Langston Hughes, New York, 1963."[7] Two questions arise. First, did Hughes simply make one more round of revisions to the script, perhaps looking to make minor changes or correct small errors, or had he reviewed the sections that involved King and updated them based on the speech in Detroit, which King delivered just after the first draft was completed? Hughes's first copy was mailed three days *before* the speech, the updated one four days *after* King's speech, so this is a plausible conjecture. Second, does the final revised version contain any evidence that this occurred? Because Hughes never kept any draft versions of the play he wrote before King delivered his speech in Detroit, these questions can only be asked of the final version. No before-and-after comparison is permitted here.

Four sections in the final script suggest that Hughes may have rewritten sections of the play to account for specific elements of King's speech. First, in the contemporary section of the play, Hughes uses Latin terms while discussing segregation: "segregation ipso facto, de facto, and every other kind of facto must go" (*Collected Works* 6: 274). King did not commonly use the term "de facto" in his speeches, but the speech in Detroit included the following: "and in the area of de facto segregation. . . . [W]e must come to see that de facto segregation in the North is just as injurious as the actual segregation in the South."

Second, something interesting appears to be happening with the list of states in this version of the play. In his speech in Detroit, King listed only three state names: Georgia, Mississippi, and Alabama.[8] Immediately after the wordplay on "de facto," Hughes's final revised script lists only Georgia and Mississippi (*Collected Works* 6: 274). Along with the earlier mention of Autherine Lucy's struggles in Alabama, Hughes has identified these three states and no others.

The third connection involves Hughes's use of "We Shall Overcome." King alluded to this song in his "I have a dream" refrain. Hughes's play blends this song into a statement—his two child-aged characters declare, "We'll walk hand in hand / We'll walk hand in hand" (*Collected Works* 6: 275)— just as King proclaimed, "I have a dream this afternoon that one day little white children and little Negro children will be able to join hands as brothers and sisters."

Fourth, as the play reaches its apex, King's name is again mentioned, and Hughes begins to develop a "dream" within the play. The young girl declares, after the mention of King by name, that "I dream a land called freedom land" (*Collected Works* 6: 278). Hughes's material on the "dream" is brief, perhaps reflecting the short revision period during which Hughes worked. Though brief, this section is significant. The line "I dream a land" leads into another singing of the play's signature song, "Freedom Land." In the lyrics of this song we can see several choices that could be connected with King's Detroit speech. Taking its inspiration from the Hebrew word "Jericho" (which means "fragrant"), Hughes's song describes a land where the seeds of freedom are planted to finally "bloom beneath the sun / where freedom lives for everyone." The three final lines read: "We are tomorrow's band—/ And friends will clasp each other's hand / In Freedom, Freedom land" (*Collected Works* 6: 270). Is Hughes borrowing ideas from King's Detroit address? On the one hand, King's reference to walking "hand in hand" had been an outgrowth of "We Shall Overcome" long before King used the phrase at the end of his speech. On the other hand, linking this land to a dream and seeing it "bloom beneath the sun" is reminiscent of the language King used in Detroit.

In the play, we can see Hughes linking his idea of "Freedom Land" with a world he has dreamed. Immediately before the song, the characters simply named "old woman" and "old man" assert in the course of their discussion that "God didn't mean for this world to be all unequaled-up like it is" and "just look at the world—all chopped up into boundaries and binaries and things, into cold wars and hot wars, great powers and no powers, into summits and valleys, black lands and white lands" (*Collected Works* 6: 270). The reference to "summits and valleys" reminds us of King's appropriation of Isaiah and his hope that the high places would be made low. Immediately after "Freedom Land" is sung, the old woman declares, "Oh, my friends, when we try to straighten out this world and make it Freedom Land, we are just carrying out God's will, that's all" (*Collected Works* 6: 270).

Hughes's play ends with Jericho falling as a result of this sustained battle. As the walls tumble down, the boy names Du Bois, Daisy Bates, Jim Peck, A. Philip Randolph, John Lewis, James Farmer, Ropy Wilkins, Martin Luther King, and John F. Kennedy as being among those who have fought against Jim Crow. Then, in the last line of the play, before music and song carry across the auditorium, the young boy says, "The Promised Land's in sight—the America of our dreams!" (*Collected Works* 6: 279). The pronoun "our" can be understood as uniting all the singers onstage with all the Joshuas who have fought against Jim Crow in America. But given Hughes's script is only finalized following King's speech in Detroit, we wonder if Hughes is recognizing his own connection with King here. The collective "our" not only acknowledges Hughes's predecessors but also establishes Hughes himself in the long line of those who have fought against Jim Crow.

Hughes's "Dream of Freedom"

This idea of a collective dream returns in Hughes's poem "Dream of Freedom," published in April 1964, less than a year after King's speech on the National Mall. "Dream of Freedom" can be read as if Hughes is reprising his role as Martel from *Troubled Island*. The tone of this poem stands as a corrective more than a declaration. The speaker offers a gentle rebuke. In five stanzas, "Dream of Freedom" states that the dream that exists in the country today needs to be collective. During this period of Hughes's life, his dominant concept is that of "the collective dream" (Harper, "Deferment" 17). Given the rise of King's rhetoric and Hughes's attentiveness to culture, it may be no coincidence that Hughes's dreams became hopeful "visions of the future" (Harper, "Deferment" 19). In the poem's sharpest rebuke, Hughes writes: "There are those who claim / This dream for theirs alone" (lines 5–6). Is Hughes reminding King of the lesson Martel had to teach Jean-Jacques in *Troubled Island*—namely, that the dream belongs to all and cannot be claimed by any one person? King's use of the personal pronoun "I" in "I have a dream" makes such a reading possible. Additional evidence to support this reading includes the fact that Hughes had been commissioned to write this poem by the NAACP, which, like Hughes, had been fighting for the collective dreams of African Americans well before King's dynamic speaking seemed to claim such dreams for himself.

Hughes in Ghana, 1962

When they are not heard, but merely read, Hughes's prose and King's oratory are surprisingly similar. One of these men had once suggested: "The most dire thought we are holding in our deep hearts is the dream of a real AMERICAN America. To shackle and muzzle this expression of that dream from Negro pulpits . . . would be to shackle the heart and deny it hope." The writer had simply asked if blacks were not expected to "believe in the American Dream, too— or is that dream just for white folks?" He concluded: "Shall we, who are the Negro people of America, have no great dreams? . . . Or shall we, with all the other Americans of foresight and good will, seek to create a world where even Alabama will respect human decency?" These statements were delivered along with the reminder that the most black Americans had "threatened to do is stage a peaceful march on Washington to petition legal redress of grievances" (qtd. in De Santis, *Chicago Defender* 26). Langston Hughes wrote these words in 1943.

The similarities in theme and focus could be seen even more clearly when Hughes traveled to Accra, the capital of Ghana, to help celebrate the opening of a new American library. Hughes himself donated more than thirty of his own books as well as several recordings of his own readings of his works. He delivered a speech that day, June 29, 1962. Though brief, his speech affords us an opportunity to examine an interesting question: How similar were King's and Hughes's dreams? What would Hughes's dreams sound like in prose? Though Hughes was not an inspiring public speaker, his speech that day reveals similarities between his dreams and King's.

Early in the speech, Hughes expresses regret over one type of interest America has had in Africa: "American businessmen, of course, have sent their surveyors and investors across the Western Ocean to Africa's rich lands. Governments and businessmen, as everyone knows, for political and practical reasons, have, in Africa, *more* than an interest of the heart."[9] Just as King did on numerous occasions, Hughes references Jefferson and America's reverence for the Declaration of Independence. Clearly conscious of the political battlegrounds in America, Hughes suggests that the relationship between America and Africa is one of exchange. Noting that it is no longer a patronizing one-way relationship, Hughes asserts that Africa has much to teach America about freedom: "Black Africa today is sending rejuvenating currents of liberty over all the earth reaching even as far as Little Rock, Birmingham, and Jackson, Mississippi."

Hughes's repeated use of the dream motif in this eight-minute speech is reminiscent of King's own speeches. In fact, dreaming is the unifying element of the speech, as Hughes asserts this idea in several different dimensions. He again links the two continents and their aspirations: "Africa's history, like America's history—and especially the Negro America's history—has been a troubled history, a seeking history, a dreaming history." He first suggests that Africa can inspire America, as the United States is seeking "a bolstering of its own basic dreams." He goes on to say that this sharing of knowledge is "no longer just a dream."

Hughes ends his speech with a twist. The final lines include his poem "Youth." King often used this poem at the end of his speeches, and it had also been used in the speech Nnamdi Azikiwe gave at his inauguration in 1960. Hughes uses this moment to offer a revision to the last three lines of the poem that brings out the focus of the speech. In the 1954 edition of *Lincoln University Poets,* these lines read: "We march / America together / we march!" (8–10). For his speech in Accra, though, Hughes typed the entire poem in capital letters and altered the ending. The final three lines of the poem, and the final lines of the entire speech, read: "WE MARCH! / OUR DREAMS TOGETHER, / WE MARCH!"

Hughes's decision to make dreams the focus of his speech reminds us of the thematic similarities between the poet and the preacher. Hughes was speaking from the heart about one of his oldest themes, yet the speech reads like one of King's. These thematic parallels remind us that these two men shared the same dream at the same moment in history. King did not simply echo the words that Hughes had written long before the 1960s; he was mirroring the way Hughes was still talking as King's contemporary. Although he lacked King's charisma and oratorical skills, Hughes, when he was asked to speak, arrived at the same dream imagery.

King's "Beyond Vietnam: A Time to Break Silence"

On April 4, 1967, one year before his assassination, King delivered "Beyond Vietnam: A Time to Break Silence" before a capacity crowd in New York City's Riverside Church. It was the most controversial speech of his life, one that would be denounced by no fewer than 168 newspapers the next day. So dire was its appraisal of the Vietnam War that the speech severed King's ties with President Johnson forever. Outside King's inner circle, the speech swayed almost everyone's opinion of King. One exception was Langston Hughes, who wrote of the public reaction in a letter to Arna Bontemps two weeks later: "At buffet for Loren Miller at the Montero's night before last . . . Roy Wilkins, Bets Garner, etc. all so *mad* with Martin Luther's they could Klux him. Me no! I Love him" (Bontemps and Hughes 486). Hughes leaves out the word "speech" immediately after mentioning King's name, but he captured the violence of other people's reactions in his use of "Klux" as a verb.

In "Beyond Vietnam," King spelled out directives for the United States to follow in withdrawing from Vietnam. Speaking in the clearest language he and his advisers could muster, King denounced the war well before it had become popular to do so. King had been waiting for more than two years to speak out against the war, but as the title of the speech suggests, he had kept silent (on advice from his closest advisers). As historian John Kirk notes, "King's decisive turning point over Vietnam came in January 1967. As he was preparing to fly to Jamaica to work on his latest book he came across an article by William Pepper" that "graphically illustrated the horrific injury inflicted" on women and children as a result of the "United States' use of chemical weapons such as napalm" (Kirk, *Profiles* 164).

In the middle section of his speech, King linked the history of the Southern Christian Leadership Conference to the ideas of Langston Hughes. After describing the formation of the SCLC in 1957, King suggests that the goals of this organization echo ideas first expressed by Hughes. "In a way we were agreeing with Langston Hughes, that black bard of Harlem," King said. Then he quoted Hughes's poem "Let America Be America Again":

O yes,
I say it plain,
America never was America to me,
And yet I swear this oath—
America will be! (233–34, lines 76–80)

By linking the formation of the SCLC to this Hughes poem, King suggests that both Hughes and the SCLC have been unjustifiably harassed because of fears of Communist subversion. The cumulative effect is to imply that the fear of Communist influence in Vietnam is equally unnecessary.

The idea of quoting from Hughes's poem in "Beyond Vietnam" most likely came from Vincent Harding. Harding, born in Harlem, wrote the first draft of this speech.[10] Years later, he offered a lengthy discussion of the poem in his essay "Is America Possible?"[11] This invocation of Hughes's poetry bears none of King's personal trademarks. It is quoted accurately rather than altered; the ideas appear verbatim rather than as an allusion; and the text appears in a more pedestrian middle section of the speech rather than echoing triumphantly at the conclusion.

As such, the direct quotation used here in 1967 vanished from King's repertoire just as quickly as it appeared. On April 30, 1967, when he delivered a sermon at his home church in Atlanta just four weeks after his speech against the Vietnam War, King used the core of this same speech for his address. After writing a new introduction by hand, King took a blue pen and excised dozens of sections from the typed version of the April 4 address. Among the passages to go was the direct quotation of Hughes's "Let America Be America Again."[12] Nonetheless, the choice to keep Hughes's poem in his "Beyond Vietnam" speech ultimately was King's alone. Many of his advisers had warned against the comments he settled on, and King took responsibility for what remained in the final draft. As a result, when viewers turned on their televisions the next evening, King's quotation of Hughes's "Let American Be America Again" was included among the excerpts.[13] Given this fact and the many reprints of this speech, this became King's most visible invocation of Hughes's poetry.

King's most recognizable acknowledgment of his debt to Hughes came less than six weeks before Hughes's death. Such a controversial subject brought Hughes out of the shadows of allusion as King broke silence on another front. In the most convincing evidence of Hughes's stature within the world of politics, with this speech, King had just quoted Hughes for the first time ever before an integrated audience. This choice had lasting repercussions. King's speech is significant because it demonstrates his use of Hughes's poetry to counter fears about Communist aggression. Delivered late in his career, it reminds us what an overt allusion to Hughes's poetry could mean when it was broadcast on a national stage. In this speech, King overtly used Hughes's reputation as a Communist sympathizer to full effect.

This anti-patriotic moment was a perfect context for Hughes's poetry. The reference to one of Hughes's most famous statements at the height of his leftist writings of the 1930s comes to us with potent resonance. First published in the high-profile magazine *Esquire* in 1936, an abbreviated version of the poem was accompanied by an illustration of a lynching (Lowney 63). It was included two years later in Hughes's most radical collection of verse. *A New Song* was published by the International Workers Order, a group directly linked to the Communist Party. In the poem, Hughes mentions dreams on no less than seven occasions. He begins "Let America Be America Again": "Let it be the dream it used to be" (lines 1–2). He continues: "Let America be the dream the dreamers dreamed" (line 6).

Using this quotation in this speech allows the reactionary response to Hughes throughout the red scare to serve as a parallel to the war in Vietnam. Though not anywhere near so devastating in its end results, Hughes was suspected of a subversion that never amounted to any genuine threat to the United States. Likewise, King's quotation suggests that Vietnam offers a similar example, as the real threat is enacting violent repression, not Russian aggression. King makes the point that America's unfounded suspicions of communism at home mirror America's zeal in suppressing communism abroad.

The subject of Hughes's Communist sympathies becomes clearer when King closes his speech by declaring that the good news of salvation is intended for both "communist and capitalist" (Washington 234). It expands when King chastises America's "morbid fear of communism" (242). It blooms in the light of King's embrace of Marxist thinking at the end of this speech when he declares that many now "feel that only Marxism has the revolutionary spirit. Therefore, communism is a judgment against our failure to make democracy real and follow through on the revolutions that we initiated" (243). Not only is Hughes a symbolic parallel, but he soon becomes a prophet who foresaw such evils forthcoming from American capitalism, for in his final paragraph King calls for a rededication to the "long and bitter, but beautiful, struggle for a new world" (243). Like Levison, King did not want a world where all people had the right to become capitalists; rather, he dreamed of a world that made capital available to all people.

King immediately paid the price for his comments. His decision not only to quote Hughes but to take a stand against American involvement in Vietnam and publicly voice the idea that communism was a corrective judgment from God received unprecedented denunciations. Johnson's advisers secretly declared that King "has thrown in with the commies" and "is painting himself into a corner with a bunch of losers" (Branch, *Canaan's Edge* 595). Having become irrelevant to the White House for communicating beliefs he had held in check for years, King "broke down more than once into tears" (597).

It is not surprising that when King thought of reacting to accusations of Communist sympathies in 1967, he spoke the poetry of Langston Hughes. It is also not surprising that Hughes was not angered by the speech. Not only was his own poetry quoted but the spirit of embracing communism mirrored his own thinking. Beginning with his "Beyond Vietnam" speech, King embraced Hughes overtly in his speeches without regard for the consequences. Within weeks, Hughes's poem "Mother to Son" would reappear at the ending of several of King's speeches.

The reactions to "Beyond Vietnam" provide clear reminders of how King had to be careful throughout his life about what to say, where to stand, and whom to quote. Invoking allusion and rewriting Hughes's poems were two of the means he used to avoid being dismissed by the establishment throughout the height of his influence between 1960 and 1965. Hughes's name and the titles of his poems simply had to be veiled in King's rhetoric during his years in the public eye. However, Hughes's ideas had already become a measurable inflection in King's voice by 1960. As a result of King's most important speeches during these years, the nation had begun to unconsciously embrace the poetry of Langston Hughes.

Notes

Abbreviations

LH Papers   Langston Hughes Papers, Beinecke Library, Yale University
MLK Archives   Martin Luther King Center Archives, Atlanta, Georgia
MLK Collection   Dr. Martin Luther King Jr. Collection, Howard Gotlieb Archival
                    Research Center, Boston University
SCLC Papers   Southern Christian Leadership Conference Papers, Martin Luther
                    King Center Archives, Atlanta, Georgia

Introduction

1. King to Hughes, November 30, 1959, LH Papers, box 96, folder 1806.

2. Spillers's essay has been reprinted in Garrow, *Martin Luther King* 3: 876–90.

3. Donna Akiba Sullivan Harper suggests this in "End of Deferment" 13.

4. For readability, all references to Dr. Martin Luther King Jr. hereafter appear without the "Jr." listed at the end of his name.

5. On several occasions (45, 61, 86), Baldwin specifically names Hughes in a long list of African American writers King enjoyed.

6. Lewis makes this comment in his audio introduction to King's March 25, 1965, address in Montgomery, Alabama. This recorded introduction is available in Carson, Holloran, and Shepard.

7. O'Neal to Hughes, February 8, 1967, and Hughes to O'Neal, Feburary 8, 1967, LH Papers, box 123, folder 2319.

8. Although the words are typed in black, Hughes underlined "history" in green ink for emphasis.

Chapter 1. "Mother to Son"

1. I thank Elaine Hall for her help in all my research at the Martin Luther King Center in Atlanta. A typed copy of this speech can be found in the MLK Archives, series 3, box 1. For the original version of "Mother to Son" see Hughes, *Collected Works* 1: 60.

2. Just before using this poem for the first time, King's personal letter sent to A. Philip Randolph three days before may have been hinting at the theme he intended to invoke in this sermon. In language that soon became intimately linked to this poem, King praised Randolph: "It is such persons as you that give us grim and bold determination to keep *going* in our struggle for first class citizenship" (Carson 3: 253).

3. A copy of this speech is in MLK Archives, series 3, box 13.

4. Eventually, even Hughes himself attributed this response to Parks when he dedicated *The Panther and the Lash* to her in 1967 with these words: "To Rosa Parks of Montgomery who started it all when, on being ordered to get up and stand at the back of the bus where there were no seats, she said simply 'My feet are tired,' and did not move" (*Collected Works* 3: 133).

5. A typed copy of this speech is in SCLC Papers, series 3, box 2.

6. A typed copy of this speech is in SCLC Papers, series 3, box 2.

7. A typed copy of this speech is in SCLC Papers, series 3, box 3.

8. What appears to be the third draft of "Normalcy—Never Again" is in SCLC Papers, series 3, box 3.

9. The text of Johnson's speech can be read at http://uspolitics.about.com/od/speeches/a/lbj_1965_15_mar.htm.

10. This speech is in SCLC Papers, series 3, box 3.

11. For more on this statement, see SCLC Papers, series 3, box 3.

12. This telegram can be found in LH Papers, box 96, folder 1806.

13. While King could now afford to reference Hughes, there are at least three reasons why Hughes might have reasonably refused an invitation to march with King. First, it is not hard to imagine that Hughes believed his best contribution to society was what he could do with words rather than with his feet. Second, by 1965, Hughes was an out-of-shape sixty-three-year-old man. Standing only five feet, four inches tall, he nonetheless weighed 185 pounds (Rampersad 2: 366). Two years earlier, Hughes had traveled extensively through Europe, where, according to his traveling partner, George Bass, he would "select a place in the midst of each of the ruins or monuments where he might sit and view the environs without taking another step" (qtd. in Rampersad 2: 366). It is likely that these two years had continued to deprive him of mobility, and the marching distance from Selma to Montgomery was over fifty miles. Third, Malcolm X was murdered in February of the same year, offering a re-minder that an investment in racial politics could result in death. Hence, Hughes conveyed his response in words by first writing an April 24, 1965, column in the *Chicago Defender*. He also relayed his excitement in regard to Johnson's 1965 speech in a telegram to the president himself, saying: "YOU HAVE MADE A GREAT AND HISTORIC SPEECH TONIGHT FOR WHICH ALL OF AMERICA MUST THANK YOU" (qtd. in Rampersad 2: 386). However, he did not accept the offer to march with King.

14. This was likely a rather dramatic reading by Coretta Scott King. Moreover, she likely said "stop now" in line fourteen in place of Hughes's original words "turn back." In fact, after King's assassination, she ended her own speech on April 27, 1968, in Central Park with a dramatic recitation of Hughes's poem that can be heard at http://fromthevaultradio.org/home/2008/02/01/091-remembering-mrs-coretta-scott-king-and-langston-hughes.

15. Lewis 289. Other celebrities were Peter, Paul and Mary, Joan Baez, Tony Bennett,

Leon Bibb, the Chad Mitchell trio, Bobby Darin, Ruby Dee, Ella Fitzgerald, George Kirby, Alan King, Mahalia Jackson, Elaine May, Mike Nichols, Floyd Patterson, Nispy Russell, and Shelly Winters.

16. This mysterious postcard acknowledgment is in LH Papers, box 96, folder 1806.

17. The speech "Transforming a Neighborhood" was delivered at the NATRA Convention RCA Dinner in Atlanta. SCLC Papers, series 3, box 3.

18. These speeches are in SCLC Papers, series 3, box 3.

Chapter 2. Black *and* Red

1. I thank Dick Reavis for bringing this event to my attention. Hughes's poem is named "Dixie" in the *Daily Worker* article about this event, but no such poem exists in Hughes's oeuvre. However, there is a possibility that this may have been "Silhouette," a poem that was later part of a larger sequence known as "Three Songs about Lynching." "Silhouette" specifically mentions "Dixie" in line 9. Of interpretive significance, if this or some version of this poem was sung and accompanied by music at the event, this might account for the very specific musical notations Hughes included in the margins of "Three Songs about Lynching.".

2. For more on these events, see Rampersad 2: 90–98, 140–44, 167–68.

3. This leaflet is literally the first item in Hughes's official FBI file, which can be viewed at http://vault.fbi.gov/langston-hughes.

4. Hughes's FBI file, 6–7.

5. Hughes's FBI file, 38.

6. Hughes's FBI file, 41.

7. Dated April 3, 1945, this information is located in Hughes's FBI file, 68.

8. This map can be viewed in Hughes's FBI file, 93.

9. By July 1948, Hoover had grown so enamored with his speech that he had "several hundred copies of this lecture" sent out around the country. References to these printed lectures can be found in Hughes's FBI file, 142.

10. Hughes obtained a transcript of Taylor's speech. LH Papers, box 315, folder 12807.

11. Hughes's FBI file, 132.

12. Dated June 16, 1948, this letter is located in Hughes's FBI file, 129–30.

13. Dated July 9, 1948, this letter is located in Hughes's FBI file, 141–42.

14. Although this photocopy of *Reader's Digest* is not included in Hughes's FBI file, Nichols's letter is located in Hughes's FBI file, 141–42.

15. Hoover's memo is located in Hughes's FBI file, 140.

16. This report is located in Hughes's FBI file, 147.

17. Dated December 3, 1948, this memo is located in Hughes's FBI file, 150.

18. Dated May 13, 1949, this information is located in Hughes's FBI file, 153–54.

19. This interview is summarized in Hughes's FBI file. During this interview at his residence, Hughes is recorded as remarking "I have a wide reputation as a leftist and only yesterday I denied being a Communist, over the radio" (185).

20. Hughes to Reeves, March 29, 1953, LH Papers, box 136, folder 2525.

21. Hughes to Reeves, April 8, 1953, LH Papers, box 136, folder 2525.

22. Cohn's comment to Hughes might have been intended to suggest why the FBI was

determined to have Hughes testify. In other words, Cohn might have been hinting that all this might have been avoided if Hughes had not embarrassed Hoover by denying Abingdon's request to reprint "Goodbye, Christ" in "Secularism—A Breeder of Crime." Once again, Hughes seems to have been unaware of this possible connection.

23. King's undated list, written in his own hand, is in the MLK Collection, box 17, folder 4.

24. Dated July 1958 but clearly written after July 14, Rustin's three-page letter is located in the MLK Collection, box 17, folder 2.

25. In a letter dated November 17, 1958, the publisher announces that more than 50,000 copies of *Stride toward Freedom* are in print. MLK Collection, box 17, folder 2.

26. Raoul Abdul to Martin Luther King, November 28, 1958, MLK Collection, box 18, folder 1.

27. Although Hughes's review was not used by King's publisher, Hughes promoted *Stride toward Freedom* in a December 27, 1958, *Chicago Defender* column. Singling out six books that would make for great last-minute Christmas gifts, Hughes called it a "deeply moving and noble book" and noted that it documented the struggles of those "who are setting a pattern and establishing a technique of protest that other oppressed peoples might effectively follow" ("Lasting Last Minute Gifts" 10).

28. For more on this reaction, see Allan H. Ryskind, "Kerry's Little Red Bookshelf," *Weekly Standard*, September 6, 2004, http://www.weeklystandard.com/author/allan-h.-ryskind.

29. For more on Santorum's retraction, see Alison Flood, *Guardian*, April 18, 2011, http://www.innovations.harvard.edu/news/1649651.html.

30. Other FBI agents agreed with Sullivan's assessment. See Garrow, *FBI* 82.

31. It is unclear what role Arnold may have had in deciding not to use Hughes's review of King's book.

32. Sarah Marquis Travel Agency to Rustin, January 19, 1959, MLK Collection, box 90, folder 3.

33. Pierce to King, January 18, 1959, MLK Collection, box 90, folder 3.

34. Reddick to Trenholm, December 19, 1958, MLK Collection, box 90, folder 3.

35. This contract is in MLK Collection, box 90, folder 4.

36. This letter is in MLK Collection, box 90, folder 3.

37. Dated February 6, 1959, a copy of this report from the *Los Angeles Tribune* is in MLK Collection, box 90, folder 4.

38. The brochure is in MLK Collection, box 134, folder 3.

39. King to Edward D. Ball, editor of the *Nashville Tennessean*, December 14, 1961, MLK Archives, series 3, box 127.

40. This letter is located at the King Center online archive, http://www.thekingcenter.org/archive/document/letter-mlk-mr-jack-h-odell.

41. Levison to King, June 3, 1958, MLK Collection, box 33, folder 4.

42. In Levison's letter to King, July 11, 1960, Levison notes this large contribution. MLK Collection, box 33, folder 4.

43. Levison to King, December 28, 1958, MLK Collection, box 33, folder 4.

44. Three checks from Belafonte of unknown sums were mailed on June 20, 1961. See Levison to King, June 20, 1961, MLK Collection, box 33, folder 4.

45. These directives from May 1961 are located in the MLK Collection, box 33, folder 4.

46. Levison to King, February 28, 1958, and December 29, 1960, MLK Collection, box 33, folder 4.

47. For example, Levison to King, December 29, 1960, MLK Collection, box 33, folder 4.

48. Just two months after his invocation of Hughes's "Mother to Son" changed Clarence Jones's life, King used Hughes's poem to culminate his address on April 10, 1960, when he spoke to the students of Spellman College in Atlanta. His subject that day was "Keep Moving from This Mountain." King invoked the imagery of the mountain from Deuteronomy 1, where Moses declares to the Israelites that they must move on to the promised land because they have been "in the mountain long enough" (Carson 5: 410). King then delineates four different mountains that must be overcome. Using these four mountains as the framework of his speech, he calls for listeners to overcome relativism, materialism, segregation, and violence. All signs seem to suggest that King is taking the mountain symbol from the Bible. However, because he ends this speech with Hughes's poem, it is noteworthy that Hughes's most important statement on his artistic philosophy used the symbol of the mountain as well. Hughes spoke of embracing one's heritage in "The Negro Artist and the Racial Mountain" (1926). For Hughes, the "racial mountain" was at once an obstacle and a destination.

Chapter 3. King and Poetry

1. For the earliest documented example of King's use of Donne's poetry, see Carson 6: 155. This sermon outline reveals that King had been quoting Donne since at least 1954.

2. King's handwritten draft, MLK Collection, box 23, folder 5. Typeset version is in Carson 5: 266.

3. The inside cover reads: "To Martin—with best wishes—Ledythe and Arthur." The book is #102 in the Morehouse College Martin Luther King Jr. Collection, Robert W. Woodruff Library, Atlanta University Center, Inc.

4. This index is located at the Morehouse College Martin Luther King Jr. Collection.

5. To locate King's comments on Wordsworth, Shelley, and Blake, see series 4.1.1.1.150_003, 4.1.1.1.150_049, and 4.3.1.60_003, respectively, Morehouse College Martin Luther King Jr. Collection.

6. For King's index card on Swinburne, see series 4.1.1.1.140_006, and for his written quotation from Tennyson, see series 4.1.1.70_50, both Morehouse College Martin Luther King Jr. Collection. For more examples of King's invocations of poems by Tennyson, see King's 1963 published speech in *The Pulpit*, where he states: "If God were only tough minded, he would be a cold passionless despot sitting in some far-off heaven 'contemplating all' as Tennyson puts it in 'The Palace of Art'" ("Tough Mind" 10). King also repeated a quotation from Tennyson's poem "The Voice and the Peak" that he first gleaned from a sermon by Robert J. McCraken (Carson 6: 199). For King's 1951 quotation of "The Voice and the Peak," see Carson 6: 118. King also quoted from Tennyson's poem "Locksley Hall" (Carson 6: 595).

7. For Browning, see 4.1.1.200_035 and 4.1.1.170_078; for Santayana, see 4.1.1.200_004; for Eddy, see 4.1.1.120_026–027; for Coward, see 4.1.1.120_009. All in Morehouse College Martin Luther King Jr. Collection.

8. In his sermon "The Three Dimensions of a Complete Life," King invokes a line from Keats's poem "The Fall of Hyperion." King reframes the poet's descriptions of pain and

misery as he claims that evil itself was "something that the poet Keats called 'the giant agony of the world'" (see Carson 5: 577). A Keats reference appeared in a King sermon as early as December 5, 1955 (Carson 6: 242).

9. For more on this issue, see King, "The Man Who Was a Fool." After citing the "poet Thoreau" early in this sermon, King lists the traits of his foolish man: "He may have books stacked up all around his library, but he may never read them. He may have access to great music, but he never listened to it. His eyes do not behold the majestic splendor of the skies. His ears are closed to the melodious sweetness of great music. His mind was closed to the insights of poets" (4–5).

10. A very brief list of some of these other poets and their works would include T. S. Eliot and his "The Love Song of J. Alfred Prufrock" (Carson 6: 596), a Francis Thompson poem (6: 561), and a quotation from Ovid (4: 318). In addition to quoting lines from Carl Sandburg on June 15, 1965, King also made use of multiple poems by Henry Wadsworth Longfellow (6: 91) as well as Shakespeare's sonnet 116 (3: 458).

11. For the first surviving copy of one of King's sermons, see Carson 6: 162. King knew of Lowell's poetry as early as 1951, when he referenced it in one of his essays written at Crozer (Carson 1: 417).

12. King doesn't always turn prose into poetry. For one example, see Carson 5: 248. Here are the original words of Tolstoy: "A man having no freedom cannot be conceived of except as deprived of life." When it came time to communicate the essence of this thought, King simply said: "Tolstoy, the Russian Writer, said in *War and Peace*: 'I cannot conceive of a man not being free unless he is dead.'" This example, from July 17, 1959, was used again on August 20, 1959.

13. King later referenced this quote from Emerson in the summer of 1959 and as late as June 20, 1965.

14. With regard to King's use of poetic langauge in his addresses, see Lischer, *Preacher King;* my reading of King's "Psalm of Brotherhood" in chapter 9; and the final two instances of poetry in King's August 11, 1956, speech, which show that he was not always "unselfconsciously talking poetry" (Lischer, *Preacher King* 125).

15. This poem always appears in references to Eros; it can be found in King's speeches as early as November 10, 1957, and as late as June 20, 1965.

16. King may have encountered this poem as early as February 1950. While the idea of such roads is clearly a common metaphor, in one of his essays composed during his time at Crozer, King wrote: "We must believe that man has the power of choosing. . . . He can choose the low road or the high road" (Carson 1: 277).

17. Typescript version located in the MLK Archives, series 3, box 2. For the corrected typescript see Carson 5: 156.

18. "Tomorrow's Light," "Keep Punching," and Douglas's letter are located in the MLK Collection, box 25, folder 1.

19. To my knowledge, King never quoted lines from an unsolicited poem.

20. Over three dozen unsolicited poems sent to King are located in various files in the MLK Collection.

21. Wilson's poem and cover letter are located in the MLK Collection, box 26, folder 4.

22. Wright's March 22, 1957, letter and poem are in the MLK Collection, box 26, folder 4.

23. King to Hughes, December 29, 1959, LH Papers, box 96, folder 1806.

24. Hughes also sent copies of "Prayer for the Mantle-Piece" to Gerald S. Pratt and Franklin Watt. Pratt received a typed message of thanks from Hughes as someone who "quires my thoughts about God," and Watt received a handwritten note in green ink wishing that his "New Year had got off to a good start." The copies sent to Pratt and Watt are located in LH Hughes Papers, box 383, folder 6846.

25. This copy of "Prayer for the Mantle-Piece" is only located in the MLK Collection, box 25, folder 2.

26. King often used this title after Hughes's death in 1967. He applied the phrase to Hughes in a speech delivered on August 10, 1967.

27. This copy of "Merry-Go-Round" is located in the MLK Collection, box 25, folder 2.

28. King's inability to receive this award in person is noted in the MLK Collection, box 25, folder 2.

29. Multiple versions of Hughes's typed comments are in LH Papers, box 481, folder 12123.

30. Though this subtitle regularly appears in an amended version in most republications, this was also Hughes's original subtitle. The multiple revisions to "Brotherly Love" I discuss here are in LH Papers, box 481, folder 12123.

31. Three examples include Simple saying that King would inspire him to sing "Love Will Find a Way," saying that King is jailed even though he loves people, and noting that King traveled to Germany with love in his heart, in Hughes's "Juke Box Melodies on Simple's Song Sheet," "Simple; Jail-Ins," and "Berlin Today," respectively.

32. King's speech almost reads as if the two men exchanged some communication within the contents of a lost letter or a personal conversation. Though no record exists, perhaps King received a copy of Hughes's poem "Brotherly Love" soon after it was published.

33. An audio recording of this event captures King trying to deliver the next few words of his prepared script. When the applause did not subside, King simply ended his speech here. Moreover, it is clear that King did not intend to end here, as a speech with the same ending from December 5, 1957, contains the words King omitted here. For the words King would have said had the applause not been so unexpectedly overwhelming, see Carson 4: 342.

34. Several of Hughes's poems can be read as if they are spoken in Simple's voice. "Brotherly Love" and "Who But the Lord" are but two examples.

35. It is unclear why none of the changes Hughes made in these contexts appeared when the poem was republished ten years later in *The Panther and the Lash*. The passing of the years or Hughes's death before this book's release are two potential explanations.

36. Hughes's article "Simple Produces a Film on an Afro-American Theme" was published on June 2, 1956.

37. These five articles appeared in the *Chicago Defender* on February 21, 1959, April 4, 1961, September 29 and October 6, 1962, and June 15, 1963.

38. These articles were published in the *Defender* on July 7, 1956, and January 19, 1963.

39. The first version of this article ran in the *Defender* on August 19, 1961, while the second appeared under the title "Long, Gone Still Hear Voices" on September 7, 1963.

Chapter 4. "Dream Deferred"

1. The numerous auditory elements in this speech can be heard in the recording of King's talk made available in the 2010 Beacon Press republication of *The Trumpet of Conscience*.

2. When Hughes first published this poem in 1951, it appeared under the title "Harlem." However, in Hughes's 1967 collection *The Panther and the Lash*, it is titled "Dream Deferred." Hughes also wrote another poem that he called "Harlem" as well. To avoid confusion, I refer to the 1951 poem here and throughout by its 1967 title "Dream Deferred."

3. This draft of "Dream Deferred" is located in LH Papers, box 316, folder 5155.

4. The last eight paragraphs of this article come word-for-word from an SCLC proposal completed in January 1966 that outlines a plan for developing a nonviolent campaign in Chicago. This proposal and King's article are likely the result of collaborative input from King's advisers, such as Clarence Jones, Stanley Levison, Bayard Rustin, and Andrew Young. While it is difficult to be certain which words King himself contributed to these documents, the presence of Hughes's poetry suggests two things. First, King's contribution was not likely the statistics offered in these documents, but rather something more like this section of Hughes's poetry, which he knew. Second, this group recognized that a reference to Hughes's poetry was one of the most convincing ways to simulate King's natural style and typical rhetoric. The original SCLC proposal can be found at http://www.thekingcenter.org/archive/document/chicago-nonviolent-action-proposal.

5. The phrase "shattered dreams" appears, among other places, in speeches King made on August 16, 1967 (Washington, *Testament* 252), and on July 14, 1965 (Carson, Holloran, and Shepard). For an address from July 26, 1965, see SCLC Papers, series 3, box 8. In both of these 1965 speeches, King is reflecting on the speech he gave at the March on Washington in 1963.

6. King repeated this statement on several occasions. For an example from September 9, 1957, see MLK Collection, box 23, folder 2; examples from January 14, 1959, and August 21, 1959, are in box 23, folder 4.

7. Although Meek does speak of dreams twice in his sermon, these references are brief and differ from King's personal diction and syntax in significant ways. King has clearly added the idea of "shattered dreams and blasted hopes" on his own. On these two brief occasions, Meek also does not emphasize the emotional disappointment of dreams but merely states that "many of us in one way or another have dreamed our dreams of going to Spain, of fulfilling some far reaching hope. . . . But we never reached the Spain of our dreams" (qtd. in Carson 6: 358).

8. This anthology is identified as book #251 in the Morehouse College Martin Luther King Jr. Collection, Robert W. Woodruff Library, Atlanta University Center, Inc.

9. Dated approximately October 1956, two of King's outlines from this sermon series can be located in Carson 6: 271–75.

10. For another example of King writing notes for a sermon on the pages of his copy of Hamilton's text, see Carson 6: 177.

11. Hughes maintained a close connection with this play from its first performance to its evolution into a film. He alerted his close friend Arna Bontemps that he expected "twenty-two curtain calls" as he prepared to attend the opening. He also sent Bontemps to the show

on a ticket he secured for the April 19 matinee. Hughes also attended a performance in May 1960 and attended the filming of the play in July 1960. In addition, he wrote captions for photographs Roy De Carava took of the Chicago performance. To learn more about his involvement, see LH Papers, box 20, folder 422.

12. For more on the relationship between "Mother to Son" and Hansberry's play, see W. J. Miller, "Foregrounding" 4–7.

13. For more on the relationship between "Dream Deferred" and Hansberry's play, see W. J. Miller, "Foregrounding" 5–15.

14. For more on this article, see Carson 6: 258.

15. Madden to Hughes, April 16, 1959, LH Papers, box 110, folder 2053.

16. McNeil would have been on Hughes's mind, as he was responsible for her breakthrough role in his play *Simply Heavenly*. In fact, McNeil wrote Hughes shortly after the opening of *Raisin* to thank him for the flowers he left her on opening night. McNeil to Hughes, March 20, 1959, LH Papers, box 110, folder 2052.

17. For more about this event, see LH Papers, box 110, folder 2053.

18. The full exchange between Ralph E. Shikes and Hughes is in LH Papers, box 126, folder 2353. For more about Hughes's notes on the public performances of this and other poems featured in "Freedom Train and Other Poems of Negro Life and History," see LH Papers, box 300, folder 4934.

19. The exchange between Hughes and Harold Scott epitomizes Hughes's stance on issues surrounding the copyright use of his poetry. On February 8, 1966, Scott sought written permission to use "Montage of a Dream Deferred" as the title of a piece he intended to stage. Two days later Hughes responded that Scott should not use this title, because it would lead people to think that the play centered exclusively on Hughes's poems. Hughes suggests Scott use "Dream Deferred" or "What Happens to a Dream" to avoid this confusion. As expected, Hughes again gave Scott free permission to use whatever title he wanted. This exchange is located in LH Papers, box 139, folder 2610.

20. Hansberry requested written permission to use this as her title on February 8, 1958, and Hughes granted it without any financial compensation in a letter dated April 5, 1958. LH Papers, box 74, folder 1426.

21. For O'Neal's letter and Hughes's response, see LH Papers, box 123, folder 2319.

22. It is interesting to note the Russian origins of Smirnoff vodka given the Communist label assigned to Hughes. Smirnoff vodka was founded in the 1860s by Pyotr Arsenievich Smirnov, the son of Russian peasants.

23. Earlier Smirnoff ads featured Cliff Arquette, Maurice Evans, Joan Fontaine, Celeste Holm, George Sanders, and Francis Sullivan.

24. It is unclear why Poitier was not featured. Already an accomplished film star, Poitier may have either required too much money, refused, been too busy, or was simply never approached.

25. Hughes refers to "Dream Deferred" as "Raisin in the Sun" on a list of his own poems he prepared to read for a radio appearance in Chapel Hill, North Carolina, in April 1960. LH Papers, box 482, folder 12156.

26. This caption appears directly below the title of the article in the table of contents of the May 1960 issue of *Ebony*.

Chapter 5. "Poem for a Man"

1. This correspondence can be found in the MLK Collection, box 33, folder 4.

2. King to Hughes, November 30, 1959, LH Papers, box 96, folder 1806.

3. Levison to King, December 21, 1959, MLK Collection, box 33, folder 4.

4. A copy of King's unsigned letter is in the MLK Collection, box 25, folder 2. The copy Hughes received is in LH Papers, box 96, folder 1806.

5. This letter was likely read by Levison but not King. LH Papers, box 96, folder 1806.

6. King's January 5, 1960, letter to Levison is misdated 1959. MLK Collection, box 33, folder 4.

7. This poem and the various drafts I discuss below are in LH Papers, box 383, folder 6824.

8. King to Hughes, November 30, 1959, LH Papers, box 96, folder 1806.

9. Hughes to Dee, January 25, 1960, LH Papers, box 53, folder 997.

10. One of the leaflets advertising the January 31, 1960, performance is in the MLK Collection, box 134, folder 7.

11. Hughes's personal calendars are in LH Papers, box 491.

12. Hughes's personal calendar, LH Papers, box 491.

13. This leaflet is located in the MLK Collection, box 134, folder 7.

14. This poem and all its drafts are in LH Papers, box 383, folder 6824.

15. Hughes sent the revised version the same day he cut out of the newspaper a photograph of King standing prominently with Pope Paul VI. The image appeared in the *New York Herald Tribune* the same Sunday morning. Hughes had also clipped another image of King from the paper a week earlier when King was pictured and quoted while in Berlin. It, too, was carefully saved and folded. LH Papers, box 572, folder 13655.

Chapter 6. "Youth"

1. In light of both Azikiwe's choice of poem and his exact words, it is interesting to note Hughes's personal letter to Azikiwe from two years earlier. On February 28, 1958, Hughes wrote to Azikiwe requesting a poem or statement for the anthology he was currently editing, titled *African Treasury*: "Know that I send to you and your Nigeria all of my very best wishes for a bright future." LH Papers, box 9, folder 221.

2. Hughes offered several titles for this poem over the course of his career. It was originally published as "Poem" in 1924, but Hughes most often simply referred to it as "Tomorrow." A handwritten copy of the poem from 1931 uses this title. Guy B. Johnson Papers #3826, series 2.1, box 8, folders 110–31, Wilson Library, University of North Carolina at Chapel Hill.

3. Sequencing is also a factor in one of Hughes's previous collections. *The Negro Mother*, a small collection of short poems from 1931, was published as a chapbook so that its entries were easily accessible for recitals. In a sequence of poems that reprise the role of Hughes's speaker in "Mother to Son," the title poem ends with a pencil drawing that depicts black and white children marching up a set of stairs toward a rising sun. The final two poems are the title poem, similar to "Mother to Son," and "Dark Youth." Published a year before *The Dream Keeper*, and with the word "Youth" also in its title, the youth in this second poem "climb to-

ward tomorrow" inspired by the mother. The sequencing reminds us that a mother's words were meant to lead to a brighter tomorrow for her children. Marching and walking were consistently metaphorical imperatives in Hughes's poetry; to the ears of Montgomery's citizens, they were everyday realities.

4. The handwritten draft featuring these floating quotation marks is in the MLK Collection, box 23, folder 1. A typeset version of these lines can be accessed more easily and just as accurately in Carson 3: 286.

5. Sometimes the title of this poem is given as "Man Was Made to Mourn: A Dirge."

6. It is not clear how King came into contact with this line from Burns's poem. No reference to this poem appears in any of King's index cards; it does not appear to be in any of the books he owned, and no clear link to another preacher's sermon has yet been noted.

7. Of course, biblical parallelism is far more complex, varied, and nuanced than this simplified introduction suggests.

8. Because King consistently used and referenced the King James Bible, I will use that translation.

9. What I am labeling "climactic parallelism" for accessibility purposes is often designated as "syntagmatic" by biblical scholars. Robert Lowth's groundbreaking analysis of Hebrew poetry used the term "synthetic parallelism."

10. For more on "iconicity," see Leff and Sachs 263.

11. For King's first invocation of Oxenham's poem in 1949 see Carson 6: 97. For his invocations of Oxenham's hymn "In Christ There Is No East or West," see Carson 6: 133, 292.

12. "The Crisis in Human Relations," undated and typed draft, MLK Collection, box 23, folder 3.

13. King's May 11, August 20, and September 17, 1959, addresses are in Carson 5: 202, 270, and 278, respectively. The January 14, 1959, address is in the MLK Collection, box 23, folder 3. The text of King's August 21, 1959, speech is in the MLK Collection, box 23, folder 4.

14. Unpublished draft of *Why We Can't Wait*, pages 41 and 43, MLK Collection, box 22, folder 1.

15. Unpublished draft of *Why We Can't Wait*, page 43.

16. For the entire sermon see Carson, Holloran, and Shepard.

17. Draft of "Unfulfilled Dreams," MLK Collection, box 10, folder 1.

18. "Paul's Letter to American Christians," page 7, MLK Collection, box 22, folder 1.

Chapter 7. "I Dream a World"

1. The entire speech is in Washington, *Testament* 208–16. As we will see in chapter 8, King's invocation of the American dream in this introduction was a set piece he built by blending his own ideas within the structure of a paragraph found in E. Stanley Jones's *The Christ of the American Road* 60. This set piece is identical to the one King delivered on September 25, 1960, and January 1, 1961.

2. That King spoke this phrase to both introduce and conclude a passage that dates back to the significant December 3, 1956, speech addressed later in this chapter makes this linguistic parallel between King and Hughes even more clear.

3. Although it is undated, Hughes's note about Martel appears to have been written before 1936. LH Papers, box 293, folder 4804.

4. Hughes's image of the pearl in this poem is central to understanding the complex imagery invoked in *Troubled Island*. Within the dialogue that precedes the passage where these lines are recited, Martel imagines a world where Haiti returns to trading with France. Dessalines's refusal highlights Hughes's vexing final image of a pearl in the poem. Hughes invests this image with an elusive resonance. On the one hand, we can read the image as something born out of the poem's basic ideology of sharing and redistribution. When wretchedness hangs its head, a pearl of charity is placed in the palms of the poor.

However, Hughes used the pearl image in two other significant (but complex) ways in the play. First, he immediately links Earth itself with the image of a pearl immediately after this dialogue. When the emperor's white mistress, Claire, enters, she entreats Dessalines to enjoy a romantic moment in the garden. She notes that "Everywhere the earth / Is drenched in color rare / By light empearled" (*Collected Works* 6: 31). Continuing to invoke the language of jewels, she notes the sky's "amethyst and gold" (6: 32); this culminates with Dessalines's refusal to engage her red lips because he has to bear the heavy burden of the crown adorned in his "ermine cape" and "scarlet cloak." He chooses ruling Haiti over "embracing" the world. Second, this choice becomes even more symbolic because Claire is described as a "pearl most rare" (6: 33) by the man she leaves Dessalines for and sails with to Paris. Like Martel, this rival chooses what the emperor rejects. As a result, true "joy" is literally anticipated as the two lovers have plans to leave for Paris (6: 34). This lover will embrace the joys of Claire, his pearl. They imagine France as a site where black and whites equally enjoin with government, commerce, and society. France becomes a symbol epitomizing Martel's dream of integration, while Haiti is the symbol of Dessalines's desire for isolation. As the scene closes, the sunset rejected by Dessalines is blooming in colors of "rose" and "gold" as Claire and her lover embrace (6: 35). Claire is the pearl symbolically linked to the larger world itself espoused by Martel. These colors are unknown to Dessalines. Thus, he loses Claire and joy as a direct result of his limited vision of his world.

Hughes's metaphor of the pearl in "I Dream a World" is also used symbolically in another poem. This intertextuality reveals that Hughes may have been thinking about one of his works for children when he drafted "I Dream a World." In the August 1921 edition of *The Brownies' Book*, Hughes published his poem "Mister Sandman." It preceded by more than thirty years the popular song of the same title recorded by the Chordettes.

In "Mister Sandman," the pearl is a simile for a dream: "'Ah,' says the sandman, 'To this little girl / I'll send a dream like a precious pearl'" (lines 9–10). This sandman does not discriminate between black and white children as he has dreams for "every girl and every boy" (line 19). Reading the image of the pearl in "I Dream a World" against "Mr. Sandman" gives us the picture of the wretched hanging their heads in sleep, to wake and find a pearl that has fallen from their eyes. Extending the metaphor, the eye is a closed shell from which the night's sand falls out in the form of a pearl. The pearl itself becomes a symbol of the joy found as a result of having been given a good dream.

5. "I Dream a World" was reprinted in *American Negro Poetry* in May 1963. The book went through eighteen printings. Hill and Wang had approached Arna Bontemps about

editing an anthology of African American poetry in May 1962. Bontemps wrote Hughes: "May I count on using at least a dozen of your finest? Actually my plan is to use some of the 'standard' ones plus some that I think should *become* standard" (Bontemps 441). Bontemps adds: "I also want to be sure to include the Raisin in the Sun passage and the I Dream a World. These are hard for the lay reader to find, but he keeps thinking about them" (448). Bontemps's comments reveal that *Raisin in the Sun* had brought such notoriety to Hughes's "Dream Deferred" that even he begins referencing the poem by the title of the play. It is hard to underestimate just how popular and readily available this book was just as King was preparing to deliver "I Have a Dream" in Detroit and Washington, D.C. Even as many as four years after its release, copies of the seventh edition "disappeared like leaves in a hurricane" and the publisher was printing yet another edition to meet the continuous demand (487). The book was so hastily completed that two simple typographical errors appear in lines 2 and 18 in all eighteen printings of Hughes's "I Dream a World."

6. For a discussion of Hughes's two separate testimonies before this committee, see Kutzinski, 185–205, as well as chapter 5 and appendixes A and B in Chinitz.

7. This copy of "I Dream a World" is in LH Papers, box 365, folder 5887.

8. For more on rhetorical techniques King studied in the classes he took with Robert Keighton at Crozer, see Lischer, *Preacher King* 64–65.

9. Although King treated Carlyle's lines as poetry here and in other instances, this line is actually from his prose piece *The French Revolution.*

10. King used the words from Holland's poem in various other places. In each context that is not addressed here in this chapter, he signaled that these words were not his own. King used this passage from Holland through 1957, and it appeared in a speech delivered on September 23, 1959. For speeches delivered on April 10 and April 25, 1957, see Carson 4: 178, 190. For the September 23, 1959, speech see Carson 5: 287.

King also used this poem on July 20, 1962, when it came time to honor Jackie Robinson. There, King recast the poem closer to its original praise of great "men" as opposed to great "leaders." King ended his speech that day without a specific reference to Holland but merely "the impassioned plea of a poet who wrote long ago." Using the poem to close his speech, King used the original first line, "God give us men!," to praise Robinson, and then he concluded: "God has given us such a man in Jack Roosevelt Robinson." King's speech is located in SCLC Papers, series 3, box 3.

King took greater liberties with this poem at the march in Chicago on July 26, 1965. He leaps back and forth through the poem, swapping lines, alternating phrases, and calling this a "prayer" rather than a poem: "I still have a dream that one day in the state houses of the North, God will answer the prayer of Joshua [*sic*] Holland: 'God give us men a Time like this demands, strong minds, true faith, willing hearts, and ready hands. Men whom the spoils of office cannot buy. Men whom the lust of office does not kill.'" Copy in SCLC Papers, series 3, box 8.

11. Rev. Ralph D. Abernathy notes that King's sermons were often "simply thrown into garbage cans" (qtd. in Baldwin, *Balm* 290).

12. Bobbitt also notes the connection between King's beloved community, this 1956 passage by King, and King's expression of the dream in 1963 (14–15).

Chapter 8. "I Have a Dream"

1. For a comprehensive discussion of King's undocumented uses of the phrase "I have a dream," see Hansen 109–16. While it is likely that King used some version of this phrase before this date, this address clearly marks the first documented use of the phrase "I have a dream." King once casually suggested he used the phrase first in Albany (Cannon 220). Some SNCC workers claim to have heard it from King on November 16, 1962 (Hansen 109–10). Wyatt Tee Walker recalls King using this phrase even earlier when he spoke in South Bend, Indiana, Louisville, and Los Angeles (Hansen 251n115). If King did use this phrase for the first time in Albany, it likely could have been at Shiloh Baptist Church. During that period he was in rhetorical contact with the dream metaphor as a result of revisiting his sermons. Because Shiloh Baptist Church was serving as campaign headquarters, its location in what was commonly referred to as the "Harlem section" of Albany raises important possibilities for connecting this context with Hughes's seminal statement on dreaming made in "Harlem."

2. Dated December 20, 1962, this draft is located in the MLK Collection, box 21, folder 1. For a transcript see Carson 6: 521.

3. Despite some startling similarities, there is no evidence that Jones knew of Hughes's poems, and his book precedes the publication of "Dream Deferred" by six years; however, it follows the publication of "I Dream a World" by three years, and Jones's book has a large number of references to African American culture. For example, Jones cites Roland Hayes (238) and George Washington Carver (239) and speaks out against racism (176). Jones valued poetry. In addition to quoting lines from Hughes's favorite poet, Walt Whitman (65), Jones wrote poetry and included one of his own poems in this text (118).

4. Garrow writes that Stanley Levison wrote most of this speech (*FBI* 26). However, the complex structure of this passage clearly bears King's rhetorical signature. This speech is located in SCLC Papers, series 3, box 3.

5. A brief list of phrases King uses as anaphora or epistrophe makes this clear. On different occasions King repeated such phrases as "How long? Not long," "We will still love you," "I can't like anybody," "There is something in the universe," and "There comes a time." His August 28, 1963, address uses "One hundred years later," "We cannot be satisfied," "Now is the time," and "Go back." Clearly, the repetition of "I have a dream" is unique in the area of metaphorical expression when read against these and other examples of verbal repetition typically engaged by King. It is the exception, not the rule. Furthermore, only borrowed phrases that are invoked and repeated by King express such metaphors. For example, King often repeated the phrases "Let freedom ring" and "Free at last." Like his use of the metaphora featuring both "world" and "dream" that are rewritten from Hughes's poetry, these expressions also originate from other sources.

6. King inverts these two phrases found in the King James Bible's Revelation 21.4–5: "[4] And God shall wipe away all tears from their eyes; and there shall be no more death, neither sorrow, nor crying, neither shall there be any more pain: for the former things are passed away. [5] And he that sat upon the throne said, Behold, I make all things new. And he said unto me, Write: for these words are true and faithful."

7. All quotes from this speech are taken from an audio recording that the author digitally preserved and then transcribed.

8. Branch identifies these churches as Mount Mary Baptist and Mount Olive Baptist (*Parting* 637).

9. In addition to Psalm 13, the phrase "how long" is also used in Psalm 35.17, Psalm 79.5, Psalm 80.4, and Psalm 89.46.

10. For other biblical questions that begin with "How long" see Habakkuk 1.2, Exodus 10.3, 1 Samuel 16.1, and Jeremiah 31.22.

11. Although the original tapes have been recorded over, King's use of the word "tonight" here highlights why some of the officers who snuck into mass meetings in Birmingham during the spring of 1963 often wrote in their reports: "I had a dream tonight" (Lischer, *Preacher King* 247).

12. As we will see in chapter 9, King's statement about the dream being rooted deeply in the American dream was an introductory statement, and as such it stands outside the chiastic structure I describe here and in the next chapter.

13. Rocky Mount was named after the mound of rocks located in the city near the Tar River. The river and stream metaphor in the quotation from Amos highlights this connection.

14. For more on Carey's original words, see Hansen 108–9.

Chapter 9. "The Psalm of Brotherhood"

1. In *Parting the Waters*, Branch notes that at this time Evers privately sought the go-ahead to invite King to "join forces" in person with NAACP leadership in Jackson, Mississippi (825). As such, this phone call most likely sought King's feedback on this strategy.

2. King's changed flight arrangements are in the MLK Collection, box 78.

3. For further discussion of these events, see chapter 2.

4. Kennedy's speech is available in text and audio at http://www.americanrhetoric.com/speeches/jfkcivilrights.htm.

5. King's speech is available in text and audio at http://mlk-kpp01.stanford.edu/index.php/encyclopedia/documentsentry/doc_speech_at_the_great_march_on_detroit.

6. Each of the June speeches reference the Emancipation Proclamation. In his only use of anaphora, Kennedy uses the phrase "it ought to be possible" five times. King says "now is the time" five times.

7. King's speech is available in text and audio at ttp://mlk-kpp01.stanford.edu/index.php/encyclopedia/documentsentry/doc_speech_at_the_great_march_on_detroit.

8. For a definition of "domestic terrorism," see W. J. Miller, *Langston Hughes* 3–5.

9. This speech is in SCLC Papers, series 3, box 3.

10. The theme of blacks and whites being equally free is also expressed in the third anaphora of Hughes's "I Dream a World." King most clearly captures the cadence of Hughes's poem in the line "I have a dream," which sounds most like Hughes's onetime variant, "A world I dream."

Chapter 10. The March on Washington

1. While the organizational structure of parallelism is not invoked, King may be using numbers symbolically in this address, just as he did in Rocky Mount. Here, he offers six anaphors of "I have a dream," followed by the names of five northern states where freedom rings and then four southern states where freedom has not been fully extended. If the numbers are symbolic, the ideal world King dreams is one step above the North, while the South is perhaps another step below the North.

2. I base this judgment on the fact that no links between Hughes's poem and King's rhetoric appear in any other of King's most accessible speeches. For a discussion of the other texts to which King may be alluding in the phrase "my people," see Sundquist 199.

3. Although they focus on different aspects, several other scholars have also noted the speech's tripartite structure. For an extended discussion, see Vail 64.

4. Several scholars have commented on King's check metaphor. For an extended discussion, see Vail 67–68.

5. This quotation can be found on page 5 of this speech, located in the MLK Collection, box 24, folder 2.

6. In the CNN broadcast "We Were There: The March on Washington, an Oral History," Boyte states: "I put my sleeping bag on my father's hotel floor. . . . I was just drifting off to sleep and I heard Dr. King's voice: 'I Have a Dream' coming through the wall clearly from the next room. And I thought, he must be practicing his speech for the next day.".

Conclusion

1. Heilner suggests that the two men split the royalties "50–50" in this letter, dated September 18, 1963. The letter can be viewed at http://www.thekingcenter.org/archive/document/request-use-i-have-dream-speech-musical-composition.

2. Heilner's letter dated September 18, 1963, the fourth and final written request, is at http://www.thekingcenter.org/archive/document/letter-irwin-heilner-mlk.

3. Bialeck to King, April 3, 1967, is at http://www.thekingcenter.org/archive/document/letter-robert-bialek-mlk.

4. This letter is available at http://www.thekingcenter.org/archive/document/letter-liabosonetto-mlk-regarding-langston-hughes.

5. This autographed script is located, but unavailable for examination, at the Morehouse College Martin Luther King Jr. Collection, Robert W. Woodruff Library, Atlanta University Center, Inc.

6. Hughes's lists are in LH Papers, box 311, folder 5063.

7. This copy is at the MLK Archives, series 3, box 131, folder 25.

8. This speech is available in text and audio at http://mlk-kpp01.stanford.edu/index.php/encyclopedia/documentsentry/doc_speech_at_the_great_march_on_detroit.

9. A typed copy of Hughes's speech is in LH Papers, box 483, folder 12221.

10. In *At Canaan's Edge*, Branch notes the complex process that led to the final version of this speech. Levison and Harding joined King in toning the speech down, and they made

the introduction more "poetic" (590–91). Branch notes that Spelman professor Vincent Harding drafted a large majority of this speech (603).

11. For Harding's discussion, which also includes a direct quotation from this stanza of Hughes's poem, see "Is America Possible?" 37–43, available at http://www.onbeing.org/ program/civility-history-and-hope/feature/is-america-possible/535.

12. A copy of this draft is available at http://www.thekingcenter.org/archive/document/ why-i-am-opposed-war-vietnam.

13. A transcript of this broadcast is available at http://www.thekingcenter.org/archive/ document/mlks-speech-civil-rights-and-vietnam.

Bibliography

Atkinson, Brooks. "'Raisin in the Sun.'" *New York Times.* 29 Mar. 1959, 1.

———. "The Theatre: 'A Raisin in the Sun.'" *New York Times.* 12 Mar. 1959, 1.

Azikiwe, Nnamdi. *Respect for Human Dignity: An Inaugural Address by His Excellency Dr. Nnamdi Azikiwe Governor-General and Commander-in-Chief.* Onitsha, Nigeria: Union Publishing Company, 1960.

Baldwin, Lewis. *There Is a Balm in Gilead: The Cultural Roots of Martin Luther King, Jr.* Minneapolis: Fortress Press, 1991.

———. *Toward the Beloved Community: Martin Luther King, Jr. and South Africa.* Cleveland: Pilgrim Press, 1995.

Baraka, Amiri. "*A Raisin in the Sun's* Enduring Passion." *Black Literature Criticism: Excerpts from Criticism of the Most Significant Works of Black Authors over the Past 200 Years.* Ed. James P. Draper. Vol. 2. Detroit: Gale, 1992. 953–55.

Barksdale, Richard. *Praisesong of Survival: Lectures and Essays, 1957–89.* Urbana: University of Illinois Press, 1992.

Bartlett, John, ed. *Bartlett's Familiar Quotations.* New York: Little, Brown, 1955.

Bigsby, C. W. E., ed. *The Black American Writer.* Vol. 1. *Fiction.* DeLand, Fla.: E. O. Painter Printing Co., 1969.

Bobbitt, David. *The Rhetoric of Redemption: Kenneth Burke's Redemption Drama and Martin Luther King Jr.'s "I Have a Dream" Speech.* Oxford, U.K.: Rowman and Littlefield, 2004.

Bontemps, Arna, and Langston Hughes. *Arna Bontemps–Langston Hughes Letters (1925–1967).* Ed. Charles H. Nichols. New York: Dodd, Mead, 1980.

Branch, Taylor. *At Canaan's Edge: America in the King Years, 1965–68.* New York: Simon and Schuster, 2006.

———. *Parting the Waters: America in the King Years, 1954–63.* New York: Simon and Schuster, 1989.

———. *Pillar of Fire: America in the King Years, 1963–65.* New York: Simon and Schuster, 1998.

Brinkley, Douglas. *Rosa Parks.* New York: Viking, 2000.

Brown-Guillory, Elizabeth. *Their Place on the Stage: Black Women Playwrights in America.* Westport, Conn.: Greenwood, 1988.

Burnham, Louis. "The Spectator: One Man's Stature." *National Guardian.* 1 Feb. 1960.

Burns, Robert. "Man Was Made to Mourn." *Collected Poems of Robert Burns*. Ware, U.K.: Wordsworth Editions, 1994. 110–13.

Cannon, Poppy. "Martin Luther King, Jr." *Heroes for Our Times*. Eds. Will Yolen and Kenneth Seaman Giniger. Harrisburg: Overseas Press Club, 1968. 201–21.

Carson, Clayborne, ed. *The Papers of Martin Luther King, Jr.* 7 vols. Berkeley: University of California Press, 2005.

Carson, Clayborne, Peter Holloran, and Kris Shepard, eds. *Martin Luther King, Jr.: The Essential Box Set*. Hachette Audio, 2009.

Chinitz, David E. *Which Sin to Bear? Authenticity and Compromise in Langston Hughes*. Oxford, U.K.: Oxford University Press, 2013.

Colbert, Soyica. *The African American Theatrical Body*. Cambridge, U.K.: Cambridge University Press, 2011.

Dawson, Michael C. *Black Visions: The Roots of Contemporary African-American Political Ideologies*. Chicago: University of Chicago Press, 2001.

De Santis, Christopher, ed. *Langston Hughes and the Chicago Defender: Essays on Race, Politics, and Culture*. Urbana: University of Illinois Press, 1995.

Effiong, Philip Uko. *In Search of a Model for African-American Drama: A Study of Selected Plays by Lorraine Hansberry, Amiri Baraka, and Ntozake Shang*. Lanham, Md.: University Press of America, 2000.

Gale, Mary Ellen. "Dr. King Buried in Atlanta: 'I Tried to Love Somebody.'" *Southern Courier*. 13–14 Apr. 1968, A1.

Garrow, David. *Bearing the Cross: Martin Luther King, Jr., and the Southern Christian Leadership Conference*. New York. Vintage, 1988.

———. *The FBI and Martin Luther King, Jr.* New York: Penguin, 1983.

———. *Martin Luther King, Jr.: Civil Rights Leader, Theologian, Orator*. 3 vols. Brooklyn, N.Y.: Carlson, 1989.

Geschwender, James A. *Class, Race, and Worker Insurgency: The League of Revolutionary Black Workers*. New York: Cambridge University Press, 1977.

Ghosh, Nibir K. "A Soul Deep Like the Rivers: Re-Visiting Langston Hughes with Arnold Rampersad." *Re-Markings* 13.1 (2014): 34–46.

Hamilton, James Wallace. *Horns and Halos in Human Nature*. Westwood, N.J.: Fleming H. Revell, 1954.

Hansberry, Lorraine. *A Raisin in the Sun*. New York: Random House, 1994.

Hansen, Drew D. *The Dream: Martin Luther King Jr. and the Speech That Inspired a Nation*. New York: HarperCollins, 2003.

Harding, Vincent. Introduction. *Where Do We Go from Here: Chaos or Community?* Boston: Beacon Press, 2010.

Harper, Donna Akiba Sullivan. "End of Deferment: Use of Dreams in Langston Hughes's Poetry of the 1960s." *Foreign Language Studies* 20.2 (2008): 13–20.

———. *Not So Simple: The "Simple" Stories by Langston Hughes*. Columbia: University of Missouri Press, 1995.

Holland, Josiah. *Garnered Sheaves: The Complete Poetical Works of J. G. Holland*. Ann Arbor, Mich.: Making of America, 1996.

Holy Bible: King James Version. Nashville, Tenn.: Thomas Nelson, 1990.

Honey, Michael K. *All Labor Has Dignity*. Boston: Beacon Press, 2011.

Hubbard, Dolan. *The Sermon and the African American Literary Imagination*. Columbia: University of Missouri Press, 1994.

Hughes, Langston. "Berlin Today." *Chicago Defender*. 3 Apr. 1965, 8.

———. *The Collected Works of Langston Hughes*. Ed. Arnold Rampersad. 17 vols. Columbia: University of Missouri Press, 2001–4.

———. "Greatest Scholar's Mistletoe." *Chicago Defender*. 5 Oct. 1963, 6.

———. "If Simple Went to Selma." *Chicago Defender*. 24 Apr. 1965, 8.

———. "Juke Box Melodies on Simple's Song Sheet." *Chicago Defender*. 8 Aug. 1957, 10.

———. "Lasting Last Minute Gifts." *Chicago Defender*. 27 Dec. 1958: 10.

———. "Let's Organize as Well as Mobilize, Says Simple." *Chicago Defender* 8 June 1957: 10.

———, ed. *Lincoln University Poets*. New York: Fine Editions Press, 1954.

———. "The Negro." *Hunger and Revolt: Cartoons by Burck*. New York: Daily Worker, 1935. 141–42.

———. *The Negro Mother and Other Dramatic Recitations*. New York: Golden Stair Press, 1931.

———. "Simple as President of All People." *Chicago Defender*. 25 May 1963, 8.

———. "Simple; Jail-ins." *Chicago Defender*. 5 Aug. 1961, 8.

———. "Simple Produces a Film on an Afro-American Theme." *Chicago Defender*. 2 June 1956: 9.

———. "Simple Says Acting Right Is Better Than Writing Right." *Chicago Defender*. 23 Mar. 1957, 10.

Johnson, James Weldon. "Lift Ev'ry Voice and Sing." *Complete Poems*. New York: Penguin Books, 2000. 109–10.

Jones, Clarence, and Stuart Connelly. *Behind the Dream: The Making of the Speech That Transformed a Nation*. New York: Palgrave, 2011.

Jones, E. Stanley. *The Christ of the American Road*. Nashville, Tenn.: Abingdon-Cokesbury Press, 1944.

King, Martin Luther, Jr. "Love, Law, and Civil Disobedience." *New South* (Dec. 1961): 3–11.

———. "The Man Who Was a Fool." *The Pulpit: A Journal of Contemporary Preaching* 32.6 (1961): 4–6.

———. "My Dream." *Chicago Defender*. 12 Feb. 1966, 10.

———. *Stride toward Freedom: The Montgomery Story*. New York: Harper, 1958.

———. "A Tough Mind and a Tender Heart." *The Pulpit: A Journal of Contemporary Preaching* 34.7 (1963): 8–10.

———. *The Trumpet of Conscience*. Boston: Beacon Press, 2010.

———. *Where Do We Go from Here: Chaos or Community?* Boston: Beacon Press, 2010.

———. *Why We Can't Wait*. New York: Signet, 1964.

Kirk, John A. *Martin Luther King and the Civil Rights Movement*. New York: Pearson, 2013.

———. *Martin Luther King, Jr.: Profiles in Power*. New York: Pearson, 2005.

Kutzinski, Vera M. *The Worlds of Langston Hughes: Modernism and Translation in the Americas*. Ithaca, N.Y.: Cornell University Press, 2012.

"Langston Hughes's Mother at 'Daily' Affair on Saturday." *Daily Worker.* 26 Dec. 1933, 2.

Leff, Michael C., and Andrew Sachs. "Words the Most Like Things: Iconicity and the Rhetorical Text." *Western Journal of Speech Communication* 54.3 (1990): 252–73.

Levine, Lawrence W. *Black Culture and Black Consciousness: Afro-American Folk Thought from Slavery to Freedom.* Oxford, U.K.: Oxford University Press, 1977.

Lewis, David. *King: A Biography.* Urbana: University of Illinois Press, 2013.

Lischer, Richard. "The Music of Martin Luther King, Jr." *This Is How We Flow: Rhythm in Black Cultures.* Ed. Angela M. S. Nelson. Columbia: University of South Carolina Press, 1999. 54–62.

———. *The Preacher King: Martin Luther King and the Word That Moved America.* New York: Oxford University Press, 1995.

Lowney, John. "Langston Hughes's Cold War Audiences: Black Internationalism, the Popular Front, and *The Poetry of the Negro, 1746–1949.*" *Langston Hughes Review* 23 (2009): 50–71.

Luker, Ralph. "Quoting, Merging, and Sampling the Dream: Martin Luther King and Vernon Johns." *Southern Cultures* 9.2 (2003): 28–48.

Miller, Jordan Y. "Lorraine Hansberry." *Black Literature Criticism: Excerpts from Criticism of the Most Significant Works of Black Authors over the Past 200 Years.* Ed. James P. Draper. Vol. 2. Detroit: Gale, 1992. 958–59.

Miller, Keith D. "Voice Merging and Self-Making: The Epistemology of 'I Have a Dream.'" *Rhetoric Society Quarterly* 19.1 (1989): 23–31.

———. *Voice of Deliverance: The Language of Martin Luther King, Jr., and Its Sources.* New York: Macmillan, 1992.

Miller, R. Baxter. "The 'Diamond Star' Within: Black Female Inspiration in Hughes's Poetry." *Critical Insights: Langston Hughes.* Ed. R. Baxter Miller. Ipswich, Mass.: Salem Press, 2013. 55–68.

Miller, W. Jason. "Foregrounding and Prereading: Using Langston Hughes's Poetry to Teach *A Raisin in the Sun.*" *Notes on American Literature* 21 (2012): 4–15.

———. *Langston Hughes and American Lynching Culture.* Gainesville: University Press of Florida, 2011.

Morrison, Allan. "Mother Role Brings Broadway Fame." *Ebony.* May 1960, 97–104.

Mullen, Edward. "Langston Hughes y la Critica Literaria Hispanoamericana." *Literatura Hispanoamericana* 17 (1978): 1395–401.

Naison, Mark. *Communists in Harlem during the Depression.* New York: Grove, 1984.

"Nonthreatening Dreamer." *Washington Post.* 16 Jan. 1983, A10.

Osborn. M. M. "The Evolution of the Theory of Metaphor in Rhetoric." *Western Speech* 31 (1967): 121–31.

Oxenham, John. "The Ways." *All's Well.* New York: George H. Doran, 1916. 91.

Parks, Rosa, and Gregory J. Reed. *Quiet Strength: The Faith, the Hope, the Heart of a Woman Who Changed a Nation.* Grand Rapids: Zondervan, 1994.

Patton, John. "'I Have a Dream': The Performance of Theology Fused with the Power of Orality." *Martin Luther King Jr. and the Sermonic Power of Public Discourse.* Ed. Carolyn Calloway-Thomas and John Louis Lucaites. Tuscaloosa: University of Alabama Press, 1993. 104–26.

Pearson, Hugh. *When Harlem Nearly Killed King: The 1958 Stabbing of Dr. Martin Luther King, Jr.* New York: Seven Stories Press, 2002.

Pitt, Nat. "Beautiful Play." *New York Times.* 5 Apr. 1959, 1.

Rampersad, Arnold. *The Life of Langston Hughes.* 2 vols. New York: Oxford University Press, 2002.

Reddick, L. D. *Crusader without Violence: A Biography of Martin Luther King Jr.* New York: Harper and Brothers, 1959.

Robertson, Nan. "Dramatist against Odds." *New York Times.* 8 Mar. 1959, 1.

Roessel, David. "The Blues I'm Not Playing: Langston Hughes in the 1930s." *Critical Insights: Langston Hughes.* Ed. R. Baxter Miller. Ipswich, Mass.: Salem Press, 2013. 176–93.

Schuchter, Arnold. *White Power, Black Freedom: Planning the Future of Urban America.* Boston: Beacon Press, 1968.

Shakespeare, William. *The Tragedy of King Richard the Third. The Complete Works of Shakespeare.* 4th ed. Ed. David Bevington. New York: Longman, 1997. 628–81.

Sharman, Nick. "'Remaining Awake through a Great Revolution': The Rhetorical Strategies of Martin Luther King, Jr." *Social Semiotics* 9.1 (1999): 85–105.

Smith, Kenneth L., and Ira G. Zepp Jr. *Search for the Beloved Community: The Thinking of Martin Luther King, Jr.* Valley Forge, Pa.: Judson, 1974.

Spillers, Hortense. "Martin Luther King and the Style of the Black Sermon." *Black Scholar* (Sept. 1971): 14–27.

Sundquist, Eric. J. *King's Dream.* New Haven, Conn.: Yale University Press, 2009.

Thoreau, Henry David. *Walden.* New York: Barnes and Noble, 2004.

Thurman, Howard. *Deep River: Reflections on the Religious Insight of Certain of the Negro Spirituals.* New York: Harper and Brothers, 1955.

Tracy, Steven C. "Without Respect for Gender: Damnable Inference in 'Blessed Assurance.'" *Critical Insights: Langston Hughes.* Ed. R. Baxter Miller. Ipswich, Mass.: Salem Press, 2013. 223–37.

Vail, Mark. "The 'Integrative' Rhetoric of Martin Luther King Jr.'s 'I Have a Dream' Speech." *Rhetoric and Public Affairs* 9.1 (2006): 51–78.

Warnick, Jeffrey. "Found in the Drama Mailbag." *New York Times.* 29 Apr. 1959, 1.

Washington, Booker T. *Up from Slavery.* New York: Doubleday, 1963.

Washington, James Melvin, ed. *A Testament of Hope: The Essential Writings of Martin Luther King, Jr.* New York: Harper and Row, 1986.

Weiler, A. H. "By Way of Report: 'Raisin' Attracts Film Buyers—Other Items." *New York Times.* 22 Apr. 1959, 1.

Wenzel, J. W. "A Dangerous Unselfishness: Martin Luther King, Jr.'s Speech at Memphis, April 3, 1968." *Texts in Context: Critical Dialogues on Significant Episodes in American Political Rhetoric.* Ed. M. C. Leff and F. J. Kauffeld. Davis, Calif.: Hermagoras Press, 1989. 167–79.

Wilkins, Fanon Che. "Beyond Bandung: The Critical Nationalism of Lorraine Hansberry, 1950–1965." *Radical History Review* 95 (2006): 191–219.

Wills, Garry. *Certain Trumpets: The Call of Leaders.* New York: Simon and Schuster, 1994.

Wilson, Kirt H. "Interpreting the Discursive Field of the Montgomery Bus Boycott: Martin Luther King Jr.'s Holt Street Address." *Rhetoric and Public Affairs* 8.2 (2005): 299–326.

Wofford, Harris. *Of Kennedys and Kings: Making Sense of the Sixties*. Pittsburgh: University of Pittsburgh Press, 1992.

Young, Andrew. "Martin Luther King, Jr.: Words That Changed a Nation." Interview with Soledad O'Brien. CNN. Atlanta. 16 Oct. 2011.

Zepp, Ira G., Jr. *The Social Vision of Martin Luther King Jr.* New York: Carlson, 1989.

Index

W. Jason Miller is associate professor in the English Department at North Carolina State University.